The London Garden Book A-Z

Abigail Willis

The London Garden Book A-Z

Abigail Willis

The London Garden Book A-Z

Written by Abigail Willis
Photography by Andrew Kershman, Susi Koch and Abigail Willis
Cover photography by Andrew Kershman
Edited by David Swindells
Book design by Lesley Gilmour and Susi Koch
Illustrations and cover design by Susi Koch

2nd edition published in 2016 by
Metro Publications Ltd, PO Box 6336, London, N1 6PY

Metro® is a registered trade mark of Associated Newspapers Limited.
The METRO mark is under licence from Associated Newspapers Limited.

Printed and bound in China.
This book is produced using paper from registered sustainable
and managed sources. Suppliers have provided both LEI and
MUTU certification.

ISBN 978-1-902910-59-8

To Clare, June and Ingrid
with thanks

About the author

Abigail Willis is an arts and gardening writer, allotmenteer and gardener. *The London Garden Book A-Z* combines her love of the capital with her passion for horticulture; the first edition was short-listed for a Garden Media Guild Award in 2012. Her guidebook *Museums & Galleries of London* is an essential guide to the capital's cultural treasures; also published by Metro, the 6th edition was published in 2016. Abigail lives and gardens in the West Country.

www.abigailwillis.co.uk
@willis_abigail

Acknowledgements

This book would not have been possible without the help of a great many people. I am enormously grateful to Andrew and Susi at Metro for commissioning the book, and for their huge enthusiasm and unstinting support, in so many ways, for the project over two editions. The beautiful photographs in the book are also down to them too, and I would particularly like to thank them for their diligence in monitoring the weather forecasts and travelling all over London in the quest to capture individual gardens (and their custodians) at their best. I must also thank Lesley Gilmour for her help designing the book, and for marshalling text and pictures so beautifully.

Researching this book through two editions has been entirely pleasurable – what could be nicer than discovering wonderful gardens and talking to fellow gardeners? My thanks to all those who responded so positively to the concept of the book from the outset and who kindly opened up their gardens to me, sometimes at very short notice, and who so generously shared their gardening experience and knowledge. It has been fascinating, not to say life-enhancing, to have met so many inspirational London gardeners, from volunteers in tiny community gardens, to head gardeners looking after historically significant gardens. 'Gardening is good for the soul', according to one gardener I met, and it's impossible not to agree.

I am also indebted to the friends and family who gave me bed and board during my research trips to London, and who good-humouredly accompanied me on garden visits, and whose companionship made work seem suspiciously like good fun.

My husband Alexander Ballinger has been a huge support to me throughout the project, keeping the home fires burning during my absences, fielding my over-excited phone calls from particularly gorgeous gardens, and casting his constructively critical editorial eyes over my work. I could not have completed the book without him.

I would also like to extend my thanks to the following for their help during the writing of this book:

Rachel Aked, Paolo Arrigo, Mark Baker, Alexander Ballinger, Caroline Ballinger, Christina Ballinger, Dick and Penelope Ballinger, Bethan Beckett, Daniel Bell, Alison Benjamin, Susan Bennett, Gillian Blanchford, Caroline Bousfield Gregory, Andrea Brunsendorf, Toot Bunnag, Tony and Tessa Campbell, Paul Carter, Angela Clarke, Fliss Combs, Alison Condie, Jane Cordingley, Alice Cottingham, Andrew Darrough, Julie Davies, Karen Douglas, Peter Foster, Sascha Foulkes, Marcus and Inky Fraser, Terri Freeman, Rosie Fyles, Pamela Gent, Paula Gent, Dani Glover, Andrew Goddard, Tania Goodman, Ingrid Grubben, Maddie Guerlain, James Hall, Celia Hammond, Paul Harwood, Emir Hashan, Darren Henderson, Tony Heywood, Lutfun Hussain, Earl Hyde, Rhiannon James, Michael Johnson, Candice Jones, Derek Kendall, Jean Langmead, Rosemary Lindsay, Janson Lotery, Gordon McArthur, Lisa McCormack, Mike McGinn, Alison McKay, Murray MacKay, David Matzdorf, Pilar Medrano-Dell, Lottie Muir, Deborah Nagan, The National Trust, Ben Nel, Open Garden Squares Weekend, Janet Payne , Linda Phillips, Nigel Phillips, Roger Phillips, Nina Pope, Clare Preston, Richard Reynolds, Tim Richardson, Paul Richens, Andy Roberts, Paul Roper, The Royal Horticultural Society, Royal Botanic Gardens, Kew, Charles Rutherfoord, Reverend Kemmyo Taira Sato, Naomi Schillinger, Tom Seaward, David and Pat Scott, Peter and Jan Simmonds, Molly St Hilaire, Wendy Shillam, Lin Skippings, Jill Smith, Michael Smythe, Penny Snell, Ben Stephenson, Amanda Stücklin, Thierry Suzanne, Ellen Swygart, Sebastian Thomas, Natasha Tidd, Jackie Tolland, Mikey Tomkins, Kay Thomson, Paul Thomson, Thrive, Aida Trabucco, TfL, Andrew Turvey, Rupert Tyler, Christopher Stocks, Roy Vickery, Lizzie Walder, June Warrington, Alison Wear, Charlie de Wet, John White, Sally Williams, Belinda Willis.

Contents

Nomura Rooftop Garden, see p.171

Introduction

This second edition of *The London Garden Book A-Z* celebrates London's thriving horticultural landscape in all its diversity, taking readers on a tour of the capital's most inspirational gardens.

As with the first edition, the book does not aim to provide an exhaustive list of every public garden in London, rather it aspires to capture a portrait of the city's vibrant gardening scene. Within these pages can be found all kinds of gardens: market gardens, therapeutic gardens, historic gardens, community gardens, independent nurseries, street gardens and pocket parks, as well as the quirky 'horticultural happenings' of the annual Chelsea Fringe festival.

A light top-dressing of practical advice on topics such as thrifty gardening and how to garden for wildlife has also been applied, to provide a useful starting point for fledgling urban gardeners. But of course the best way to learn about gardening is to just do it, a process memorably described to me by one gardener as "trial and effort".

Energy, commitment and passion are what make great gardens; in many ways gardens are more about people than they are about plants. Researching *The London Garden Book A-Z* has confirmed this to me. Creative, tenacious, and adaptable, London gardeners see opportunities in the most unlikely of places, from rooftops to roundabouts, from sidewalks to skips. In the following pages a few of them generously open up their gardens to the reader, along the way sharing their plant choices and gardening philosophies, and revealing what remarkable gardens thrive in London's notoriously unyielding clay.

Abigail Willis

Laburnum Tunnel, Hampton Court Palace Gardens see p.126

LONDON GARDEN HISTORY

London Garden History

With over 3,000 parks and open spaces covering some 67 square miles, London is revered as one of the world's greenest capitals. But famous as they are, London's parks are only one aspect of the city's green and pleasant demeanour – Greater London contains an estimated 3.8 million domestic gardens, covering one fifth of its area. It is also home to an impressive array of publicly accessible gardens, such as the centuries-old, former monastic gardens belonging to Westminster College (see p.236) and Inner Temple (see p.134). Even London's squares and cemeteries often have the prefix 'garden' attached to them, suggesting the fondness for informal, domestic-style open spaces in the capital.

At the heart of royal and fashionable court life, and the trade hub of an expanding Empire, London was naturally a centre for high-powered gardening. The hottest design trends and the latest plant discoveries landed in London first, and it was in London's botanic gardens, nurseries and private homes that new species were raised, studied and tended, endowing English gardeners with a degree of plantsmanship that was admired throughout Europe.

From the late 16th century the capital's busy river wharves and docks received an influx of exciting plant discoveries from the Levant and the Americas. The John Tradescants, a father and son gardening duo who successively held the post of 'Keeper of his Majesty's Gardens, Vines and Silkworms', were each responsible for several new introductions and their well-stocked garden in Lambeth became a London landmark. *Tradescantia virginiana* is named in honour of Tradescant the Elder, while it is the Younger that we must thank for Michaelmas daisies, phlox and magnolia.

Taking up the Tradescants' mantle, 18th-century London merchant Peter Collinson was the conduit for many American plant species entering British gardens, working in collaboration with the Philadelphia-based botanist John Bartram. Collinson employed Bartram to seek out new species, the seeds of which were duly shipped over to London and distributed to subscribers. Loddiges' Nursery in Hackney and Philip Miller, head gardener at the Chelsea Physic Garden, were among the pioneers who subscribed to 'Bartram's boxes', the first of which arrived in London in 1734. At Osterley Park a special 'American border' was created to showcase newly discovered North American trees, shrubs and flowers, ordered by Osterley's plant-collecting châtelaine, Mrs Child.

This being the Age of Reason, serious research accompanied the quest for novelty and London became home to a succession of horticultural establishments such as the Chelsea Physic Garden (founded 1673, see p.56) and the Royal Botanic Gardens at Kew (established 1757, see p.206). The

Westminster College Garden

Chelsea Physic Garden, see p.56

5

Horticultural Society of London was set up in 1804 with the aim of collecting plant information and encouraging best horticultural practice, and became the Royal Horticultural Society in 1861. Among its eminent founder members were the botanist Sir Joseph Banks and royal head gardener William Forsyth – the Society's first meeting was held at Hatchard's Bookshop, on Piccadilly.

It was in London too that modern horticultural literature was born, with early publications including the list published in 1596 by John Gerard of the plants in his Holborn garden and *Paradisi in Sole Paradisus Terrestris,* a horticultural manual written in 1629 by the apothecary John Parkinson, who had a sizeable botanic garden in Long Acre. Although the Deptford-based diarist John Evelyn failed to complete his great work on British gardening, the *Elysium Britannicum,* his published works include the *Kalendarium Hortense* of 1664 (one of the earliest gardening almanacs) and a monograph on salads. The book was published in 1699 and includes Evelyn's recipe for salad dressing – revealing that the culinary use of olive oil in British households was by no means a 1960's innovation.

The emergence of the terraced house with its enclosed back (and sometimes front) garden as London's default residential unit during the city's rapid expansion in the 18th and 19th centuries really turned London into a city of gardeners. With

The Hill Garden & Pergola, see p.130

their own little patch of London soil to cultivate, Londoners got busy planning and planting beds, enthused by practical guides such as Thomas Fairchild's 1722 publication *The City Gardener,* written specifically for a London audience. London's infamous smog made growing conditions difficult for most plants (they usually died after flowering), but this obsolescence suited the city's burgeoning nursery trade and those such as Loddiges' and James Gordon's in Mile End did a roaring trade. Carlyle's House in Chelsea (see p.42) displays a typical London back garden layout of the 19th century (although the house itself dates from the previous century). In the early 1830's London was the birthplace of one of horticulture's most significant inventions, the Wardian Case, a kind of portable greenhouse that enabled plants to survive long sea journeys and which facilitated the 19th century boom in plant hunting and a mass influx of new and exotic plants.

The rustic and romantic Arts and Crafts garden developed by William Robinson and Gertrude Jekyll was the dominant garden style of the late 19th and early 20th centuries. Essentially designed for a country house setting, the style could be transplanted to the city but only by those wealthy enough to afford the generous plots of land it demanded. In London, two delightful essays in the style are The Hill Garden and Pergola (see p.130), designed by TH Mawson for Lord Leverhulme, and Eltham Palace (see p.90), whose Arts & Crafts gardens temper the Art Deco glamour of the

Thomas Carlyle's Garden, see p.42

Chiswick House, see p.60

Palace's interiors, installed by the millionaire couple Stephen and Virginia Courtauld. The masses were also able to enjoy a taste of this gracious style of gardening thanks to JJ Sexby, who was appointed London County Council's first superintendant of Parks in 1889. Sexby installed 'Old English Gardens' in several of the parks he laid out, including Peckham Rye Park, Southwark Park and Brockwell Park – whose Sexby-designed walled garden has recently been restored (see p.234).

Gardening became a national necessity during the two world wars of the 20th century, when food shortages prompted a huge increase in allotment plots and motivated the population to 'dig for victory'. In London the Blitz was a catalyst for early community gardens, with some bomb sites being turned into impromptu gardens by local workers and residents. A few became permanent fixtures and former bomb sites in the City, such as the Goldsmiths' Garden (see p.148) and the Cleary Garden (see p.68), flourish to this day (although considerably smartened up since their original make-do-and-mend guise). The desire to cultivate

derelict land lives on in 21st-century London, in community enterprises such as Bonnington Square (see p.26) and Culpeper Community Garden (see p.86), or in guerrilla gardens like the Lavender Field in Lambeth (see p.116).

The current surge in popularity of gardening as a pastime has been accompanied by a growing appreciation of London's horticultural heritage. Two of London's most significant gardens have recently been the subject of extensive restorations – Chiswick House (see p.60), the birthplace of the Landscape Movement, and Myddelton House Garden (see p.160), the home of renowned 20th-century plantsman, E A Bowles. It is surely no coincidence that the first museum in the world to be devoted to garden history should be in London, and more precisely in Lambeth, one-time home to the pioneering, plant-hunting Tradescants. A celebration of four centuries of British gardening, the Garden Museum (see p.106) is a fine place to start any exploration of London's gardens.

LONDON GARDENS A-Z

Golf Course Allotments

A Allotments

After years in the doldrums allotment gardening is back on the agenda – and in a big way. In London demand far outstrips supply, with some boroughs' waiting lists stretching far into the future (in Wandsworth prospective allotmenteers face up to a 12-year wait while in Hackney, waiting lists have been frozen since 2008).

History has shown that when the going gets tough, the tough get digging, and UK allotment numbers peaked at 1.75 million during the 'dig for victory years' of WWII. Today, runaway food prices, concerns about food security, pesticides and the dominance of supermarkets, have all contributed to the resurgence of allotment gardening. The quaint, old-fashioned concept of eating fresh food in season has also made a comeback, along with a desire to cut food miles, 'eat local' and reconnect with nature.

Those lucky enough to have an allotment can't rest on their laurels though, since according to a government report (commissioned in 2006, but buried until 2011) the number of UK allotments fell by over 50,000 in the previous decade; the figure is currently around 330,000. On this land-limited island of ours even allotments with 'statutory' (as opposed to 'temporary') status aren't guaranteed protection. In London, where pressure on open space is acute, allotments have been at the centre of some notable planning battles. Manor Gardens allotments in east London, which had been bequeathed in perpetuity for the benefit of local people in 1900 by Major Arthur Villiers, were obliterated in 2007 to make way for the new Olympic Park, despite a strong campaign to save them. But bulldozers aren't always a foregone conclusion and in 2010, allotmenteers at Fortis Green were able to buy their site from their landlord, Thames Water, thus saving it from development. The site is now run by the Fortis Green Community Allotments Trust.

Much cherished by their members, London's allotments are vibrant, multicultural, cross-generational mini-communities. Some sites are more utilitarian than others, but some lucky plot-holders can enjoy mod-cons such as composting toilets, cafés, trading huts, manure bins, wildlife areas and events such as seed swaps, barbecues, flower shows, and even horticultural speed-dating. Most allotments are usually closed to the public but some – such as the Golf Course Allotments in Haringey – participate in the NGS Open Gardens scheme (see The Yellow Book, p.270) and the London Open Garden Squares Weekend in June (see p.170) allowing visitors to see behind the scenes of these productive urban plots. It's always fascinating to observe so many different approaches to growing in one place – even if everyone else's veg invariably looks healthier than your own.

At Stanley Road Allotments in Sutton, visitors can even take part in the harvest, since the site shares three of its ten acres with Carshalton Lavender, a not-for-profit community project devoted to reviving the once thriving, centuries-old, local lavender industry. The volunteer-run project, which was set up in 1996, celebrated its first harvest in 2001 and in 2009 distilled the first lavender oil in Carshalton for a century. Impressively, the field was entirely stocked with plants grown from locally sourced cuttings of *Lavandula intermedia*, believed to be from the original lavender fields. The project continues to offer plenty of scope for involvement, from regular workdays and foster-a-cutting schemes, to the Community Harvest at the end of July, when the field is opened to the public to pick their own lavender.

And this being London, even humble allotment sites with their patchwork of plots and ramshackle sheds can come dripping in history, such as those at Fulham Palace Meadows, founded in 1916 on a site that previously played host to Roman, Anglo-Saxon and Viking settlements. The Royal Paddocks allotments at Bushy Park have an even grander provenance, having been granted to the 'labouring poor' by Royal Warrant in 1921 on Crown land

Pudding Mill Lane

formerly used as paddocks for the king's horses. In Brixton the 26 plots of the Windmill Allotments flourish in the shadow of a recently restored historic 19th-century windmill; while in Hampstead, the Branch Hill allotments are picturesquely sited on the former garden of the mansion belonging to John Spedon Lewis, founder of John Lewis stores – the 32 plots here are presumably 'never knowingly under-sowed'.

Those in search of a plot of their own should contact their local borough council in the first instance, since most allotments are council owned and restricted to local residents. The London Allotments Network (www.londonallotments.net) is a useful second port of call and holds a waiting list of people who want plots and who live in boroughs where there are no allotments or who are already on a borough waiting list but prepared to take a plot in another borough.

However there's no need to sit idly by while you grow old waiting for an allotment to become vacant. Check out Project Dirt's networking website for opportunities to get involved in a community growing project near you (www.projectdirt.com) or Capital Growth (p.40) for details of training and food growing and volunteering opportunities around London (www.capitalgrowth.org). Edible Landscapes (www.ediblelandscapeslondon.org.uk, a community project based in Finsbury Park that aims to help Londoners grow more of their own food), holds regular informal workdays teaching volunteers the fine art of forest gardening – including vital skills of plant identification, propagation and how to cook the produce once it's been harvested.

Resources in brief

www.capitalgrowth.org

www.carshaltonlavender.org

www.ediblelandscapeslondon.org.uk

www.foodupfront.org

www.fortisgreenallotments.co.uk

www.fpmaa.com

www.gcaa.pwp.blueyonder.co.uk

www.golfcourseallotments.co.uk

www.landshare.net

www.london.gov.uk

www.londonallotments.net

www.mgs-puddingmill.org

www.paddocks-allotments.org.uk

www.projectdirt.com

www.srags.org.uk

www.sustainweb.org/londonfoodlink

www.wimbledonfoodgroup.co.uk

www.windmillallotments.org.uk

Cable Street Community Garden

"Regular deliveries of horse manure from the police stables nearby keeps the soil fertility levels high."

Cable Street Community Gardens

With its patchwork of productive plots enclosed by residential buildings and the brick arches of a railway bridge, the Cable Street Community Garden is a latter day, inner city version of the traditional walled kitchen garden. These gardens, however, were never an adjunct to a big house, but were created in the 1970s as a far-sighted Friends of the Earth initiative to reclaim derelict land for community use. From the early days of a few dedicated pioneers, the gardens have grown in popularity and today boast around 100 members, of all ages, different walks of life and cultural backgrounds.

The gardens have always been run organically and over the decades have developed a lively biodiversity, nurtured by the absence of pesticides, the wide range of vegetables, fruit and flowers grown on site, and by wildlife friendly features such as ponds, wildflower areas and a native hedgerow. Two bee hives have recently been introduced, and are looked after by long-standing member Jane O'Sullivan and Emir Hasham, a plotholder for eight years. One hive is tucked away on Emir's spacious plot by the railway arches with the bees being housed in a plastic modern hive, the 'Beehaus' made by Omlet. As a new beekeeper he finds this design easy to use and the bees settled in well. The allotment is Emir's relaxation away from his career working in special effects for TV advertising – 'I try to grow things that I like eating but that look nice as well.' His eclectic choice of crops includes chillies, peppers and aubergines, black kale, several varieties of chicory, a kiwi fruit and hops.

www.cablestreetcommunitygardens.co.uk
www.omlet.co.uk

Emir Hasham

B Barbican

As divisive as Marmite, this residential quarter in the heart of the City, has attracted more than its fair share of criticism since its official opening in 1982. It is now recognised as a bona fide architectural icon, having been listed (Grade II*) by English Heritage in 2001.

It's all too easy to dismiss the Barbican as a concrete carbuncle but the Brutalist vision of architects Chamberlain, Powell and Bon is actually a good deal greener than is often credited. Over half the Estate's 15.2 hectares is open space, of which 5.25 hectares is given over to public and private landscaped gardens, ponds and the Conservatory. There are potentially 12 kilometres of window boxes and residents deploy these to great effect, while the highwalks are punctuated with wooden tubs and concrete troughs gardened by the City of London and members of the Barbican Horticultural Society respectively. Some containers serve as resident's allotments and their rows of Swiss chard, onions, asparagus and beetroot strike a homely note on the ultra-urban highwalks.

Although Le Corbusier's Unité d'Habitation was a strong influence on Chamberlain, Powell and Bon's Barbican designs, the classic London garden square was also a reference point.

Thomas More Garden and Speed Gardens (the Barbican's two private gardens), are defined by the surrounding residential blocks. Beech Garden, a publicly accessible garden, follows a similar format but is effectively a container roof garden on a large scale, made up of formal beds sunk into the tiled surface of the Barbican's 'podium' level. Beech Garden has recently been completely replanted by ecological plant expert Nigel Dunnett with a beautiful palette of sustainable and wildlife-friendly plants that can cope with the three distinct micro-climates within the site and its scanty three feet planting depth. Visit in midsummer and you will be rewarded with a vista of subtly woven threads of sisyrinchium, allium, salvia, white rose campion, sedum, stachys, red hot poker, Jerusalem sage, *verbena*

Beech Garden

"The Barbican Conservatory is less well known, despite being the second largest of its kind in London after Kew."

bonariensis and clump-forming grasses. In spring bulbs bring colour to the garden and in autumn seed heads ensure a long season of interest for residents and visitors. Fourteen newly planted tree specimens add height and interest, and include multi-stem amelanchier, black elder and viburnum. Whereas the previous planting arrangement had relied on irrigation to succeed, Dunnett's new scheme is designed to be low maintenance with plants that can cope with minimal watering.

Probably the best-known public open space in the Barbican is the Lakeside Terrace in front of the Arts Centre. Here visitors experience the Barbican's hard landscaping at its most uncompromising, albeit softened a little by containerised palm trees and the shallow green waters of the lake. The latter is planted with yellow flag iris and is home to shoals of rudd and golden orfe (the carp that previously lived in the lake fell victim to a mischievously introduced pike).

The Barbican Conservatory is less well known, despite being the second largest of its kind in London after Kew. An idiosyncratic afterthought, it was built around the fly tower of the Arts Centre theatre and opened in 1984, with a cacti-filled Arid House being added two years later. The Conservatory is currently open to the public every Sunday 12.00-17.30, offering a chance to admire over 2,000 species of tropical and sub-tropical plants, plus resident terrapins and an aviary.

The Barbican's Fann Street Wildlife Garden is home to wildflowers, small mammals and various bird species and has been designated a site of Borough Importance for Nature Conservation and is managed by the volunteers of the Barbican Wildlife Group. Only open to Barbican residents, the garden usually takes part in the London Open Garden Squares weekend (see p.170). Invertebrates however are free to check in and out of the recently installed insect hotel.

Barbican, Silk St, London, EC2Y 8DS
www.barbican.org.uk   T: 020 7638 4141

This page: Fann Street Wildlife Garden (above),
Lakeside Terrace (below)
Opposite page: Barbican Conservatory

B | Battersea Flower Station

This charming, independent local garden centre set up shop in 2012, and has been welcomed by locals and not-so locals (as well as the national press) with wide-open arms. Even if you're not immediately in the market for any of its wares, the Battersea Flower Station is the most delightful place to visit for an inspirational mooch.

This verdant strip of land is discretely set in a wooded snicket beside the railway and between Battersea Park Road and Winders Road, where once barrows from Battersea market were stored. The Flower Station was the brainchild of Lisa McCormack, Scott Melville, and John Schofield who quit their jobs (in marketing, logistics and large chain garden centres respectively) to realise their dream of creating a place of beauty that had real value to the local community.

Drawing on her previous life in advertising, Lisa had come up with the Flower Station's brilliantly punning name before they had even found premises, and says of the trio's endeavour, "people talk about the death of the high street, and there's no doubt independent retailing is a challenge, but we're so proud of what we do here. It's all about offering people something above and beyond just a product - we live or die by our customer services ethos. Locals have thanked us for making Battersea feel like a village again."

Beneath the shade of the sycamore trees, Battersea Flower Station sells not just flowers (there's a resident florist), but all kinds of trees, plants, houseplants and shrubs, as well as stylish and useful gardening paraphernalia in the well-stocked garden shop, including a good range of pots, large and small. Its tin shed carries tempting garden gifts and the friendly staff can advise on what plant goes where (essential information when planning tricky London gardens, balconies and window sills). Customer care is high on the BFS's list of priorities, and always evolving in response to feedback – they offer local delivery, a window box planting service and came up with the brilliant wheeze of selling compost by the scoop for those small scale gardeners who don't need and can't store a great big sack of compost. All Battersea Flower Station products are locally sourced, and the staff are all Wandsworthians too. Utterly captivating.

16 Winders Road, SW11 3HE
(entrance next to 318 Battersea Park Road)
T: 020 7978 4253
www.batterseaflowerstation.co.uk
Mon-Thurs 9.00-17.00, Fri until 19.00
Sat 9.30-18.00, Sun 11.00-17.00

B Bees

Honey bees may be in decline in some parts of the globe but in Britain, at least, the beekeeper population is on the rise – the British Bee Keepers Association's (BBKA) current membership stands at around 24,000, up two-fold since 2006.

In London beekeeping is all the rage, with as many as 5,000 hives believed to be located within the M25. Concern at the plight of *Apis mellifera*, a desire to connect with the rhythms of the natural world and interest in locally produced food are some worthy motivators behind this increase, but it's also true that London is a great place to raise bees. London's status as one of the world's greenest capitals (with over 3,000 parks and open spaces) favours the urban beekeeper, providing a long season of bee-friendly forage, a warm microclimate and a low incidence of the agricultural pesticides used in rural areas.

A symbol of industry and prosperity, it is not surprising that honey bees reside at some of London's most prestigious addresses. The grounds of Buckingham Palace and Clarence House have beehives, as does Regent's Park. Fortnum & Mason's have hives above their Piccadilly store, as well as on the roof of White Cube gallery in Bermondsey and at St Pancras International Station. Regardless of the location, all the Fortnum and Mason bees live in bespoke, architecturally themed, hives – painted in Fortnum's signature eau de nil. London's cultural institutions have got in on the act too, with the Royal Festival Hall, Tate Modern and Tate Britain and the Victoria & Albert Museum all hosting rooftop bee hives.

The London Beekeepers Association runs its own training programme and recommends that novice beekeepers are mentored for a season and learn the fundamentals of handling livestock with a sting in their tail. Regional London beekeeping associations also offer training, as do outfits such as Urban Bees, the London Honey Company and Capital Bee. In Hackney, the Golden Company, whose training hive is based at St Mary's Secret Garden (see p.198), is a social enterprise, training young people in beekeeping and entrepreneurship.

Not everyone can be a beekeeper, but there are other ways in which Londoners can address the potentially disastrous decline in bee numbers. Initiatives such as the BBKA's 'Adopt a Beehive' and the Bumblebee Conservation Trust's 'BeeWatch' project aim to support bees, without whose pollination skills we would all be scuppered. Everyone can do their bit to help honey bees and other threatened species such as bumblebees and solitary bees by converting their garden, allotment, balcony or window box into a bee-friendly glade. The best ways to do this include installing 'bee hotels' and planting a seasonal succession of nectar-rich trees, herbs and flowers, such as apples, rosemary, sunflowers and foxgloves and not forgetting important early and late sources of pollen such as spring crocuses and autumn ivy (see p.251).

A truly seasonal, local product, London honey comes on stream in late summer and autumn and is highly sought after, with different boroughs producing their own distinctive flavours and textures, from the dark runny 'Tate Honey', to the pale, lime scented honey made by bees 'working' the London parks. Borough Market, farmer's markets and select delis are a good source of London honey, as is Fortnum's, while Tate honey can be brought from the gallery's website. Reflecting the current buoyancy of the capital's beekeeping scene, the London Honey Show is held every October at the Lancaster London hotel (whose rooftop bees make the hotel's breakfast-time honey), with various prizes being given out, including the coveted 'Beekeeper of the Year' award.

Fortnum's Beemaster Steve Benbow tends the hives on the roof of the Piccadilly store

Beekeeping Resources:

British Beekeepers Association
www.bbka.org.uk

London Beekeepers Association
www.lbka.org.uk

The Golden Company
www.thegolden.co-op.com

Pure Food
www.purefood.co.uk

Urban Bees
www.urbanbees.co.uk

The London Honey Company
www.thelondonhoneycompany.co.uk

Bees for Development
www.beesfordevelopment.org

Capital Bee
www.capitalbee.org.uk

Beehaus beehives
www.omlet.co.uk

The National Honey Show
www.honeyshow.co.uk

London Honey Show
www.londonbees.com

B   Beekeeping on RFH

Beehives don't come more stylish than the one tended by Mikey Tomkins and Barnaby Shaw on top of the Royal Festival Hall. The meticulous scale model of the iconic 1950s concert hall was built by sound artist Dr Robert Mullander using the original architects' drawings, and in 2008 the bees moved in.

The roof of the world-famous venue is a prestigious site but not necessarily the easiest one for the urban apiarist, with bees, honey and associated paraphernalia having to be carried through the Hall's main public spaces and up and down five floors. But a privileged view of the capital, across to the Houses of Parliament, St Paul's and down the Thames, makes up for this, along with the therapeutic effects of the bees themselves. According to Mikey, an enthusiastic practitioner and advocate for urban agriculture, beekeeping is a great lesson in learning to slow down and appreciate the complexity of things – 'no matter how hard one works at life, a colony of 50,000 female insects seems invariably better organised!'

Spring is a busy time for his charges as they prepare for their annual population explosion by collecting pollen and nectar. Throughout the summer Mikey and Barnaby look in on the three RFH hives once a week. The honey harvest usually takes place in August with the small but delicious yield (usually around 12-14 kg per hive) being sold at public and private events.

www.mikeytomkins.co.uk
www.royalfestivalhall.org.uk

"Urban beekeeping feels like you're doing something despite all the best intentions of the city to deny you it. You discover that its hard concrete shells harbour a soft vegetative core and bees find this much quicker than we do."

B Bonnington Square

Bonnington Square Pleasure Garden

Named with a nod to the Vauxhall Pleasure Gardens of old, this resident-run garden square may not have all the diversions offered by its famous forebear but what it lacks in orchestral performances, balloon flights, acrobats and masked balls it makes up in community spirit and charm. The site was developed in its current form in the mid 1990s, when residents successfully lobbied the council to save and redevelop the garden (at that point a derelict children's playground) for local people. Designed by 'committee', Bonnington Square's enclave of artistically inclined residents fortunately included garden designers Dan Pearson and James Frazer, who between them devised a luxuriant planting scheme, combining semi-tropical and Mediterranean plants with English natives.

The semi-tropical feel of the garden remains today, with lofty palms, Zealand flax, bananas, bamboos and mahonia providing the garden with its architecture and foliage. A small lawned area basks in the garden's sunlit centre, with benches for relaxing on, a picnic table and a children's play area among the amenities. Roped border edges and the odd anchor lying around add a faintly nautical feel to proceedings, while a giant iron slip wheel salvaged from a local marble works makes a dramatic sculptural contribution against the far wall. Such is the garden's exuberance that it has spilled out onto the Square's surrounding pavements, which have been planted with trees, shrubs and climbers as part of the Bonnington Square Garden Association's ongoing Paradise Project. Vistors to the square should not miss the opporunity to visit the Bonnington Café which is just around the corner and very much part of the community.

www.bonningtonsquaregarden.org.uk
www.bonningtoncafe.co.uk

Bonnington Café,
11 Vauxhall Grove, SW8 1TD
Open daily 12noon-14.00, 18.30-22.30

Harleyford Road Community Garden

Begun in the 1980s, this community garden developed more organically than its neighbour, with no overriding design. As a result it is more jungle-like, with a relaxed feel compared to the orderly Bonnington Square. Here, winding mosaic pathways lead to several distinct areas, including a recently installed pond, children's play area, herb and vegetable beds, and a wildlife area (those nettles are there for a reason). Its 1.5 acres are gardened organically by regular volunteers, with the more experienced helping the less so, and its plants include well-established roses as well as more exotic specimens. Both gardens take part in the Open Garden Squares weekend with live music and a variety of stalls (see p.170).

A 'secret' passage connects Bonnington Square with Harleyford Road Community Garden

29

B Brunel Museum Garden

This quirky Thameside garden comes with its own rather lovely museum, which celebrates the achievements of father and son engineers, Marc and Isambard Brunel, who created the world's first under-river crossing here in 1843. The audacious and dangerous undertaking was young Isambard's first major project while his last, the construction and launch of his revolutionary 22,500 ton steamship the *SS Great Eastern*, was also accomplished near here in 1858.

With its workmanlike chimney and no-nonsense brickwork engine house, the Brunel Museum is a beacon of the Industrial Revolution, but it's a treasured local landmark too. Its gardens may be small but they are open to the public daily, with a ship-shape picnic table, well-stocked community herb beds, and benches made by local school children representing some of Brunel's iconic bridges.

The 50ft diameter circular roof garden that sits on the top of the tunnelling shaft was created in spring 2012 by Capel Manor student Lottie Muir over just two months with help from local residents. She even had one day's help from Fenton House head gardener Andrew Darragh and several people undertaking community service. They re-energised this enclosed space into a productive plot whose raised wooden beds

brim with a generous abundance of vegetables and herbs, now tended by members of the Museum's gardening club who meet weekly.

Originally designed as a potager garden, the planting plan is now focused on plants to drink rather than to eat. Every Friday and Saturday Lottie transforms the roof garden into a party potager to host Midnight Apothecary. In her guise as the Cocktail Gardener, her seasonal pop-up serves an irresistible menu of some of the prettiest cocktails in town, to a laid-back clientele who sip their botanically inspired drinks surrounded by plants and birdsong and toasting the odd marshmallow round the firepit.

Lottie alchemises natural botanics into delicious 'alcoholic prescriptions' that are infused with herbs and flowers picked from the garden, or foraged from around London. She marries her exquisitely balanced flavours with locally sourced alcohol wherever possible (nearby Bermondsey is a particular hot spot for low-booze-miles artisanal gin and beer). Her imbibable menu established the 'Chelsea Fringe Collins' (created specially for the festival, see p.53) and Woodland Martini (whose ingredients include Douglas fir needles and sage) as instant classics. Teetotalers are not forgotten, with delicious non-alcoholic concoctions such as lavender honeysuckle fizz to excite the tastebuds. Served in elegant vintage glassware, with floral garnishes and nary a gaudy cocktail umbrella in sight, Lottie's cocktails make the perfect city sundowner in the city.

And for those who want to try this at home Lottie's signature recipes have been distilled into a book, *Wild Cocktails*, and she can also be seen working her magic on Jamie Oliver's cocktail channel, Drinks Tube.

The Brunel Museum
Brunel Engine House, Railway Avenue, SE16 4LF
www.brunel-museum.org.uk

Meet the Cocktail Gardener

Lottie's entrée in to the world of cocktails came about more or less by accident, when she was asked by the Brunel Museum to devise a nocturnal event for Museums at Night. Lottie's idea of botanical cocktails around the fire in the community garden was an instant hit. "It was at the time of the Olympics, and although pop-ups and cocktails were trendy, no-one was doing botanicals – now they're all the rage!" says Lottie. Her new career was born, but being a cocktail gardener isn't necessarily all that it's cracked up to be, "I don't actually drink that much" admits Lottie, "and when I'm designing new cocktails, I have to stay sober so I can remember the recipe, so I just have a few sips and then test drive them on friends." Lucky friends, say we.

Drawing on a lifetime's experience of foraging – her mother was an avid gardener and the family were practically self-sufficient in food – Lottie grew up with the knowledge that hedgerows are full of free food. In London one of her favourite foraging haunts is Walthamstow Marshes, which according to Lottie have an incredible array of food, from walnuts to wild fennel, and wild cherries. "Rich pickings!"

As a professional gardener (she was top of her year at Capel Manor when she studied there), Lottie is well placed to advise would-be cocktail gardeners on the best botanicals to grow in a small London garden. "I would suggest growing things you can't easily buy – chocolate mint, things like jasmine and honeysuckle (which make beautiful syrups), blackcurrant sage and pineapple sage, and then I would grow masses of fennel, and structural plants such as rosemary and lavender. If you don't mind a wilder look, I'd also recommend angelica, lovage and alexanders."

Although many botanicals are Mediterranean plants, with a corresponding love of sunshine and lots of drainage, Londoners who have shady gardens and heavy soil don't have to miss out. For these situations, Lottie has found that "all the different kinds of mints, lemon verbena and lemon balm are quite happy in semi-shade, while Alpine strawberries and sweet woodruff are lovely to look at and really like the shade." Oh, and they make a pretty mean cocktail ingredient too…

Lottie Muir
www.thecocktailgardener.co.uk

Spring Colour in Cannizaro Park

C Cannizaro Park

What was once known as plain old Warren House acquired the altogether more exotic name of Cannizaro House when its then leaseholder inherited the Dukedom of Cannizaro in Sicily in 1832.

While the original 18th-century mansion played host to the great and the good over the years (George III used to breakfast here after military reviews on Wimbledon Common), its residents were, when not entertaining, putting their stamp on the expansive gardens that roll out behind the house. Their efforts were not in vain – the 34-acre park is home to many unusual trees and shrubs and was designated a Grade II* listed Garden of Historic Interest in 1987. Today the house is a privately owned luxury hotel but the park has been open to the public since 1949, having been taken into council ownership in the previous year.

A cherished local resource, the park's lawns, woodlands and distinct garden spaces are a magnet for wildlife, picnickers and strollers (dogs are allowed on leads) and in the summer the area around the Italian Garden vibrates to the sounds of Cannizaro Festival.

Council run, albeit with energetic support from an active Friends organisation, Cannizaro still feels like a private garden, attractively scruffy in places and with a quirky variety of features – from the exuberant Millennium Fountain at the entrance to the gothic style aviary with its population of budgies. Notable statuary within the garden includes a bust of Haile Selassie, located in the Old Tennis Court area, commemorating the Ethiopian Emperor's exile in Wimbledon and a white marble depiction of the goddess Diana with a faun. Remnants of the garden's past can be glimpsed in Lady Jane's Wood, which was planted in 1793 by Viscount Melville to commemorate his marriage, and still forms part of the area known as the Azalea Dell. What is now the Italian Garden was once part of the Old Kitchen Garden, which provided the sociable household with fruit and veg.

Diana and Faun

Newer developments include the rustic-style Water Garden, which was added in the post-war period, and a herb garden, recently installed by the Friends.

Cannizaro comes alive in the spring, when its lush camellias, magnolias, azaleas and rhododendrons erupt into flower – the colourful legacy of Kenneth and Adela Wilson, who owned Cannizaro between the two world wars and who lovingly restored the garden. They planted many of the rare trees and shrubs that Cannizaro is known for, choosing species such as camellia and rhododendrons, which relish the acid soil and free-draining subsoil of the site. In spring the sunken garden near the hotel is jolly with serried ranks of tulips and spring flowers, while autumn colour doesn't disappoint either, courtesy of acers and maples, and other mature broad-leaved trees.

Set up in 1997 to help maintain the garden in the face of dwindling council budgets, the Friends actively care for and improve the gardens and have initiated major replanting in the Azalea Dell, Iris Beds and Water Garden. Some 80 new rhododrendrons were planted in the winter and spring of 2008-09.

Cannizaro Park
West Side Common, Wimbledon, SW19
www.merton.gov.uk   www.cannizaropark.com
Open daily all year
Admission free

C Capel Manor Gardens

Cradled within the noisy embrace of the M25, just off junction 25, Capel Manor is a revelation, a thriving horticultural and animal husbandry college set in 30 acres of inspirational themed gardens. Visitor friendly features such as a restaurant and gift shop, and an animal corner stocked with cuddly alpacas and Shetland ponies make Capel Manor a great destination for family outings – even the family dog can join in the fun (as long as it's on a lead).

Like the Chelsea Flower Show, but without the irritating crowds and TV crews, Capel's imaginative show gardens are the main attraction, with a comprehensive array of different styles and themes to explore. Those with a historical bent should relish the nicely observed period features of the formal 17th-century style garden, the intricate Italianate maze, and the Victorian garden, with its serpentine lines, gazebo and colourful bedding schemes. To add a little perspective to these modern day interpretations it's worth remembering that the Capel Manor estate itself dates back to the 13th century, making the existing Georgian manor house virtually a new build in comparison.

For gardeners in search of inspiration there are plenty of practical garden layouts and ideas to filch – from a low-allergen garden (planted entirely with insect-pollinated plants as opposed to high-allergy wind pollinated ones) to a security conscious family garden complete with a 'police approved' hedge. Of particular relevance to London-based gardeners is the 'terraced house back garden' with its appealing sequence of well-defined spaces maximizing a typically long narrow city plot.

The small gardens of 'Sunflower Street' showcase the talents of seven former Capel Manor College students with styles ranging from minimalist to Mediterranean, via a traditional blowsy cottage style garden. The College enjoys a deservedly high reputation, with graduates often going on to enjoy glittering horticultural careers – popstar-cum-gardening-guru Kim Wilde is one such an alumna and her 'Jungle Gym Garden' here is great fun. Another creation by successful Capel graduates is 'Le Jardin de Vincent' – a beguiling evocation of a sun-soaked Provençal plot that won a medal at Chelsea Flower Show before being rebuilt on a larger scale at Capel.

As with all the best gardens, things don't stand still at Capel and new elements are regularly added. The Old Manor House Garden, with its ersatz 'Elizabethan' ruin, was opened in 2010 with a regal planting scheme celebrating Queens Elizabeth I and II, the latter monarch turning up in person to open the garden to the public. Bringing things up to date, this garden is bordered by a contemporary 'moat' – a state-of-the-art natural swimming pond, which is enjoyed by Capel students on hot days. Other updated features include a redevelopment of the ½-acre Victorian Walled Garden to feature a display of 'instant gardening' as well as an ongoing collaboration between Capel Manor and Robert Mattock Roses that will establish the Walled

Le Jardin de Vincent

Garden as home to a new historical collection of British-bred traditional roses. Another gem here is the aromatic collection of scented pelargoniums in the greenhouse.

The rear of the Walled Garden is earmarked for a display of modern and heritage fruit and veg. In the meantime, visitors with a taste for edible gardens are well-catered for elsewhere with the Thompson & Morgan fruit garden, experimental 'no-dig' vegetable plots, and trial gardens run by *Gardening Which?*.

More esoteric gardens include the meditative 'Growing Together in Faith' garden, which uses a rose motif to highlight the commonality of the four world religions. Built around a well-stocked koi pond, the Japanese Rock Garden offers an interpretation of eastern horticultural aesthetics while the Sensory Garden with its refreshing rill of running water, fragrant plants and easily accessible raised beds makes the point that gardening is for everybody. This philosophy is put into practice with hands-on workshops for physically disabled Enfield residents.

The gardens are divided into three areas for maintenance and with a ready supply of experience-hungry students it's perhaps no surprise to discover that Capel's grounds are beautifully tended, with an abundance of clearly labelled plants to ease identification. As befits a centre of learning, Capel holds several specific plant collections, including salvias, penstemons and the recently expanded National Collection of Sarcococcas. Students are set to work on key seasonal tasks like planting bedding, applying mulches and pruning roses.

Although sited at the outer limits of London, this 30-acre horticultural haven is well worth braving a trek across town and the somewhat lacklustre public transport links at the Enfield end. You may even find yourself signing up for a course...

Capel Manor College & Gardens
Bullsmoor Lane, Enfield, Middlesex, EN1 4RQ
www.capelmanorgardens.co.uk
T: 08456 122 122
See website for opening times and transport links

C   Capital Growth

In a city where allotment spaces are rarer than the proverbial hens' teeth, Capital Growth has conjured and coaxed new fruit and veg growing spaces out of the most unlikely places – on roof tops, in skips, on canal barges as well as in schools and housing estates.

A joint initiative between London Food Link, the Mayor of London, and the Big Lottery's Local Food Fund, the project launched in November 2008 with the aim of creating 2,012 food-growing spaces in London by the end of the Olympic year, 2012. This milestone having been achieved and then some (CG's food growing spaces total currently stands at 2,564), the project runs as a food growing network, offering support and training to GYO-ers in London, as well as organising annual events such as the Big Dig in spring (which sees hundreds of volunteers turning out to help community gardens get ready for the new season), and a Grow Well, Feel Well day in summer which focuses on the well-being benefits of gardening.

Capital Growth hosts many of its training sessions at the allotment garden in Regent's Park, a site which it runs in partnership with The Royal Parks and Capel Manor College (see p.36). This spick-and-span allotment (no tatty sheds or improvised CD bird-scarers here, thank you very much) features smart raised beds, and practical paving slab pathways, and with its array of produce, is an inspiring and informative showcase for the joys of growing your own. The site hosts open days, as well as training sessions on topics as various as understanding the sex life of plants, and on soil life and how to make compost and wormeries. Capital Growth also work closely with community growing projects such as Glengall Wharf Garden in Burgess Park, north Peckham, and Cordwainers Grow in Hackney.

www.capitalgrowth.org

Regent's Park Allotment Garden
Corner of Chester Road & the Inner Circle
Open weekdays 8.30-16.30

Glengall Wharf Garden
54 Glengall Road, SE15 6NF
www.burgessparkfoodproject.org.uk

Cordwainers Grow
www.cordwainersgrow.org.uk

This page & opposite: Glengall Wharf Garden

C Carlyle's House

Clocking in at just 79 x 20 feet (24 x 6 meters), this is a historic garden on a scale that most of us can relate to. Tucked away behind an early 18th-century terraced house, the garden's claim to fame is that it was once tended by Victorian 'celebrity' literary couple Jane and Thomas Carlyle. They moved into 24 Cheyne Row in 1834, spending the rest of their married lives here.

Back in those days, Chelsea was not the pukka postcode it is today and the house provided affordable accommodation, where the 'sage of Chelsea' penned his epic (and today largely unread) historical studies, and the couple received the leading artists and writers of the day.

The marriage was not the most straightforward or happiest of unions but both Jane and Thomas shared a passion for their modest back garden. Responsibilities divided along traditional gender lines: Thomas was keen on vegetable growing and buying tools while Jane was in charge of flowers and nurturing, often introducing cuttings and plants from her native Scotland. One mystery seedling she transplanted turned out to be a gooseberry, another a nettle; their lowly horticultural status did not deter Jane from fussing over them like sickly children.

The couple's letters and journals reveal an ongoing devotion to what they called their 'gardenkin' and both worked enthusiastically to transform the barren patch. Their frustrations and preoccupations are familiar to anyone gardening today – bizarre weather patterns, unresponsive plants, overzealous hired help, and frantic garden tidy-ups before the arrival of visitors. Although Jane lamented that 'Mr C. does not know a myrtle from a nettle', Thomas enjoyed gardening and also liked escaping to the garden to enjoy a quiet smoke. Carlyle was fond of writing in the garden – setting up his table on the lawn, beneath an awning which, pictured in photographs of the time, looks for all the world like the 'sails' favoured by modern garden designers.

Today the garden is tended by custodian Lin Skippings, with additional help from Linda Chinnery, the assistant custodian. The present layout was planned by Anthony Lord in 1980 and includes many features that would have been familiar to the Carlyle's – such as the box-edged borders enclosing the fig and pear tree by the privy, and the rectangular patch of lawn with gravel path skirting around it. Linda and her team garden in the spirit of the Carlyles rather than being strictly historically accurate. A vine and the all-important gooseberry have been reintroduced, while the recent loss of an overbearing walnut tree in the far corner has opened up light and space for a veg patch. In keeping with Mrs Carlyle's fondness for plants with sentimental attachment, Linda has also added bluebells, aquilegia and even a nettle from Jane's childhood garden in Scotland. Also in keeping with historical accuracy is Lin's microscopic budget – a shade over £100 for the year at the time of writing – visitors who bring cuttings and seeds are welcomed!

The borders are probably a little fuller and prettier than they were in the Carlyle's day – the shady border that runs alongside the lawn features popular Victorian plants like ferns and laurel as well as *Geranium phaeum* and climbing hydrangea while on the sunny border opposite a pink rose winds through a trellis. Lighting up the shade beneath the pear tree are woodland stalwarts like dicentra, foxglove, and pulmonaria. In late spring deep pink peonies and purple lilac bloom against the warmth of the far wall. Being walled and near the river, the garden enjoys a warm microclimate but unlike many walled gardens it doesn't – according to Linda – suffer too badly with slugs and snails, which is probably just as well since the garden is run as organically as possible.

Carlyle's House
24 Cheyne Row, SW3 5HL
www.nationaltrust.org.uk
T: 020 7352 7087
Open: Wed-Sun 11.00-17.00 (Mar-Oct)

Carlyle's House Garden

C Centre for Wildlife Gardening

Proving that cities and the natural world need not be mutually exclusive, CWG leads by example, its 0.25ha site in downtown Peckham is full of great ideas for boosting urban biodiversity.

Its collection of demonstration mini-habitats shows that the urban jungle can also be home to wildflower meadows, woodland copses, mini-beast villages, as well as more traditional cottage gardens. Four ponds suitable for gardens big and small are nestled around the site including one making creative use of a recycled bath tub. Taking advantage of these tailor-made environments on their door-step are songbirds, common toads, newts, foxes, endangered invertebrates like stag beetles (for whom London is something of a stronghold), as well as picnicking mums and their hungry broods. Throughout the site use is made of natural materials grown in situ. Fences are woven from osier fresh from the willow bower, hurdles are made from split hazel and logs stand tall as stag beetle loggeries.

Managed by the London Wildlife Trust, the site is a productive one too – vegetables are grown year-round in a cluster of sturdy wooden raised beds while two beehives produce 'Peckham Honey' that is much in demand with local hay fever sufferers. Plants, trees and seed raised on the site can be purchased for modest sums from the on-site nursery and come with useful information about each plant's wildlife garden credentials.

Various community groups engage with the wildlife and growing space on the site, including groups of green-fingered older adults and local family groups with parents and children learning together. A hard-working educational resource, the Centre is popular with school groups and offers hands-on activities like pond-dipping, bush beating, mini-beast hunts as well as open days including 'frog day' in early April. During 'Play Out Days' over the summer children from the local streets run free around the Centre and the Marsden Road is closed to cars for a few hours after school.

The friendly team of volunteers who help run the garden also benefit from a structured programme of on-site training and happily pass their knowledge on to visitors, dispensing tips about how to achieve a chemical-free wildlife garden (including how to deter the wildlife you don't want). Got a slug problem? Try putting down used coffee grounds to deter the little blighters. And as for unwanted foxes, lion dung is apparently the answer. Keeping your soil in good heart is crucial if you want to garden organically and if you're unsure about how to convert your kitchen and garden waste into compost, there's a comparative display of bins to help make your mind up – from no-nonsense 'Daleks' to state-of-the-art wormeries, which are ideal for small-garden households.

At the hub of all this activity is the centre's funky, award-winning visitor centre, which sports an expansive 'living roof', and houses the London Wildlife Trust's Southwark office. The centre is also furnished with some aesthetically pleasing art works, including bollards by Antony Gormley and a pair of intricate, wildlife-themed wrought iron entrance gates by Heather Burrell

Centre for Wildlife Gardening
28 Marsden Road, SE15 4EE
www.wildlondon.org.uk
T: 020 7252 9186

For some it's the first cuckoo, for others it's the evenings drawing out but for many the real harbinger of summer is the Chelsea Flower Show. Every May this well-heeled corner of London goes gardening mad as the RHS's premier show takes over the grounds of the Royal Hospital, transforming them beyond recognition with stunning 'instant' gardens, floral marquees and retail opportunities by the barrow load. Even the shops on Sloane Street and the King's Road get into the spirit of things with extravagant floral themed store fronts (see p.50).

The show gardens and the famous Floral Pavilion are the big crowd pleasers here, showcasing the skills of designers and plantspeople from Britain and around the world. The horticultural equivalent of an haute couture catwalk, Chelsea is the place to spot the hottest trends, from eco-chic to vertical planting, before they filter down to the mass market.

The show gardens are the work of some of the biggest names in international garden design and

the mega-bucks fantasy gardens they create for Chelsea seem to spring up as if from nowhere, belying months, if not years, of preparation. Incredibly, most of them look as if they've been in-situ forever. Newly introduced in 2012, the Fresh show garden category replaced the Urban Gardens of previous years and promises innovative, cutting-edge gardens, with designers being freed from some of Chelsea's usual judging restrictions. By contrast, the Artisan Garden category puts the emphasis on natural, sustainably sourced materials and traditional craftsmanship.

Whatever the category of show garden (and these are subject to change from time to time), the free planting plans that are dished out at every turn are worth picking up for their take-home design ideas and plant lists. And for those whose idea of gardening is more spectator than contact sport, there are always of plenty of inviting 'garden structures', from humble shed to trendy 'pod'.

Heavily covered on television by the BBC, Chelsea is insanely popular – be prepared to wade your way through heavy crowds with a holiday atmosphere. Some 157,000 visitors come to the CFS every year, so expect to queue, or stand on tip-toe, to see some exhibits. Like the Wimbledon tennis tournament, you probably actually get to see more of the show gardens on the box than you do in real life, but it's a different story inside the Great Pavilion. This wonderfully scented arena is the place to admire expertly staged plants at close quarters, many of them blooming unseasonably early, and to meet some of the nurserymen and women who coax perfection from flora as various as pelargoniums, dahlias, sweet peas and roses. Some well-known nurseries such as Kelways, Notcutts and Avon Bulbs have been coming to Chelsea for years and the floral pavilion is a testament to their horticultural prowess. Exhibitors are usually very approachable and happy to answer questions. The talent is not all home-grown, and displays from further afield – the Cayman Islands, Bermuda, South Africa – overflow with exotic plants. Here, as with the show gardens, exhibitors vie with each other for a coveted RHS medal (either bronze, silver, silver-gilt or gold), awarded by a panel of eagle-eyed judges.

Although on a smaller scale to the Great Pavilion, the Floral Design Marquee can be an equally intense experience. Over 150 NAFAS (National Association of Flower Arranging Societies), individuals and groups compete to create the ultimate floral arrangement. The resulting inventive, intricate floral creations are always worth seeing, as the queues suggest, and are likely to make those whose normal approach to floristry is plonking a bunch of blooms in a vase of water feel rather inadequate.

Retail opportunities, needless to say, are never far away. If you haven't blown the budget on a Pimms and a sandwich (quite possible at Chelsea), then head for the stalls ranged in the shade of the London plane trees on Eastern Avenue. This is your opportunity to stock up on all manner of goodies, from upmarket gardening attire to the latest pruning gizmo or all-singing-and-dancing water features, or even a work of art. The legendary plant sell-off at the end of the last day has something of the Harrods' sale about it, but there are some amazing specimens to be had if you can beat off the competition and find a way to transport your prize home safely.

Chelsea Flower Show Royal Hospital Road, SW3
www.rhs.org.uk

C Chelsea in Bloom

Whatever the fickle finger of fashion might be dictating, florals are always à la mode in Chelsea, in May at any rate. While the grounds of the Royal Hospital are given over to the horticultural haute couture of Chelsea Flower Show, the high-end shop fronts of Sloane Square and environs are likewise transformed, with fun and fabulous displays of floral art.

There's a different theme each year (2016 was 'Carnival') and over 30 retailers usually take part in the competition, which is organised by the Cadogan Estate in association with the RHS. Whatever the theme, colour, glamour and pizzazz are the order of the day and retailers vie with each to produce the most stunning display. The arrangements are scrutinised by an expert panel of judges, with various categories being awarded, including 'Best Floral Display', an 'Innovation' Award, along with the usual gold, silver and bronze.

Floral foot soldiers can embark on a self-guided tour of participating stores by picking up a map from the Chelsea in Bloom Information Point in Sloane Square, or consulting the website, but the fashion-forward floristry can also be savoured from the comfort (or otherwise) of a complimentary rickshaw tour. The website also has details of other floral themed events, pop-up bars and special menus designed to compliment the event, and this is where you can also cast your vote for the 'People's Champion Award'.

www.chelseainbloom.co.uk

This page: Robert Bradford, *Flower Poodle*, 2016
Opposite page: *Bonsai Kai* at Fenton House

C Chelsea Fringe

Timed to coincide and overlap with the Chelsea Flower Show, the Chelsea Fringe bills itself as the 'alternative gardening festival' and since its inaugural edition in 2012 has unleashed a heady mix of horticultural happenings across the capital, and beyond.

Founded by the garden writer and journalist Tim Richardson, the festival is completely independent of the RHS Chelsea Flower Show and its freewheeling, creativity-on-a-shoestring ethos is a world away from the megabucks show gardens and corporate sponsorship that characterises Chelsea. It's street gardening as opposed to haute-couture horticulture – there's room for both, of course, but the speed with which the Fringe has grown shows that there's a huge appetite for a more inclusive, dressed-down style of gardening.

'It's a true fringe festival', explains Tim, 'events are not curated and as long as it's legal, on topic (ie about gardens, plants and landscapes), and above all, interesting, it's in!' A community interest company run by volunteers, the Fringe is entirely in the spirit of the contemporary gardening scene in London, embracing everything from grass roots community garden projects to avant-garde art installations, and work by horticultural professionals as well as enthusiasts. Events are usually free to enter and there is no such thing as a typical Chelsea Fringe event, in fact 'the quirkier, the better', says Tim. In 2016, the fifth anniversary of the Fringe, the programme included a vegetable puppet theatre, pop-up crate gardens, weed walks in Camden Town, knitted landscapes, botanical dye workshops, topiary master-classes and a floating garden.

And it's no 'little Londoner' either – from very early on the Fringe has been a festival without frontiers, inspiring other cities in the UK and across the globe to get involved. Bristol, Brighton and Kent were early adopters, but cities as far afield as Vienna, Ljubljana, Melbourne and Nagoya have all discovered the fun of the Fringe and embraced Londoners' 'can-do' approach to conjuring beautiful community gardens out of previously unloved spaces. Event registration is open right up until the end of the two week festival, meaning that the best way to keep track of the ever-evolving Chelsea Fringe is via its website.

www.chelseafringe.com

Tim Richardson

Archimedes had his bright idea lying in the bath, Tim Richardson, the man behind the Chelsea Fringe, didn't even get out of bed. The idea came to him fully formed early one morning during Chelsea Flower Show week; a year later the first Chelsea Fringe was born. Hailed as 'the fastest growing fringe festival ever' by the World Fringe Festival Network, the Fringe instantly captured the imaginations of London's free-spirited community and guerrilla gardeners and the festival has grown from 100 events in the first year to over 350 in 2015.

During the festival Tim goes to as many events as he can ("I love it, there are new things every year"). The best events, he has noticed, are those which involve "an intense moment", the chance to connect with other people and learn new skills, be it dry-stone walling, exploring the herbal history of Southwark or making a botanical cocktail. It's an observation that chimes with the Fringe's own mantra: "It's all about the gardeners, not the gardens".

Tim even came up with the idea for a choir of gardeners so he can take part in the Fringe himself. 'The Diggers' are led by choirmaster Wendy Lanchin and their number also includes Inner Temple gardeners Andrea Brunsendorf and Amanda Dennis. They take their cue from Gerrard Winstanley's 17th-century guerrilla gardening movement, whose anti-establishment 'Diggers' Song' is part of their repertoire, along with other 'on-topic' radical gardening tunes such as 'Jolly Ploughboys'.

For all the fun and festive atmosphere of the Chelsea Fringe, there is a serious purpose underlying the festival. "It's all about expanding the remit of gardening", says Tim, "and harnessing the power of gardens to enhance communities, improve the environment and transform people's lives. After all, everyone likes to see a garden."

Tim Richardson

"It's all about expanding the remit of gardening and harnessing the power of gardens to enhance communities"

Clockwise from top left: Paper making with artist Lucy Baxandall using native plants, Horticultural installation artists Heywood & Condie's Greenhouse, Dalston Curve Garden, Scented Shells at the Town House, Spitalfields

Statue of Sir Hans Sloane

London's historic gardens don't come more venerable than this, the Chelsea Physic Garden. Occupying a 3.8 acre site of prime Chelsea riverside, the CPG has been cultivating plants here since its foundation in 1673, when the Society of Apothecaries needed somewhere handy to park their state barge and a place where they could grow and study medicinal plants.

Today, this jewel of a botanic garden remains a centre for horticultural research and conservation as well as a living showcase for the amazing medicinal resource that is the plant world. It's a great place to unwind too – a gentle stroll around its tranquil paths makes the perfect counterpoint to a hectic shopping spree on the King's Road.

With over 300 years of experience behind it, the CPG effortlessly combines beauty with educational purpose and contains several themed areas to explore. The Garden of Medicinal Plants opened in 2014 and guides visitors on a health-conscious journey around the world, via some 500 plant species. Designed by Head Gardener Nick Bailey, this neatly ordered garden is the place to discover the monastic origins of the *officinalis* suffix attached to so many healing plants, to learn how the pyramid builders of ancient Egypt fought infections (by eating garlic, since you ask) and to compare different cultural approaches to plant based medicine, from Oceania to Asia, Europe and the Americas.

It's fascinating to see familiar garden plants in a new light – be it *Sedum spectabile* as a decoction for sore throats (in Chinese medicine), *Echinacea purpurea* as an American snakebite treatment, or *Artemesia afra* as a tonic for gastro-intestinal complaints (Zulu and Xhosa tribes, Africa). But before the urge to self-medicate takes hold, there are also some stark reminders of the plant world's power to harm as well as heal; the label that accompanies *Berberis vulgaris*, which has been used as a diuretic in Indian medicine, contains a stern health warning: 'deaths have been recorded'. The ethno-botanical beds are complemented by a pharmaceutical garden, featuring plants that yield therapeutic compounds

of proven value in modern medicine. These beds include plants such as *Filipendula ulmaria*, *Ephedra altissima* and *Taxus baccata*, and highlight respectively their role in alleviating pain, treating ear, nose and throat conditions, and assisting the fight against cancer.

But it's not just medicines that plants provide for us. The Garden of Edible and Useful Plants reveals the extent to which we rely on plants for every aspect of our lives: from foods to building materials, clothing and cleaning to arts and ritual. It includes an intriguing and beautiful amphitheatre of plants used in perfumery and aromatherapy, including the gorgeously scented *Pelargonium odoratissimum* and *Rosa centifolia*, the source of attar of roses.

The latest addition to the CPG, the World Woodland Garden, opened in 2015 and introduced 150 new plants into the garden to explore the longstanding debt (both medicinal and in other spheres of life) that we owe to plants from forest environments. Divided into three distinct geographic regions, the planting here demonstrates traditional and modern uses of plants from North American woodlands, Europe and East Asia respectively.

To the south of the garden Fortune's Tank Pond is a focus for the CPG's teeming wildlife – water boatmen, damselflies, newts and leeches. During the summer

it is surrounded by a mini wildflower meadow of British native species such as *Centaurea cyanus* (cornflower) – and a popular port of call with the Garden's bee population. Their hives can be seen in the Mediterranean woodland area and the honey can be purchased in the shop (subject to availability).

Over on the western side of the garden, the Historical Walk recounts the story of the CPG through the plants introduced by some of its key players. This amounts to a roll call of some of the biggest names in gardening history, including explorer and naturalist Sir Joseph Banks, William Forsyth (who gave his name to Forsythia) and the 19th-century plant hunter Robert Fortune, who introduced tea production to India from China. A statue of another major figure in the CPG is given pride of place, slap bang in the centre of the garden – Sir Hans Sloane (1660-1753), the great physician, scientist and collector. Sloane ensured the survival of the CPG when he granted the Apothecaries a

lease on the site for an annual rent of £5 – on the proviso that the garden was kept in perpetuity as a 'physic garden'. The peppercorn rent is still paid to his descendants. Sloane's collections went on to form the basis of the British Museum and later the Natural History Museum, but he is also remembered (with gratitude) for bringing the first recipe for milk chocolate to these shores.

Blessed with a free-draining soil that most London gardeners can only dream of, a southerly aspect and a balmy microclimate, the garden is home to many unusual, tender and endangered species. The largest outdoor-grown olive tree in Britain is found here, while the beds just inside the Swan Walk entrance are devoted to tender plants from the Canary Islands, such as the rare *Echium wildpretii*, whose native habitat is atop a volcano in Tenerife. Protected by a fleece in winter, this exotic border really kicks off in June, when the 8ft (2.4m) blue flower spikes of *Echium pinniana* are in full bloom.

Glasshouses have been a feature of the garden since its earliest days, and today the greenhouses of the Tropical Corridor house spectacular south American orchids and tender rarities such as *Brighamia insignis,* a native of Hawaii. Fashioned from an unlikely combination of Icelandic lava and stone from the Tower of London, the 18th-century rock garden is possibly the earliest of its kind in Europe and is the backdrop to a collection of Cretan plants including *Petromarula pinnata (*Wall Lettuce).

Seasonal changes make this a garden to return to time and again – from bud burst to leaf drop. The serried ranks of specimens displayed in the old-fashioned plant 'theatre' encapsulate this progression with plants as diverse as snowdrops and chillies, depending on the time of year. Annual membership buys various privileges, chief amongst them year-round access to the garden (the general public are usually only allowed in April-October). And although children are limited to two per accompanying adult,

there's plenty for budding young gardeners to enjoy within the CPG walls, with points of interest including sinister-looking carnivorous plants, mysterious mandrakes and delicious dinosaur fodder in the Cool Fernery. Lectures and the ever-popular compost clinics offer more grown-up appeal but the CPG is not all about education – there are leisure opportunities aplenty. On warm summer days the lawn is filled with languid, Chelsea picnickers while the in-house café serves top-notch home-cooked light lunches and teas whatever the weather. The well-stocked shop is full of good books, rich smells and gardening goodies – seeds, soaps, plants and preserves, as well as the odd useful implement.

The Chelsea Physic Garden
Swan Walk, SW3 4HS
www.chelseaphysicgarden.co.uk
T: 020 7352 5646
Open: April-October (dates vary from year to year);
Tues-Fri, Sun & Public Holidays 11.00-18.00

A view of the Exedra taken from inside Chiswick House

Popular with local dog walkers (who even have their own association, the wittily named CHOW), the 65 acres of gardens of Chiswick House are also revered as the birthplace of the English Landscape Garden. It was here in the 1720's and 1730's that, working alongside the architect-owner of Chiswick House Lord Burlington, William Kent pioneered the 'picturesque' garden, creating playful, Arcadian vistas after the manner of Poussin and Claude's landscape paintings. Although subsequent residents of Lord Burlington's neo-Palladian villa also put their stamp on the terrain, many of Kent and Burlington's innovations have survived and are looking better than they have for a long while, thanks to a multi-million pound restoration completed in 2010.

Classical references abound: Kent and Burlington had met on the Grand Tour and enthusiastically set about recreating what they had seen in Italy at Chiswick. A Doric column (today surmounted by a freshly carved Venus de Medici) rises majestically from the rose garden. An equally emphatic obelisk spikes the circular pond at the heart of the Orange Tree Garden, itself overseen by a dinky Ionic temple. The Exedra, a semi-circular yew hedge at the rear of the house, is punctuated with niches filled with Roman statues and classical urns, while strategically placed sphinxes and lions patrol the area like latter day guard dogs.

Burlington looked to ancient Roman precedents in the garden's layout too, using a device known as a 'patte d'oie' (goose-foot) to create trios of avenues radiating out from a central hub, each spoke terminating in an eye-catching feature such as the quaint Rustic House. Renaissance gardens provided the inspiration for the Cascade, Burlington's last major work at Chiswick. This tumbling waterfall, at one end of the serpentine River, never worked properly in Burlington's time but modern technology has finally overcome the centuries' old teething problems and today water gushes dramatically down the rocky descent. The graceful balustraded stone bridge which arches over the River is actually a canalised

stream, formerly known as the Bollo Brook. It post-dates Burlington's time, having been installed by the 5th Duke of Devonshire in 1774, but is a perfect focal point, forming the shared terminus of two interlinking patte d'oies.

One of the most mutable art forms, gardens by their very nature never stand still. Luckily for us Lord Burlington was so proud of his creation at Chiswick that he commissioned a set of eight paintings by Pieter Rysbrack. These views – reunited finally after their dispersal in the 1950s – are displayed inside the house and offer a fascinating picture of Kent and Burlington's gardens in the early 18th century, with their painterly arrangements of allées, woodland and classical ornament. A major resource for the restoration team, the paintings also record features that have been lost, including various garden buildings designed by Burlington and the estate's original Jacobean manor house.

Despite their historic significance, the gardens slid into decline in the 20th century, having become a much loved but rather neglected public park in the late 1920s. Ever dwindling local authority budgets meant that whilst hedges and lawns were cut, Chiswick's carefully designed woodland glades grew dense with self-sown trees and shrubs, Kent's artful vistas became distorted and the footfall of over one million visitors a year took its toll on pathways and lawns. In 2005 the independent Chiswick House and Gardens Trust was set up to oversee the £12.1 million restoration, which would respect the key elements of Kent and Burlington's work whilst embracing the wider history of the gardens and their contemporary role as a recreational space for locals and visitors.

Today the gardens are well on the way to recovery. A campaign of tree felling has been balanced by the planting of new specimens in areas such as the Grove, the Northern Wilderness and the Camellia Shrubbery. The Western Lawn – now liberated from its municipal clutter of rubbish bins, railings and random benches – once again sweeps expansively down from the house to the river; roses bloom in the Rosary as they did in the 19th century, and the amous octet of Cedars of Lebanon in the forecourt have been renewed with young specimens, propagated from the surviving originals.

Once deemed unsafe for the general public, the Grade I listed Conservatory – designed by Samuel Ware for the 6th Duke of Devonshire in 1813 – has been comprehensively repaired and conserved. Its historic and rare collection of camellias is celebrated in an annual Camellia Show, held each spring (see p.327). A precursor of the great glass structures of Kew and Chatsworth, the Conservatory has a further claim to fame in being one of the locations (along with the Exedra) used in The Beatles, 1966 'Paperback Writer' pop promo. The 96 metre long glass structure looks out over the manicured, geometric flower-beds of the Italian Garden, which was laid out in 1812 by Lewis Kennedy and has likewise been restored to its Regency pomp.

The walled garden that lies behind the Conservatory originally served as the kitchen garden to nearby Moreton Hall and was purchased by the 6th Duke in 1812. Now once again operating as a productive space for fruit and vegetable growing, it is used for community gardening projects and is open to the public on selected days.

Thankfully, the unique ambience of the house and garden has survived the restoration. Built as a party pad-cum-art gallery by Lord Burlington, Chiswick House has been the scene of some memorable parties over the centuries, hosting Tsars, Shahs and any number of British royals and aristos, and it is still a fun place to visit. The laid-back atmosphere can best be absorbed over coffee and cake in the award-winning café designed by Caruso St John; energetic youngsters can burn off excess energy in the adjacent play area while their elders can conserve theirs in comfort. A dog-friendly destination since Lord B's day, the garden features all manner of pooches on parade and hosts a popular annual dog show, complete with celebrity judges. If the season and weather permit, visitors might want to watch a cricket match, play a game of tennis, catch an outdoor movie screening or perhaps enjoy a picnic on the refurbished (dog-free) Wilderness Lawn.

Writing to Lord Burlington in 1731, apropos of his architectural interests and projects, the poet Alexander Pope advised the earl to 'Consult the genius of the place in all'. Like Kent and Burlington before them, the restoration team at Chiswick have clearly taken this advice to heart and their work here has triumphantly revived one of Britain's most iconic gardens, whilst sympathetically equipping it for the demands of a 21st century public.

Chiswick House & Gardens
Burlington Lane, W4 2RP
chgt.org.uk
T. 020 8742 3905

Chiswick House
Open March-Oct, Sun-Wed & Bank Hols
10.00-18.00 (17.00 March & Oct)
There is a charge for admission to the house.
English Heritage & National Art Pass members free

Gardens
Open daily from 7.00-dusk
Free entry

Conservatory
Open daily from 10.00-16.00
Free entry

Annual Camellia Show – Spring

The restored rosary & Doric column,
Chiswick House

C City Gardens

There's more to the City than fat cat bankers and shiny office blocks. Built up as it is, the Square Mile is also home to a quirky collection of gardens, planted highways, churchyards and burial grounds.

Although most of the gardens themselves are post WWII creations, history is unavoidable in London's most ancient quarter, with sites incorporating everything from Roman remains to plague pits alongside the latest in contemporary architecture.

Most of the City's 200 open spaces are managed by the Corporation of London, with biodiversity high on the agenda. Wildlife friendly initiatives include insect hotels, bird and bat boxes, green roofs, nectar rich planting, and the use of pheromone traps instead of chemical pesticides. It's a strategy that seems to be working because in recent years the City has become a habitat for rare species such as the Peregrine Falcon and is a stronghold for the country's Black Redstart population. The Barbican Estate is home to a healthy population of the once common but now endangered house sparrow while strategically placed log piles have been created in gardens such as Finsbury Circus, in the hope of enticing stag beetles into the City.

City gardens flourish in the face of considerable adversity. The air is polluted and the soil is poor, compacted and of limited depth – beneath its scanty surface runs a Swiss cheese labyrinth of communications cables, power lines, sewers, railway lines, cellars and basements, not to mention burial sites and archaeological remains. Although there's a toasty microclimate that favours exotic species, some native plants resent the generally dry conditions, while the City's tall buildings create destructive wind tunnels and vortexes. One third of the City has been redeveloped in the past 30 years, and this relentless change causes its own problems too, particularly for trees, which need time to mature and which are susceptible to damage or removal by reckless contractors.

But its not all doom and gloom; over the past three decades the number of green spaces in the City has increased tenfold as all new building developments have to show an environmental gain. It also helps that the City's open spaces are protected by their own Acts of Parliament and that over £1.5 million a year is lavished on their upkeep. A walk around the City quickly confirms that its well-used and much-loved gardens are as much a part of its identity as chalk stripe suits, and telephone number salaries.

The Gardener statue by Karin Jonzen, Brewers' Hall Garden

City Gardens Map

Carter Lane Gardens

Hard by the funky folded-metal structure that is the City Information Centre, Carter Lane Gardens makes a good start point for a garden themed walk through the City of London. The gardens were re-landscaped in 2009 with an eco-minded scheme of orderly evergreen hedges, accompanied by swathes of bee-friendly and drought tolerant lavender and *Gaura lindheimeri*. With benches and closely cropped lawns for lounging on, it's tempting to linger, but other treasures await…

St Paul's Churchyard

The garden here was first laid out as an Open Space in 1878 and combines the burial grounds of the various churches that have occupied this area over the centuries (St Paul's, St Gregory by St Paul's and St Faith the Virgin under St Paul's). Today the garden comprises a formal rose garden, planted in 1976, grassed areas and mature trees, with benches and a few venerable tombs. This being St Paul's Cathedral the garden hardware is a cut above, and includes rare early 18th-century iron railings, the 19th-century St Paul's Cross and a memorial to Londoners killed in WWII. The statue of John Wesley is always accompanied by a red and white planting scheme, the traditional colours of the Methodist movement. The tree population features a weeping mulberry in the North garden, two *Ginkgo biloba* trees and several walnut trees (with attendant squirrels).

Festival Gardens

Built on the site of the 13th-century thoroughfare, Old Change, this formal sunken garden was designed by the classically inclined architect Sir Albert Richardson to celebrate the 1951 Festival of Britain. Like so many City gardens it occupied land cleared courtesy of the Luftwaffe ten years previously and the garden follows the footprint of the Livery Hall that stood on the site until 1941. The garden is enclosed on three sides by pleached limes and has recently been renovated – its Portland stone fountain scrubbed clean and its newly laid lawn made fully accessible to the public for the first time with additional benches also part of the new spec.

25 Cannon Street Garden

Although you would never guess it, this elegant ½ acre garden sits atop an underground car park and is officially classed as a roof garden. Its central space is a crisp oval lawn, smartly mown with business-like stripes, which is offset by a predominantly green and white planting scheme in the surrounding borders. Good use is made of foliage plants such as fatsia, magnolia and rhododendrons, which are underplanted with numerous bulbs and lilies of the valley.

Cleary Garden

This hillside garden has a rich history having been a Roman bathhouse, a piggery, a medieval vineyard and a newspaper print works. In 1940 the latter was destroyed, and the resulting bomb site was turned into a garden by Joseph Brandis, a shoemaker, who used mud from the Thames and soil and plants from his home in Walthamstow to effect the garden's transformation.

A visit from the then Queen in 1949, and its position above a section of the District Line, assured the makeshift garden's survival. In 1982 it was comprehensively redesigned to commemorate the centenary of the Metropolitan Parks and Gardens Association and named in honour of one of the Association's movers and shakers, Fred Cleary. Following a further overhaul in 2007 the garden has returned to its vintner's roots, with the addition of vines from the Loire Valley. Arranged over three levels the garden descends, via a sturdy brick and timber pergola, to a lawn, beneath which lie the remains of the Roman baths. The pergola is festooned with roses, wisteria and clematis and on street level is accompanied by a bed of peonies, gifted by the Shimane prefecture in Japan. The planting is beefed up by some fabulous trees, including *Taxodium ascendens* (pond cypress), *Metasequoia glyptostroboides* (dawn redwood) and the drought-loving *Pinus strobus* (eastern white pine). Benches cater for human visitors while an insect hotel and bird boxes help the City's wildlife.

Carter Lane Gardens

Cleary Garden

St Paul's Cathedral Churchyard

Festival Gardens

Christchurch Greyfriars Garden

Postman's Park

Brewers' Hall Garden

Aldermanbury Square

Christchurch Greyfriars Garden

This pretty garden, laid out within the walls of a ruined Wren church (itself built on the site of the medieval Franciscan church of Greyfriars) has recently been replanted as a cottage garden, although some roses from its previous incarnation as a rosary remain. The ten wooden towers, home to adventuresome clematis and assorted bird boxes, represent the pillars of the nave whose footings can still be glimpsed amongst the wildlife-friendly mounds of gaura, lady's mantle, agapanthus, heuchera, geranium and catmint. Although reputedly haunted by two highborn murderesses, the site is relatively tranquil today, with visitors more likely to be disturbed by passing traffic than any paranormal activity.

Postman's Park

Not quite the 'hidden London' find it once was, thanks to the film of Patrick Marber's *Closer*, in which the park features in several key scenes, but a historic and interesting City garden nonetheless. The site became a public garden in 1880 and was much beloved of local postal workers but, as the gravestones dotted about suggest, it was once a churchyard. The tiled panels of the memorial wall by GF Watts record heart-rending acts of bravery by ordinary people – the latest addition dates from 2007. Being dark and shady it's a difficult spot to garden, but an eclectic collection of plants thrives here, including tree ferns and bananas and the City's only publically accessible horse chestnut tree. Seasonal highlights are delivered by snake's head fritillaries, Japanese anemones and, in June, the dazzling white bracts of the handkerchief tree, *Davidia involucrata*.

St Mary Staining

This simply laid out garden is sited on a former burial ground and surrounded on three sides by buildings designed by the 'big three' of contemporary British architecture: Richard Rogers, Nicholas Grimshaw and Norman Forster. The curving and sloping façade of the latter's building is a result of the architect having to accommodate an existing plane tree, protected by a preservation order.

Monkwell Square

Part of the surrounding development, designed by Terry Farrell in the 1980s, this small garden has a strong personality. Essentially a large brick and stone raised bed, with matching balusters and stone obelisks, it is boldly planted with mophead hydrangea, broad leaf trees in each corner, and a double avenue of yew topiary cones with a strip of lawn at either side. A number of 'Flowers in the City' plaques attest to its popularity.

Aldermanbury Square

Not a garden in the conventional sense, but its cool, contemporary use of trees, grasses and hard landscaping is worth a look. The current layout dates from 2006, when traffic was excluded from the square. It features a grove of 14 hugely expensive 'table-pruned' London planes along one side, beneath which bubble water features placed in the sleek granite paving. On the opposite side, silver birch trees are under-planted with alliums and grasses, whose seeds provide food for birds. Part-funded by a nearby development project, the square exudes quality, right down to its stylish scattering of wooden chairs and its memorial to the Millennium, a standing stone inscribed by David Kindersley.

Brewers' Hall Garden

Just off Aldermanbury Square, this street-side garden consists of three brick-built raised beds, planted with resilient perennials like ladies' mantle, bergenia and periwinkle and evergreen shrubs such as sarcococca. A statue by Karin Jonzen depicting a gardener at work illustrates why bad backs and knees are a common complaint among horticulturalists.

St Mary Aldermanbury

A peaceful garden with three distinct areas, standing on the former site of the church and churchyard of the same name. The Wren church, which replaced a 15th-century predecessor, was damaged in the Blitz and subsequently relocated to Fulton, Missouri as a memorial to Winston Churchill (he made his famous 'Iron Curtain' speech in Fulton). The swamp cypress at the far end of the garden was given by Fulton in return for the church.

Remnants of the medieval church remain within the garden, and the lawn is studded with the footings of the columns that once defined the nave. The church has no shortage of historical associations – the infamous Judge Jefferies was buried here, and it was in this parish that John Heminges and Henry Condell, Shakespeare's first publishers, worshipped. A memorial, topped by a bronze bust of the Bard, reminds us of the debt we owe these 'heroes of the First Folio'. This stands as the centrepiece of a raised, paved seating area, with drought-tolerant planting, in what was once the churchyard. A pretty knot garden completes the trio of gardens.

St Lawrence Jewry

An awkward corner site outside the Corporation of London's official church – a Wren creation extensively rebuilt following war damage. It has been ingeniously transformed into a water garden. The pond is planted with water lilies, irises and bulrushes and is home to a large resident carp. Blocks of evergreen hedging tactfully indicate the garden's street boundary.

Girdlers' Hall Space

Although the Girdler's Company is in possession of an award-winning walled private garden behind their classically styled livery hall, it's the open space in front of it that will perhaps be more appreciated by workers in search of somewhere to enjoy their lunchtime sandwich. Owned by the Corporation of London, the site, at the intersection of Basinghall Avenue and Coleman Street, is a lovely example of their 'green corners' policy with its crisp arrangement of parallel lines of box hedging, interplanted with soft, billowy grasses, ferns and acanthus, multi-stemmed trees, and possibly the lushest stretch of lawn in EC2. Seating for weary City folk takes the form of granite blocks or more forgiving wooden benches and chairs. From here the doll's house like proportions of the Girdlers' Hall can be admired, against the backdrop of City Tower, which looms in the distance.

St Dunstan in the East

St Dunstan in the East

Contained within the ruined stone walls of St Dunstan in the East, this romantic and pleasantly melancholic garden was opened to the public in 1971 and it remains a popular sanctuary for those in search of a bit of p&q amid the hubbub of the City, even at close of play on a Friday afternoon when the City's drinking holes begin to fill up. Like so many churches in the City, St Dunstan's was a double victim of the Fire of London and the Blitz, but the tower and steeple by Sir Christopher Wren survive, along with the walls and window tracery, through which climbers meander in search of the sun. As befits a garden of this age, mature trees add further character to the scene; specimens include acer and Japanese zelkova, with several palm trees injecting an exotic air.

The recently renovated planting scheme is in restful green and white, and features deliciously fragrant philadelphus, white hydrangea, hebes and hostas, with stands of white peace lily. A soothing water feature plays in the centre of the garden, which is well-provisioned with wooden benches, and a neatly mown lawn perfect for lounging. A collection of massive lead planters, smartly embossed with the Corporation of London's coat of arms, are prettily planted with seasonal colour.

CAMDEN GARDEN CENTRE

Bursting with inspiration!

CAMDEN GARDEN CENTRE is an unusual, award winning Garden Centre. We not only supply quality plants and gardening products and give expert guidance and customer advice but we are also a charitable organisation offering employment, training and educational opportunities and donate funds to our parent charity.

Our training scheme has been tremendously successful since we opened in 1982 and has helped more than 300 trainees from a variety of backgrounds. Many of our trainees have gone on to set up their own successful businesses.

Winner
GardenRetail
AWARDS
2012
2006
2002

OPENING HOURS:
April-Sept: Mon-Sat 9am to 5.30pm, Sun 11am to 5pm
Oct-March: Mon-Sat 9am to 5pm, Sun 10am to 4pm

2 Barker Drive, St Pancras Way, London NW1 0JW
T: 0207 387 7080 www.camdengardencentre.co.uk

C Clifton Nurseries

Whether you're commissioning a bespoke garden for your house or just after a pot of basil for your kitchen windowsill, Clifton Nurseries have got all the angles covered.

Hidden behind the blandly elegant white stucco houses of Little Venice, the nursery is a haven for horticultural shoppers, offering a comprehensive portfolio of services – from irrigation systems to 'Assisted DIY' garden maintenance, flower arrangements and even a plant storage facility (for when you've got the builders in). And it's no johnny-come-lately either, tracing its origins as a 'nursery ground' as far back as 1851; its enterprising owner in the late 1800s did a roaring trade hiring plants out to London's hotels, theatres and, later,

film studios. However by the late 1970s Clifton was facing an uncertain future until Lord Jacob Rothschild bought the nursery in 1979. Since then the nurseries' historic premises have been graced by an award-winning shop building (designed by Jeremy Dixon) and a new Palm House, built in the spirit of a predecessor on the site. In recent years the nursery's horticultural expertise has also been awarded five Gold Medals from Chelsea Flower Show (see p.46).

For all the impressive architecture, this is still a great place to buy plants – the Palm House is home to an eclectic stock of indoor plants including fragrant gardenia, jungly palms and ferns, cacti and carnivorous plants as well as some flamboyant

imitation blooms. Outside, the main plant display area caters for city gardeners with grasses and evergreens, topiary, seasonal herbaceous plants, bulbs and herbs. If they don't have what you're looking for, the nursery can order it for you and also offer advice on the right plant for the right place.

In summer the glass-topped arcade that extends out from the palm house shelters a colourful mass of bedding plants, including deluxe hanging baskets, and is also home to a luxuriant grape vine, whose edible fruits dangle temptingly at harvest time. For those in search of containers, there's a comprehensive selection of pots from sturdy frost-proof salt-glazed ceramics to classic wooden Versailles planters and trendy zinc tubs. Lifestyle

needs are further addressed in the shop, which deals with the furnishings, cushions and candles side of gardening, as well as nitty-gritty gardeners' fare like composts, tomato feed, tools and seeds. An on-site café with outside seating completes the set up.

Clifton Nurseries
5A Clifton Villas, Little Venice, W9 2PH
www.clifton.co.uk   T: 020 7289 6851
Open: Mon-Sat 9.00-18.00 (Apr-Oct),
Mon-Sat 8.30 to 17.30 (Nov-Mar),
every Sun (except Easter) 11.00-17.00

Cloistered away next to the historic Priory Church of St John, this fragrant garden is part of the Museum of the Order of St John, which tells the 900 year-old story of the Knights of St John. As members of an Order of the church, the Knights also had medical and military roles, setting up hospitals in the Holy Land and Europe, while fighting in defence of Christendom. Today, the modern Order of St John is best known for establishing the St John Ambulance.

The garden's planting scheme was devised by London-based designer Alison Wear, to fit in around the existing hard-landscaping, and is packed with references to the Order's long peregrination around Europe, with silver-leaved Mediterranean sun-seekers like *Phlomis fruticosa* (Jerusalem sage) and medicinal herbs such as *Hypericum calycinum* (St John's Wort), *Lychnis chalcedonica* (Maltese or Jerusalem cross), and a white rose, *Rosa* 'St John'. Aromatic herbs such as wormwood, thyme, oregano, fennel and lavender, further recall the Knights' medical endeavours, while creating a soothingly aromatic environment for the visitor.

Working within the constraints of the layout, Alison designed for colour and texture rather than harmony or sophistication, using citrus and olive trees in strategically placed tubs to break up the formal setting. Winter interest is provided by aromatic evergreens such as *Daphne odora*, bay and box. When it came to planting in April 2011, Alison found that the soil was "nothing but dust", so an 'enormous amount' of compost and manure was applied to the narrow beds. The strategy is working and with museum staff undertaking to water the fledgling plants in the absence of an irrigation system, the garden already appears remarkably well-established.

Museum of the Order of St John
St John's Gate, St John's Lane, EC1M 4DA
www.museumstjohn.org.uk   T: 020 7324 4005
Admission free (small donation suggested for tours)

Alison Wear Garden Design
www.alisonwear.com

Columbia Road Market is a London institution – a photogenic relic of the old East End that has somehow survived into the 21st century. A true hardy perennial, this flower and plant market is open every Sunday of the year (unless Christmas Day falls on a Sunday), and is a favourite haunt of budget-conscious London gardeners. Over the past few years this unique market has become popular with tourists too, and teeming crowds can at times make this shop-lined Victorian street difficult to navigate, particularly if you've got an armful of plants to deliver safely home.

The market runs from 8am until around 3pm but is at its busiest between about 10.30am and 1pm. This presents shoppers with a dilemma: early birds get a clear run and the pick of the stock, latecomers have less choice and elbow room but more bargains, as prices plummet as the day draws to a close. This is a great place to kit your garden out on the cheap as some of the impressively well-stocked gardens in the immediate vicinity suggest – there's a particularly verdant example on the corner of Chambord Street. With about 50 stalls there's a surprisingly adventurous range of plant life on offer – from citrus trees to colourful seasonal bedding to elegant orchids and trusty herbaceous perennials. If your cutting garden is yet to come on stream, there are plenty of specialist cut flower stalls too, selling keenly priced, great quality blooms and foliage for spectacular arrangements. An eclectic range of independent shops complements the market stalls – a choice which embraces cafés, milliners, contemporary furniture, art galleries, garden equipment and vintage bric-à-brac.

Stall holders are a friendly lot and, when not belting out their sales patter, are happy to dispense advice and growing tips. Most of the traders hail from Essex where many have their own nurseries, like David Williams of Oak Royal Nurseries in Cranham. He has been doing Columbia Road since 1972 and deals in unusual shrubs, perennials and alpines – his stock includes ornamental grasses such as *Pennisetum orientale*, perennials like

Heuchera 'Blackberry Jam', and *Leptospermum*, (from New Zealand, where it is more commonly known as manuka). His regular customers include gardening clubs who visit the market by the coach load. Market representative George Gladwell has a nursery at Langdon Hills, Basildon – and is the go-to man for bulbs or perennials or to arrange a spot of filming (the market is a popular location). Another grower is Lyndon Osborn, whose nursery is in High Barnet. Lyndon specialises in what he calls 'London plants' – mainly shade loving or tolerant plants which can cope with London's built-up landscape, which he sees as a giant woodland. Being grown so close

to the city his plants have a low carbon footprint and are acclimatised to London's growing conditions; antipodean tree ferns are the showy stars on his stall but you can also spot the likes of *Aeoniums*, *Salvias*, *Plectranthus* (hardy and tender varieties) and *Artemisia*. Stall holder Anthony Burridge (one of many Burridge's on the market) takes a different approach, buying 'leftovers' from Dutch wholesalers to sell at a discount on the market. His stock changes every week and is a great place to look for plant bargains.

To make the most of the market come prepared with cash, suitable bags or a trolley and a good idea of what you want to buy – otherwise you will get seriously led astray with impulse buys. There are lots of deals for buying in bulk and things get even cheaper as the day goes on. It's a great idea to go with a friend and combine your buying power.

Columbia Road Market, E2 7RG
www.columbiaroad.info
Open: Sundays 8.00-15.00

A few things to look out for when buying plants (whether you are buying them at a market or not):

- Plants that look healthy probably are – choose plants that have strong, even growth and a nice shape; check for signs of pests or disease such as discoloured leaves, holes in leaves or ragged edges.

- Check for healthy roots that fill the pot (if roots are growing out through the bottom the plant is pot bound and should be avoided). Carefully upend pot and pull away from plant – while inspecting roots also look for signs of unwanted insect life.

- Plants should be clearly labelled; varieties awarded the RHS Award of Garden Merit (AGM) are particularly good buys as they have been rigorously tested for hardiness, as well as pest and disease resistance.

- Don't be afraid to buy plants in bloom – you can see exactly what you're getting and whether or not it's going to work in your garden.

- When buying bulbs – check that bulbs are firm with no signs of pests or disease.

C Container Gardening

Window boxes, balconies and roof gardens… where would the garden-less Londoner be without containers? Even those lucky enough to have a garden of their own often choose to supplement their borders with a strategically placed container or two, for an extra kick of seasonal colour, to fill in a bald patch, or simply because they have a beautiful plant pot to show off.

And whether they be a traditional hand-thrown terracotta long-tom or a rusty old dustbin, containers are ideal for gardeners who like to change their planting schemes on a whim or who enjoy mixing it up with plant combinations that wouldn't be possible in nature. Container gardening is tailor-made too for London's serial renters – moving your garden is a cinch if your plants are housed in portable pots.

Of course, there is a price for all this versatility; like having a demanding pet, container gardening requires commitment. Your plants will be totally dependent on you to water and feed them, a daily chore (twice daily in hot weather) that can make holidays and weekends away fraught with anxiety. Capillary matting and automatic irrigation systems are one solution, reciprocal watering arrangements with like-minded neighbours another.

C Coriander Club

For the ladies of the Coriander Club there's no taste like home and here in the raised beds and polytunnels of Spitalfields City Farm is where they can find it, growing the Bangladeshi vegetables and herbs that are hard to source in the UK.

In Bangladesh it is traditional for women to grow their own food but this is not so easy in Tower Hamlets, one third of whose population is Bangladeshi. Coriander Club founder Lutfun

Hussain set up the women-only group in 2000 as a place where Bangladeshi and other women could get together to socialise and exercise whilst gardening: 'It's good to share and it's really nice to work with others in the garden.'

Lutfun brings with her years of expertise in raising Bangladeshi crops such as kodu, snake gourd, Indian mustard, chillies and even rice in Britain's cool climate. From a farming background, she has been gardening in London since her arrival in 1969 and by trial and error has worked out what succeeds in this country. Crops like aramanth, aubergines, chillies and enormous kodu gourds are cosseted in the cosy confines of the polytunnels, while coriander, climbing beans and mooli (a kind of giant radish) are hardy enough to grow outside. Other outdoor crops include veg plot stalwarts like potatoes, carrots, onions, tomatoes and pumpkins (which race like unruly children through the raised beds and well beyond). Produce is shared amongst members, but word-of-mouth ensures any surplus finds ready buyers. A spirit of generosity pervades the garden and Lutfun says, "Sometimes people come to find food for a sick relative and I always try to save some for these people. It is always a comfort to taste food from home when you are not well."

Sustainability is central to Lutfun's approach and she runs the garden organically, making full use of the farm's manure, and saving seeds for sowing the following year. Cheerful blooms such as tagetes, calendula, sunflowers and dahlias appear in profusion around the site, keeping the insect population happy. Such is the garden's productivity that it is a regular winner at the annual gathering of community gardeners at Capel Manor in September (one of Lutfun's favourite gardening events along with the Chelsea Flower Show). The farm's proximity to the City makes it popular with corporate volunteers, who get stuck in helping Lutfun with gardening tasks or undertake bigger team challenges like fencing.

Pick-and-cook sessions are held twice monthly and Lutfun often prepares food on site to show visitors more about her native cuisine. The Coriander Club has also produced a cookbook with recipes showcasing the Bangladeshi ingredients it grows at the farm.

Spitalfields City Farm, Buxton Street, E1 5AR
www.spitalfieldscityfarm.org T: 020 7247 8762

Lutfun Hussain

Culpeper Community Garden

From derelict bombsite to multi-award winning garden, the Culpeper has come a long way since the early 1980s when the site began to be developed as a public garden.

Transformed by the community for the community, this triangular plot of land now brims with plants and buzzes with wildlife, a verdant oasis in the depths of urban Islington. The layout is a model of clever planning, serpentine paths weave around the garden offering a choice of routes, each one as beguiling as the next, making the space feel bigger than it is. On your journey you may pass a rockery, a picnic lawn, a herb garden, a frog-filled pond, as well as the 40 or so mini allotment-style plots tended by community groups, children, disabled gardeners and local people who don't have a garden of their own. In spring snowdrops and bluebells usher in the new season while in June the pergola is festooned with roses and the garden is saturated with the colourful blooms of annuals and herbaceous perennials. Insects and birds love it here, the diversity of plants, from vegetables and herbs to native trees and shrubs provide a great range of habitats. Woodpeckers, finches – green and gold – and dragonflies are just some of creatures who have made this their home. The garden has an organic

and sustainable approach and in 2008 a new community centre was completed. The centre fully embodies the garden's philosophy with eco-features such as a green roof, and a water collection system to keep the pond topped up with rainwater.

People as well as plants flourish in this atmospheric garden – on any given day you may find groups of friends or families just chilling on the picnic lawn, children hunting for ladybirds or pond dipping, gardeners tending their plots or enjoying a cuppa and a chat at the tea hut. Events such as musical performances, gardening workshops, talks and plants sales make the Culpeper a social hub too, and the community ethos is still strong with an annual pensioners strawberry tea and projects to cater for community groups, schools and disadvantaged groups such as asylum seekers.

Culpeper Community Garden
1 Cloudesley Road, N1 0EJ
www.culpeper.org.uk
T: 020 7833 3951

Overseen by a buzzy, beanbag strewn café that's popular with all age groups, the Curve Garden is a welcome green hiatus in this ultra-urban part of town. The garden was created in 2010, on the derelict site of the old Eastern Curve railway line, and where goods trains once trundled, wildlife friendly trees and hedgerows now flourish. Copses of homely natives such as wild cherry and hazel, alder and birch create a calm and cosy ambience, and even when the trees are bare in early spring, copious plantings of spring daffodils, hellebores and grape hyacinths ensure the presence of cheery colour.

Café tables, many of them sustainably made from reclaimed wood and recycled pallets, are dotted among the raised beds where fruit, vegetables and herbs are grown by local residents. At the far end of the garden, there's a slightly more open space which serves as a low-key children's play area.

The funky timber pavilion that houses the café (designed by the architectural collective Exyzt) also provides a rainproof focal point for community events, workshops and gatherings. The conservatory style Pineapple House with wood-burning stove hosts year-round nature-inspired design workshops, many of whose creations are displayed throughout the garden. The Eastern Curve Gardeners get together on Saturday afternoons to look after the plants before enjoying herb-topped fresh pizzas baked in the community built clay oven. Run as a social enterprise, and open to all, this friendly neighbourhood garden is a lovingly nurtured space that in turn nurtures the community it serves.

Dalston Eastern Curve Garden
13 Dalston Lane, E8 3DF
www.dalstongarden.org
Open Mon-Thurs 11.00-19.00, Tues till 23.00
Fri-Sun 11.00-23.00

E · Eltham Palace

Gardens don't come much more glamorous than the one which wraps itself around the heady architectural cocktail that is Eltham Palace.

Surprisingly rural in feel, given their SE9 location, the gardens gently complement the exotic union of the Great Hall built by Edward IV in the 15th century and the Art Deco mansion created for millionaire couple Stephen and Virginia Courtauld by architects Seely and Paget in the early 1930s. While there's more than a hint of Hollywood about Eltham's grande-luxe interior (a vision of sleek wood veneers, endless bathrooms and sweeping staircases) the garden is of the old-fashioned English Arts and Crafts variety, albeit one with its own moat and archaeological remains.

Despite the expense and care they lavished on Eltham, the Courtaulds only lived here for 8 years, moving out in 1944, so they never saw the gardens which they had planned come to maturity. English Heritage assumed responsibility for Eltham in 1995 and since then the gardens and house have been nurtured back to their 1930s glory. The garden retains a checklist of period features, including the obligatory herbaceous border and *ne plus ultra* of inter-war horticulture – a rock garden. However, while the Courtaulds employed a dozen or more gardeners, Eltham's 19 acres today are kept in trim by just three garden staff, with help from volunteers and outside contractors.

In high summer the 260ft (80 metre) long herbaceous border, which unfolds along the foot of the south moat wall, puts on a high spirited display with puddles of soft purple-blue nepeta and acid yellow lady's mantle spilling out on the gravel path. Spires of electric blue delphiniums nod in the background, interspersed with sunny accents of achillea, golden rod and day lilies. White lupins and asters provide cooler tones, fiery notes come courtesy of geum and red crocosmia. The border was redesigned in 2000 by Isabelle van Groeningen and the artistry of the scheme can be savoured

either at ground level or from on high – the wooden bridge that spans the dry southern stretch of moat supplies a handy viewing platform. The ancient stone and brick walls of the moat soak up the summer heat, creating a toasty microclimate which makes weeding the back of the border hot work on sunny days, though it's clearly enjoyed by legions of butterflies.

Following the now dry course of the western moat, the sunken rose garden is another survivor of the Courtauld era. Planted with monoculture beds of hybrid musk and early hybrid tea roses and a surrounding lavender hedge, the rose garden is at its best in the summer. The two 'garden rooms' which follow on from it come into their own in the spring, when they are filled with the scent of *Daphne bholua*, with further colour provided by clusters of cream, dusky mauve and deep purple hellebores. Elsewhere in the garden scillas, daffodils, snowdrops, primroses, and wood anemones lighten up the otherwise bare terrain in the spring. Other classic 30's features include an island in the moat planted with a solitary weeping willow and, on the north bank of the moat, a precipitous Japanese rock garden, which has recently been restored.

The stone loggia at the rear of the house offers an elevated vantage point over this part of the garden and is decorated with relief-carved roundels celebrating the enthusiasms of its wealthy creators – Ginie's for horticulture and Stephen's interest in mountaineering (although he also was a keen horticulturalist, with a passion for orchids). The 19th-century Ionic columns which support the wisteria clad pergola here are a piece of suitably up-market architectural salvage, having been rescued from the Bank of England when it was redeveloped in the 1930s.

The garden is managed as organically as possible, with the occasional spritz of glysophate on paths to keep weeds at bay. In spring a generous mulch of leaf mould or well-rotted manure is applied around the garden, with several tons of mulch going on the herbaceous border alone. As in the Courtauld's day, the far moat bank and parkland grasslands are managed traditionally, being left to flower and set seed before being cut for hay. In the summer this area is loud with insects and the garden as a whole is rich with wildlife – from the carp that silently patrol the moat to the dragonflies that skim across its surface, to woodpeckers, sparrowhawks and green parakeets that compete for airspace.

Designed as a place for entertaining (even in its Tudor incarnation the palace played host to foreign dignitaries and jousting tournaments), Eltham Palace still radiates an air of moneyed leisure. The Courtauld's home movies show how much they and their friends enjoyed Eltham's gardens, the outdoor antics usually being accompanied by a menagerie of assorted dogs, ducks, geese, goats and Stephen and Virginia's pet lemur, Mah-Jongg. Dogs (and presumably lemurs) are no longer welcome but visitors can still enjoy a picnic in Eltham's grounds. There is no better place in which to switch off from modern life and recapture those lost days of a pre-war English summer.

Eltham Palace
Court Yard, Eltham, Greenwich, SE9 5QE
www.english-heritage.org.uk
T: 020 8294 2548
Open Sun-Wed 10.00-18.00 (April-Oct), 10.00-16.00
(Nov-March), closed Jan

F Fenton House

Tucked away in leafy, affluent Hampstead, Fenton House Garden is one of London's 'paradise' gardens. Like the original 'pairi.daêza' of the ancient Middle East, the garden is walled and it is home to an orchard, kitchen garden as well as a formal lawned garden, topiary, brimming flower borders and at least five wells.

Dating from the late 17th century, the garden's time-mellowed red brick walls were built at the same time as the comfortable four-square merchant's house itself. But like most properties with a bit of age, its grounds have evolved over the years, with the apparently timeless topiary being added by the National Trust in the 1950s, while the orchard has been in situ for some 300 years.

The garden is broadly arranged over two levels, with the orchard tucked below the higher formal garden. The latter makes good use of the old brick walls, whose sheltering embrace provides a pleasing backdrop for tidily trained climbing and rambling roses, such as 'Veilchenblau' and 'Chevy Chase', and scented climbing honeysuckle. Topiary enthusiasts will enjoy the clipped yew hedge, holly lollipops and cones that define three sides of the lawn; all this restraint is offset by the exuberant drifts of orange helianthemum, white rose campion and

sisyrinchium that spill over the gravel path that runs alongside the lawn. On the other side of the lawn, the Lawn Border undergoes a colour metamorphosis as the year unfolds, the soft pink and blue 'bridal' tones of spring giving way to the full-bodied late summer colour of dahlias and the eye-catching annual climber, Spanish Flag (*Ipomoea lobata*).

Gardener-in-charge Andrew Darragh has been in post for five years and relishes the freedom that comes with a historic but not set in aspic garden. Colour is an important focus for him ("I have the borders in colour all year round", he enthuses) and he has also gradually introduced a more informal, romantic feel to the planting, bringing in old-fashioned favourites such as foxgloves, peony poppies and verbascum and allowing them to self-seed where they will. On the nepeta-lined terrace that overlooks the lawn and orchard below, a line of elegant terracotta planters from Whichford Pottery add pops of colour according to season, in summer singing out with cheerful specimens such as orange Californian poppies and indigo coloured salvias. In June the intimate, enclosed sunken rose garden is heady with the scent of old-fashioned roses and lavender but softened with a more haphazard country house style planting of alliums, geraniums, foxgloves, poppies, white valerian and alchemilla. The north terrace is home to statuesque beauties such as alliums, cardoon, verbascum, phormium and some of the towering *Echium pininana* that feel so at home at Fenton House that they are beginning to naturalise around the garden.

One recent change in the garden has been more dramatic – the removal early in 2016 of the overgrown robinia avenue in the front garden. The robinia had no historic precedent and had outgrown its welcome, making the approach to the house dark and oppressive. Its less bombastic replacement, an avenue of Japanese flowering cherry (*Prunus amanogawa*), a compact and upright variety, has allowed more light to flood into this south-facing garden and will provide clouds of spring blossom followed by richly coloured foliage in the autumn.

Very much a place for living and working, the garden is run with sustainability in mind. Peat has been banished, so Andrew grows vegetables and annuals such as cosmos from seed, and buys in bulbs and bare root plants in the autumn. The soil here is free draining and this combined with the garden's location at the top of a hill means that mulching is a vital part of the regime at Fenton House, along with a pragmatic 'right plant in the right place' policy. "You can tell the difference when a border has not been mulched", says Andrew and the group of hard-working compost bins discretely tucked away in the corner of the vegetable garden testify to a commitment to husbanding the garden's resources and maintaining optimum growing conditions.

Down in the Orchard abundance is the order of the day; in spring the fruit trees float above a succession of colourful bulbs, while in the summer the grass is allowed to grow unchecked, with paths being mown through the haze of seed heads. Amazingly, this modestly sized orchard contains thirty different varieties of apples from historic types like 'Devon Quarrendon' (introduced 1676) to newfangled varieties like 'Discovery' (1949); 'Glow Red Williams' and 'Ovid' are some of the pear varieties that have been trained against the orchard walls and even the vegetable beds are surrounded by espaliered fruit trees. Harvested fruits are sometime sold at the entrance porch to the house and there is also a small selection of plants for sale near the wooden-framed glasshouse, charmingly operating on an 'honesty box' system. The garden hosts a popular Apple Weekend every year on the first weekend in October, with lots of different apple varieties to taste and compare, kids' activities, a bar for the grown-ups and deckchairs on the lawn for a family-friendly village fête style day out.

Fenton House
Hampstead Grove, Hampstead, NW3 6SP
www.nationaltrust.org.uk
T: 01494 755563 (Info line)
Open Wed-Sun 11.00-17.00 (Mar-Oct);
Sat-Sun 11.00-16.00 (Dec)

Once the epitome of 60's cool, the London mews has lost none of its allure since the dashing days of Simon Templar and John Steed. Prestigious locations and picturesque architecture add to the cachet, as does the prosaic fact that mews houses often come with a garage, the holy grail of central London housing stock. What they don't tend to have is gardens – a bit of a downer for the horticulturally inclined resident.

At Bathurst Mews Tony Heywood isn't letting a little thing like that stand between him and the chance to create a garden. Since 2000 he has gradually been 'foresting' his pretty mews with giant containerised olive trees, in the process transforming the entire street into not just a magical city oasis, but also a more sociable place to live.

Initially Tony and his partner Alison Condie started with the space outside their own house, populating it with a gnarly old olive, a pyracantha, a Japanese maple and a regularly changing assortment of interesting potted exotics, such as *Cardiocrinum giganteum* (Giant Himalayan lily), *Colocasia esculenta* (Giant Elephants' Ears) and *Equisetum*. A parthenocissus, planted some years earlier, had already powered its way over the nearby mews entrance arch, creating a lush green proscenium against which other plants, such as a scarlet-flowered bottlebrush, could be placed to create a living picture.

Tony and Alison soon realised that lovely as it was to have a garden outside their home, it would be even more fantastic to be able to see them elsewhere along the mews. Luckily their fellow residents felt the same way and were already asking Tony to source olive trees for their houses. As the olive population grew, Tony hit on the idea of 'zoning' individual trees to create a woodland landscape, with a variety of containerized plants forming a colourful forest floor.

Olives makes the ideal foundation plant for this urban forest, chosen by Tony for their sculptural qualities ("like giant bonsai"), evergreen habit, hardiness and readiness to live in containers. Indeed so happy are the olives in west London that they fruit, producing a small harvest that is painstakingly preserved in jars by Tony and Alison. The forest is necessarily containerised since the mews' foundations are too shallow to tolerate direct planting, and plants must be easily portable to allow maintenance contractors access to buildings. Although Tony's idea of 'easily portable' is probably not yours or mine – moving a mature olive tree requires advance planning and a crane or, when needs must, a car, a tow-rope and plenty of willing muscle. The equine residents of Bathurst Mews (www.hydeparkstables.com) haven't yet been co-opted for olive moving duties, but provide assistance in other ways, generating a handy local source of manure.

Fully grown olive trees are eye-wateringly expensive but as a professional gardener Tony is able to get the olives at a trade discount, nonetheless the trees represent an extremely generous personal contribution to the streetscape. Plant arrangements are generally masterminded and maintained by Tony and Alison (no small task given that watering alone can take all evening in the summer) but residents are free to add their own personalised touches.

Nasturtiums, alliums and lilies have proved successful companion plants, as have fragrant herbs such as lemon verbena and prostrate rosemary, while tomatoes and strawberries were just too tempting for the local foxes. A recent mass planting of 3,000 tulips (including fringed, parrot and Mendel varieties) was a big hit, resulting in what Tony calls "an insane blaze" of colour and crowds of camera-toting sightseers. Less flamboyantly, he is also introducing native deciduous trees to the forest, with containerised birches and copper beeches being deployed alongside the olives.

Over a decade on, Tony is able to credit the forest with some powerful knock-on effects, "You start with a tree and that supports a whole host of other activities". Attracted by the trees and well-stocked feeders, birds such as robins, blackbirds, greenfinches, great tits and even a tawny owl have flocked to the mews. The forest has also eroded the usual city reserve between its human occupants, with al-fresco dining and socialising beneath the illuminated olives becoming something of a way of life. Neighbours look out for each other more now and residents at the far end of the street (beyond the reach of Tony and Alison's hard-working hosepipe) set up their own watering rota to ensure their bit of the olive grove thrives.

Until recently the mews enjoyed a tranquil vehicle-free aesthetic that seemed to have evolved symbiotically with the forest. However, the Forested Mews has fallen victim, like so many other desirable locations in London, to the execrable trend for digging ever-deeper basements. Negotiating Travis Perkins delivery lorries, skips and scaffolding has meant headache and heartache for Tony and Alison. While work is ongoing many of the olives have had to be removed to protect them from damage, and with the evergreens gone, the birds too have made themselves scarce. It's a bitter pill to swallow, but as Tony notes "this is contemporary London and it's a fine example of the challenges gardeners face with the hard realities of being surrounded by people with too much money". But gardeners are nothing if not resilient, and in the spring of 2016 in spite of the construction carnage, the narcissus and tulips made a great show, a beacon of hope awaiting the return of the olives, and the birds.

Bathurst Mews, W2 2SB

"You start with a tree and that supports a whole host of other activities"

F Front Gardens

Do Londoners love their cars more than their front gardens? In some boroughs it appears that they do – according to an influential report carried out by Ealing's Local Agenda 21, nearly a quarter of the borough's 74,300 front gardens are completely hard surfaced with no vegetation at all. And the problem is exacerbated by a 'domino effect' whereby the more front gardens are converted into parking spaces the less on-street parking is available, leading to more gardens being paved over. The trend looks set to continue, despite the 2008 planning regulation requiring planning permission for impermeable surfacing of more than 5 square metres.

However, with a bit of thoughtful design and the use of permeable materials such as gravel, reinforced lawns and carefully chosen plants, it is perfectly possible for cars and front-gardens to cohabit. The 2011 RHS publication *Gardening Matters, Urban Series: Front Gardens* has some great ideas for car-friendly gardens. Ealing Front Gardens Project hope to reinstate three front gardens in 2012, working with home-owners who want to restore their hard-surfaced gardens back to something softer.

They may be small but London's estimated 1.8 million front gardens cover some 9,400 hectares and have a big contribution to make to the capital's environmental and aesthetic well-being, providing important habitat for urban wildlife and a valuable focus for neighbourly interaction. Conversely, impermeable surfaces bring with them the increased risk of flooding, the creation of localized heat islands (which intensify the effects of heat waves), and contribute to a decline in biodiversity. Perhaps most importantly, paved gardens are just plain ugly.

In Islington one community-gardening scheme has harnessed the positive potential of front gardens. The Blackstock Triangle Gardens Project was started in 2009 by neighbours Naomi Schillinger and Nicolette Jones and initially focused on treepits in the local roads. The following year, thanks to Capital Growth funding, they added a food growing dimension, with grow bags and free seeds being issued to 50 participants enabling them to raise sweetcorn, squash and beans in their front gardens. In 2011 the number of participants doubled to 100 and in an exciting development, funding was found for ten front gardens to have their concrete removed and be reinstated as productive spaces. The project, which is still going strong, has boosted community spirit with people getting to know their neighbours through their gardens, and friendships cemented over tea and cakes at popular 'Cake Sunday' events. In spring seeds and plug plants are distributed to encourage front garden veg growing.

Recently, inspired by a visit to Chartres in France, Naomi has introduced hollyhocks to the Blackstock streetscape; they have, she says, proved to be a winner, a brilliant treepit plant and very easy to grow. Naomi shares her 'community growing' experience in her book *Veg Street* (which includes month-by-month advice on what to grow as well as great low-cost ideas for protecting, labelling and watering your plants) while a further book, Grow *All You Can Eat in 3 Square Feet*, capitalised on her talent for growing delicious food in tiny spaces.

www.outofmyshed.co.uk/btg/
www.ealingfrontgardens.org.uk

> Garden greenspace in the capital's gardens has been lost at a rate of two and a half Hyde Parks per year driven by recent trends in garden design

Naomi Schillinger

F Frugal Gardening Tips

Once the gardening bug has bitten it can be a surprise to discover how much your new addiction can cost – garden infrastructure, tools, plants and seeds can all be expensive to acquire and naturally there are no end of specialist companies eager to part you from your cash. Horticulture may be big business nowadays but there are plenty of ways of gardening on the cheap – and in fact, as allotment plots all over the land testify, most gardeners (and their gardens) thrive on the ingenuity required by a make-do-and-mend approach. Here are a few tips to get you started:

Collect seed from your plants

- Grow plants from seed – it may take longer but it's far cheaper and more satisfying and you can choose exactly the variety you want (for inspiration read *A Garden from a Hundred Packets of Seed* by James Fenton, Viking 2001.)

- Seed exchange events are a great place to pick up seeds for free or a small donation. If you're buying seeds, the chances are you won't use all of them in a season so get together with gardening friends to swap seeds – that way you'll get more varieties and perhaps try out ones you wouldn't normally grow.

- Collect seed from your plants to use the following season (see left); surplus seeds can be swapped with friends or via a seed exchange forum like www.gardenswapshop.org.uk.

- Plant stands at your local horticultural society or gardening club can often be a great place to pick up cheap and unusual plants (though don't be shy about checking the root ball for unwanted weeds or pests).

- Ditto car boot sales, jumble sales, church fêtes.

- Take cuttings – don't be afraid to ask friends with established gardens. Propagating from plants is straightforward and can be quicker than growing from seed. Roses, lavender, penstemon and pelargoniums are all dead easy to propagate, and with the advantage that because you are essentially making a clone of the parent plant you know exactly which variety you are getting (not always the case with seeds).

- Once they get going, plants are amazingly good at reproducing – cottage garden favourites like poppies, pot marigold, nasturtiums and columbines are prodigious self-seeders. Dig up the unwanted seedlings and plant elsewhere, or swap or sell them.

- Clump-forming herbaceous perennials like sedum, geraniums, asters, daisies, grasses and oriental poppies can be divided in spring (and sometimes autumn) to make more plants to fill your garden – or to swap and sell.

- Terracotta pots are beautiful and their porosity makes them perfect for raising plants but they can be pricey. Be imaginative about containers – as long as there are drainage holes in the bottom anything from an old olive oil can to a wellington boot can become a 'plant pot'. Rubber tyres make good raised beds for the allotment or veg patch.

An old bath can make a great container

- Yes, it is perfectly possibly to germinate seeds on your window sills but you may find that your gardening ambition will quickly outgrow the available space around your own home. Your dreams will be haunted by visions of gleaming greenhouses, packed with pristine produce and radiant blooms. There's no need to splash out on a new one though – scour your local small ads or Freecycle for unwanted greenhouses in search of a new home (I got my little lean-to greenhouse from a neighbour who had bought a larger one). Polytunnels are a cheaper alternative to greenhouses and the web is awash with instructions on how to make your own if you want to save even more money.

Wheelbarrow – a movable container!

- Harvest your own water. It may cost a little to install a water butt or two but it's better for the environment (and for your plants) to recycle rainwater for garden use. If you are on a water meter, you may even save some money.

- Make your own compost – it's an eco-friendly way of adding goodness to your garden soil and getting rid of kitchen waste (but not cooked food or meat). If you don't have a garden, a wormery on your balcony or in your backyard will produce small quantities of top quality compost that can be used for potting purposes.

Make your own compost

Fulham Palace Garden

The gardeners at Fulham Palace have a good excuse for not double-digging the veg beds at Fulham Palace gardens: they're simply not allowed to. Packed with archaeological interest, and home to the Bishops of London for over 1,000 years, Fulham Palace is a protected site and that goes for its soil as much as its venerable Grade-I listed buildings. Within the two-acre walled garden the permitted digging depth is 30cms, while in the 11 acres beyond its mellow brick walls the limit is a scant 10cm. It's not, however, a restriction that's cramping anyone's style – this is a garden that's reclaiming its rightful place in horticultural history.

Once spoken of in the same breath as the Chelsea Physic Garden, Fulham Palace was an important botanical garden in the 17th century, visited by the likes of John Evelyn and Hans Sloane. It was Henry Compton, the Bishop of London, between 1675 and 1713, who put Fulham Palace on the horticultural map. The botanising Bishop grew over 1,000 exotic species in his stovehouses and sourced seeds and plants from the Colonies (territories that, handily for Compton, were under his jurisdiction as Bishop of London). *Magnolia virginiana* and Black Walnut (*Juglans nigra*) were two of Compton's American introductions and are still represented at Fulham Palace today - albeit by modern specimens. Such were the garden's horticultural riches that Hans Sloane collected specimens here for his eponymous herbarium (now in the care of the Natural History Museum). Compton's entrepreneurial head gardener George London was a skilled plantsman, and went on to found the famous Brompton Park Nursery.

Compton's collection was largely dispersed after his death and the garden altered by subsequent incumbents to their own taste. Thus in the 1760s Bishop Terrick had the grounds re-landscaped in the Romantic style while in the 1830s Bishop Blomfield planted a knot garden; in the early 20th century sports-mad Bishop Winnington-Ingram

installed a grass tennis court. The 1970s saw the departure of the last resident Bishop of London at the Palace and the garden went into decline. Its current renaissance – part of a larger redevelopment programme at the Palace – has seen the triumphant restoration of the once derelict Victorian vinery and bothies in the walled garden and the replanting of Bishop Blomfield's knot garden to its original 1830s design. The botanising bishops are further celebrated in a planting scheme that utilises the whole range of 'Bishop' dahlias, including that old favourite 'Bishop of Llandaff'.

Although the garden is most associated with Bishop Compton, other bishops of London played a significant role in botany in this country – such as Bishop Grindal who introduced the tamarisk to this county and who may have planted the holm oak, the oldest tree in the garden which is now designated a Great Tree of London. The museum's regular 'Garden Walks' are a great way to get to know the garden better and discover the fascinating stories that lie behind its many unusual and historic tree specimens.

Progress in the restored walled garden is tangible. Young fruit trees have recently been planted along the mellow brick walls and will be trained into traditional fans and espaliers. Varieties include the 'Boston Russet', the earliest known American apple. The south-facing veg beds are once again productive, the orchard's apple and pear crop gets dispatched to a co-operative cider maker, while the two beehives installed in 2013 have also covered themselves in glory, producing a decent crop of runny honey that scooped first prize at the National Honey Show.

It's an exciting time to be gardening at Fulham Palace – Head Gardener Lucy Hart (and her team of two senior gardeners, three student gardeners and a band of volunteers), get to work in a garden that is extremely old but, through their efforts, at the same time is always new and evolving.

For its many visitors, however, Fulham Palace Garden is simply a place of leisure – and this too is in keeping with historical precedent. In the days of the Bishops the Palace hosted pageants and garden parties while today its extensive lawns are a popular picnic venue during the summer months. It's no coincidence that among the finds unearthed during a recent archaeological dig in the walled garden was a Swiss army penknife, complete with champagne cork still imbedded in one of its many blades. A garden with a sense of history, yes, but one that knows how to enjoy itself too.

Museum of Fulham Palace
Bishops Avenue, SW6 6EA
T: 020 7610 7165
www.fulhampalace.org

The Knot Garden

G The Garden Museum

A redundant church on a congested intersection in Lambeth is a surprising venue for this museum celebrating the joys of gardening, past and present. In some ways, however, the location is perfectly fitting, for its churchyard contains the tomb of the Tradescants, pioneering 17th-century plant hunters and royal gardeners. Their 'Ark' or collection of curiosities and specimens became the basis of Britain's first university museum, the Ashmolean (whose eponymous founder, Elias Ashmole, is also buried here). The churchyard of St Mary-at-Lambeth is also home to another significant tomb with a botanical connection: that of the infamous Captain Bligh, whose mission to transport over 1,000 breadfruit plants from Tahiti to the West Indies ended so disastrously.

The Garden Museum has been based here since 1977, hosting a small but entertaining display of its permanent collection of tools, paintings and gardenalia alongside temporary exhibitions exploring the work of key gardening figures such as Russell Page, Beth Chatto, and Charles Jencks, and topical subjects such as the 'green city' movement. The museum's pretty and peaceful 17th-century style knot garden – designed by the Dowager Marchioness of Salisbury – was another popular draw, along with its cosy vegetarian café and thoughtfully stocked shop.

But the demands of the museum have outgrown the limitations of its historic site and an ambitious redevelopment scheme is currently underway which will increase the exhibition and education spaces, and provide a new Archive of Garden Design. Part of this expansion will be achieved by means of three new pavilion buildings in the churchyard, which will house a Garden Classroom, a Learning Studio and a larger café. The gallery space will be doubled, meaning that many more items from the permanent collection can be displayed, along with a recreation of John Tradescant's Ark featuring objects from the Tradescant Collection. The gardens are set for a major redesign too - according to the pre-publicity a 'leading contemporary designer' will be bringing the garden and churchyard together to create a new public garden – and the church's medieval tower will also be opened up, allowing visitors to enjoy the views across the Thames and the north bank. The new museum is scheduled to reopen in the spring of 2017.

The Garden Museum
Lambeth Palace Road, SE1 7LB
T: 020 7401 8865
Info@gardenmuseum.co.uk
www.gardenmuseum.co.uk

G Geffrye Museum Garden

Best known as the museum of the home, the Geffrye has another, rather less well-publicised string to its bow. Its evocative collection of period rooms – housed in a gracious early 18th-century almshouse – is complemented by a suite of historic gardens and an abundantly stocked herb garden, tucked away behind the museum.

With outside space at a premium these historic gardens are necessarily compact but offer a succinct 'edited highlights' tour of the English urban back garden through the centuries. Developed in 1998, the garden rooms – like their interior counterparts – focus on middle-class taste and although not recreating any individual gardens, care has been taken to ensure planting choices and relationships are historically accurate. In a further symmetry, whilst the museum's furniture collection reflects this part of London's association with the furniture industry, the gardens and herb garden reference the market gardens and nurseries for which this area was also once renowned.

A 16th-century knot garden is the first in the sequence – its sinuous knots are described by grey-leaved *Santolina chamaecyparissus* and wall germander (*Teucrium chamaedrys*), and its intricate design derived from Renaissance decorative arts. With our modern interest in growing vegetables, deep bed growing and herbs, the Late Elizabethan garden looks reassuringly familiar with its sturdy raised wooden beds, planted with useful flora – aromatic herbs for culinary, medicinal and cosmetic purposes and 'pretties' such as peonies, cowslips and roses.

Showing off your prize specimens was the name of the game for mid-to-late Georgian gardeners – the town garden recreated here is simple but decorative, reflecting the garden's increasing role as an 'outside room'. Three circular box-edged beds are planted with a central box ball and a few choice seasonal specimens such as candytuft (*Iberis sempervirens*) and *Fritillaria imperialis* – unlike modern gardeners,

the Georgians were not dismayed by the sight of bare earth between their plants. An auricula theatre is another opportunity for the display of rare and valued plants – May is the ideal time to inspect these orderly blooms grandstanding in their specially constructed playhouse.

The Victorians, however, liked nothing more than densely planted carpet bedding – preferably using the brightest colours available. The mid-19th century garden evoked at the Geffrye has an annual bedding display which has recently included a 'pelargonium pyramid' – an early take on today's mania for 'vertical planting'. A small-but-perfectly-formed glasshouse – the kind gardeners then and now would kill for – completes this picture of cosy domesticity. Containing African violets, pelargoniums and ferns, its contents reflect the Victorians' enthusiasms for tender and exotic plants.

Relaxed and cottagey are the key words for the Edwardian garden – a pastoral rejection of the formality of the preceding era. Visitors in May can inhale the intense perfume of the blowsy purple wisteria on the Lutyenesque brick-pillared pergola, those in June can admire its companion, a climbing rose, in bloom (the latter a favoured nesting place for resident blue tits). The border here features the likes of *Geranium x magnificum*, Bergenia, Aquilegia, and a lovely Rose 'Irene Watts' and Peony 'Baroness Schroeder'.

Returning back through the enfilade of period garden rooms, one comes to the Herb Garden – the most established of the Geffrye gardens, having been planted in 1992. This walled space – once derelict land adjacent to the museum – is a traditionally arranged herb garden, centred around a specially commissioned bronze fountain by Kate Malone. Now beautifully mature, the garden contains over 170 different herbs with a variety of different applications from the medicinal to the cosmetic.

Auricula theatre

Nectar-rich plants such as anise hyssop, golden rod and sage attract visiting bees and there is also a section devoted to dye plants such as rose madder and lady's bedstraw. With the 21st century's new-found enthusiasm for herbal medicine, the red warning labels flagging up poisonous herbs such as monkshood are a useful warning to novice herbalists that nature's larder should be exploited with caution.

Overlooked by Hoxton station, the garden cannot claim to be the quietest in town. But the new East London Line station has benefited the museum with visitor numbers increasing thanks to nosy travellers having their curiosity piqued as they look down on the Geffrye gardens from the elevated railway platforms. The diverse plant life and a chemical-free regime, means that the Geffrye garden is a popular destination too for local wildlife – including butterflies, foxes and assorted bird species, from tiny darting wrens to starlings bathing themselves with joyful abandon in the herb garden fountain. Blackfly are less welcome visitors but numbers are managed using a spray solution of Ecover washing up liquid. The gardeners here (two full-time, plus several volunteers) also have to cope with soil that is typically heavy London clay. An annual mulching of around 20 tons of farmyard manure, delivered in the depths of winter, helps ramp up the organic content.

The historic gardens are open 1 April-31 October but the museum's spacious front garden can be enjoyed year-round. It has recently been renovated to bring its appearance more in line with its days as an almshouse – and its lawns and mature trees are a green space much valued by locals and visitors.

The Geffrye Museum
136 Kingsland Road, E2 8EA
www.geffrye-museum.org.uk   T: 020 7739 9893
Gardens open: 1 April-31 Oct during museum hours
Museum open: Tues-Sat 10.00-17.00,
Sun & Bank Hols 12.00-17.00
Admission free

G GROW London

Held at the end of June in a huge white marquee on Hampstead Heath, this contemporary garden fair puts paid once and for all to the notion that gardening is the exclusive preserve of the fuddy-duddy. Founded in 2014 by Affordable Art Fair entrepreneur Will Ramsay, GROW London is aimed at a young design-savvy audience with a showcase of around 100 handpicked exhibitors catering to the urban gardener's every need and aspirational desire.

The aesthetically pleasing wares on offer range from des res sheds to posh planters and vertical planting pods, as well as embracing wildlife-friendly birdhouses and bee hotels, along with outdoor leisure goods such as hipster hammocks and cast iron firepits for those long not-so-hot summer nights in the city. Top of the range gardening implements by brands like Sneeboer and Niwaki will ensure that your tool kit combines form with function, while for those who aim to look good even as they wrestle with the weeds, this is the place to finally track down some chic gardening attire.

Blending style with substance, the fair does not neglect gardeners who prefer to put plants first, rewarding plantaholic visitors with a carefully curated selection of nurseries from London and further afield who grow unusual and beautiful plants that thrive in city gardens. Interspersed around the venue, a handful of inspirational 'feature areas' are, in effect, mini-show gardens, providing ideas to steal for your own plot, and on a diminutive scale that most urban gardeners will appreciate.

A mercifully tat-free zone, GROW London offers plenty of temptation to loosen the purse strings, but also intellectual stimulation in the form of free talks by expert speakers. Hands-on workshops impart practical and creative skills such as flower arranging or wood-whittling, while the buzzy in-house café and champagne bar add to the festive atmosphere.

GROW London
www.growlondon.com

G Guerrilla Gardener

Since he first began blogging about his illicit gardening activities in 2004, Richard Reynolds has almost single-handedly turned the underground business of being a guerrilla gardener into a high-profile occupation.

Recently voted the 24th most influential gardener in Britain, Reynolds (aka @Richard_001) has taken the Duchess of Cornwall on a tour of guerrilla gardens in London, designed a GG themed installation in Selfridges, and had his book *On Guerrilla Gardening* translated into French, German and Korean.

Reynolds defines guerrilla gardening as gardening land without permission – this is usually public land but in some cases more adventurous guerrilla gardeners have trespassed onto private land to wield their hoes. Reynolds undertook his first covert mission in the neglected flower beds outside Peronnet House, the residential block in Elephant & Castle where he lives. He recalls, "I thought, right,

I'm going to sort this out: I don't want to complain about it, I want to have the fun of doing it myself." With gardening in his DNA – both his mother and grandmother are avid gardeners – Reynolds was unfazed by the challenges of unauthorised urban gardening. Once embarked on cultivation of obviously neglected land, he found the powers-that-be were usually happy to turn a blind eye. Indeed, on occasion, they have even been known to take the credit for the hard, often nocturnal, work put in by Richard and his fellow guerrillas.

As more troops have rallied to 'fight the filth with forks and flowers', Richard's forthright approach to his obsessive hobby has evolved into something that might even be termed 'responsible guerrilla gardening'. Careful now not to overcommit himself too far from home, he ensures local guerrillas are in place to care for new gardens being created, since well-maintained plots are less likely to be a target for vandals and litter.

"My main aim is to provide some sort of inspiration for other people, for them to just go and do it in their area, as befits their motivations and their particular landscape."

"Cheap, colourful and low-maintenance stuff is what I'm after – the kind of things you wouldn't expect local authorities to plant".

Lavender Fields, Lambeth North Tube Station, SE1

Frustrated by the 'professionalisation' of gardening as seen on TV, Reynolds has harnessed the informality of social networking media to encourage would-be guerrillas to "just get stuck in – learn from your mistakes and if something dies, try something else". His snappy website has become the global hub of the guerrilla gardening movement from where Reynolds launched 'Pimp your Pavement', a campaign to liven up London's sidewalks through the power of plants.

Consistent aftercare aside, cheap, practical plant choices are essential to successful guerrilla campaigns, and Richard recommends easy, gently invasive annuals such as calendula, nigella and Californian poppies that provide lots of colour over a long season. Sunflowers are another GG favourite and the focus of International Sunflower Guerrilla Gardening Day, held every May Day. Richard's own preferred guerrilla plant is fragrant, evergreen lavender and it features in his favourite stealth garden, the 'lavender field' near Lambeth North tube – "it's the largest one I look after and the most spectacular. It's the best place to garden because of the conversations I have with passers-by. They are so happy with it, particularly when the lavender is in full bloom and covered in bumble bees. You can smell it before you see it!"

www.guerrillagardening.org
www.pimpyourpavement.com

H Hall Place and Gardens

Bexley's excellent local history museum is also a compelling destination for garden lovers. Hall Place itself is a historic house with a split personality – one half a flint-and-rubble Tudor hall, the other a smart, red brick 17th-century mansion. The 65 hectares of award-winning gardens that surround it also reflect this diversity.

Close to the house is a series of formal gardens – a knot garden, a white border, two lengthy herbaceous borders, and a topiary lawn guarded by a procession of heraldic beasts sculpted in yew. This unusual menagerie was planted in 1953 to celebrate the Queen's Coronation – the animals depict royal genealogy, the Falcon representing the Plantagenets for example. The yews have been trimmed and tied three times a year since their planting and were in good shape to celebrate the Queen's 90th birthday in 2016. These fearsome creatures overlook a well-stocked rose garden, whose glorious colours and delicious scents make this a must-see (and a must-smell) attraction in June. Elsewhere, simple arrangements of lavender hedges, pleached trees, and stripy lawns strike a more modern note.

The river Cray is the watery dividing line between the manicured gardens and the stately unfolding of landscaped parkland beyond. Here can be found, amongst other things, a wildflower meadow, mature specimen trees, oodles of wildlife and a heather garden (at its best in early spring). As if this wasn't enough, the old walled gardens are laid out with a sequence of 'demonstration' gardens, a well-labelled kitchen garden and a small orchard. The palm house is modern and functional, but crammed with exotics including crops like peanuts, sweet potatoes, coffee, avocados and kumquats. On an educational note, there is a planted timeline showing the sequence of botanical introductions to the Western world and – harking back to Hall Place's origins – a 'really useful' Tudor herb garden.

Bourne Road, Bexley, DA5 1PQ
www.hallplace.org.uk   T: 01322 526574
Historic House, visitor centre, glasshouse & café open daily 10.00-17.00
Gardens & parkland: Open daily 9.00-dusk
Admission free to gardens, visitor centre & Café
Wheelchair access

Above: Topiary lawn and the Queen's heraldic beasts
Opposite: Knot garden

H | Ham House

Back in the day – the 17th century to be precise – this imposing Thameside mansion was a hotbed of political intrigue.

During the Commonwealth, the beautiful and wily Duchess of Lauderdale played a daring game, secretly working for the Royalist cause whilst openly pursuing a friendship with Oliver Cromwell. With Charles II restored to the throne the house became an important hub of the Restoration court, its fine interiors and stately gardens a reflection of the family's status at the heart of the royal court. Today Ham House is run by the National Trust, which began restoring the gardens to their 17th-century layout in 1975.

Approaching from the Thames, the visitor is greeted by a statue of Old Father Thames, stationed outside the Jacobean front of the house like a grizzled old family retainer. Neatly clipped bay drums and yew cones patrol the perimeter of the entrance front garden, overseen by stern-looking busts set in the surrounding wall. The Coade stone pineapples on the front fence sound a more welcoming note, the exotic fruit being a symbol of hospitality and a signal of the Lauderdale family's love of entertaining.

Moving clockwise around the grounds the Cherry Garden is the next space one encounters. Named for the fruit trees which were once grown here, it's a dignified essay in topiary with diamond-shaped box hedged compartments, punctuated with neat hand-clipped cones and soft mounds of grey-leaved lavender and santolina. A marble statue of Bacchus hovers centre stage, where the gravel paths intersect. Visitors arriving on a hot summer's day will appreciate the shady sanctuary of the twin pleached hornbeam tunnels running along either side of the garden.

The south terrace – which fronts the Carolean side of the house – ushers in a change of mood and scale. This broad gravel path is edged on the house side by a border planted in sequenced 17th-century style and filled with period plants such as lychnis (rose campion), echinops and echinacea interspersed with slender cones of yew. To the left of the house is a weathered brick wall, to the right, an evergreen hedge – both perfect foils to the rosy pink accents of the flowers in the herbaceous border. A collection of large-scale terracotta pots ramps up the drama of the terrace, below which lies the expanse of the 'plats' – a quintessentially 17th-century garden feature consisting of eight immaculate squares of lawn, intersected by pale gravel paths. Beyond the plats lies another period garden, the 'wilderness'. This slightly misleading term (many of us will wish our wildernesses looked this tidy) actually denotes a formal wooded garden divided up by a Union Jack style arrangement of radiating grassy paths, bordered by hornbeam hedges, behind which are concealed compartments containing four circular summer houses.

To the west of the house lies the Orangery Kitchen garden; only half of its original plots have been planted up so far (in its heyday the garden would have been twice as big, with a further 16 beds extending beyond the west wall). Vegetables, herbs and espaliered fruit are attractively grown here, on organic lines using companion planting and avoiding chemicals. The fresh produce is put to good use by the café, which is based in the elegant 17th-century Orangery. One of the oldest examples of its type in the country, in early summer the Orangery's mellow brick facade is clothed in billowing clouds of purple wisteria, making the outside seating option particularly appealing.

Ham Street, Ham,
Richmond-upon-Thames, TW10 7RS
www.nationaltrust.org.uk/hamhouse
T: 020 8940 1950
See website for opening times and admission prices.

H Hampton Court Flower Show

The extrovert younger sibling of the Chelsea Flower Show came of age in 2010, celebrating its 21st birthday with a bumper crop of show gardens, a gigantic floral marquee and a major new 'Home Grown' exhibit.

Luxuriating in the spacious grounds of Hampton Court Palace the event has grown into the UK's biggest gardening show, covering a whopping 34 acres and pulling in annual crowds of over 160,000. The operation may be on a grand scale and the RHS standards as rigourous as ever but the vibe is relaxed – Hampton Court is noticeably less stuffy than Chelsea and has a greater emphasis on inclusivity, the environment, and growing your own. And – good news for plantaholics – unlike at Chelsea, plants are freely available for sale throughout the duration of the show, and there are even handy plant and product crèches where purchases can be parked for the day.

With over 600 hundred exhibitors vying for your attention, it can be difficult to know where to turn first; most visitors tend to spend around five hours at the show, so be strategic and pace yourself. The catalogue may seem an unnecessary extra expense on top of the ticket price but it's worth picking one up to really get the most out of a visit.

As at Chelsea, on arrival most visitors make a bee line for the Show Gardens; these meticulous installations will have taken three weeks to build, months to plan and are tended assiduously throughout the show so that visitors as well as the judges see them at their best. Once the judging has been completed and medals awarded the gardens are opened up to the public who can walk through them and admire them in detail – another welcome point of difference with Chelsea.

Conceptual show gardens are a particular feature of Hampton Court, with designers flexing their creative muscles to create more avant-garde gardens – offerings have explored challenging themes such as homophobic hate crime, landmine injuries and breast cancer. In recent years, the Small show gardens (currently known as Summer gardens) have explored literary themes to good effect.

Should the July weather be less than kind, there are plenty of undercover exhibits to mosey around. Clocking in at over 6750 metres square, the **Floral Pavilion is the** mother of all marquees and like a village flower show gone mad. The immaculately ordered displays of flowers and plants are a unique fusion of art and nature and a testament to the growers' dedication to the pursuit of perfection. With displays from top nurseries like Fibrex Nurseries, Avon Bulbs and Hardy's Cottage Garden Plants, there is quite literally a world of plants to admire, from alstroemerias to alliums, fuchsias to ferns, hostas to hardy bamboos, and cacti to carnations.

The Show's annual rose festival is a sumptuous, sensuous celebration of the flower that defines the British summer, with delectable presentations from top rose growers like Harkness, David Austin, and Peter Beales. The festival is a chance to get acquainted with new rose cultivars, as well as sink your nose into some fragrant old favourites.

Lovely as the show gardens are there's no denying that horticultural-themed retail therapy is also high on most visitors' agendas – and in terms of quantity and quality, Hampton Court Flower Show takes some beating. As well as the nursery stands there are exhibitors selling everything from the gardening nuts and bolts like decking, fencing and fruit cages to desirable 'lifestyle' products and fancy ornamental extras like weather vanes and sundials. The show's carnival atmosphere makes it all too easy to get carried away, but why not? The sun's shining, the jazz band is striking up, the Pimm's is delicious and that bespoke Italian water-feature would look just fabulous in your garden…

www.rhs.org.uk

H Hampton Court Palace Gardens

You've got to hand it to Henry VIII, he certainly knew how to think big. When not wreaking havoc on the monasteries or dispatching wives, he was busy collecting palaces. Hampton Court was just one of dozens acquired in his lifetime, and the one most closely associated with this mercurial monarch.

Conveniently sited by the Thames, Hampton Court Palace became a favourite honeymoon destination for Henry and he expanded its already lavish accommodation with no expense spared. Very much the sporty type, the king kitted out his favourite palace with tennis courts, bowling greens and a tiltyard for jousting, as well as a 750-acre park for deer hunting. Henry's tiltyard lives on in name,

home to a café and subdivided into several smaller gardens, including the Magic Garden, a high-spec Tudor-themed children's playground that opened in 2016. Designed by landscape architect Robert Myers the Magic Garden ticks all the Tudor boxes with strange topiary, a disappearing lion, 'king' and 'queen' helter-skelter towers, a moat, heraldic dragon's den, and a playful 'perspective pergola' – great fun in a garden setting for children aged 2-13.

Henry's mania for martial arts was not shared by some of his successors and in 1689 joint monarchs William and Mary converted the tiltyard into a six-acre walled kitchen garden. One acre of this has recently been restored to its 18th-century appearance, when it majored in salad production

The Tiltyard Rose Garden

(a royal salad typically comprising a minimum of 35 ingredients). Fruit and vegetables from this super-abundant patch can be purchased from the garden's stall on Tuesdays in the summer, and then fortnightly from November through until Christmas.

Other monarchs also put their stamp on Hampton Court – Charles II romantically followed in Henry's footsteps by honeymooning here with Catherine of Braganza (more pragmatically, he also installed one of his mistresses in special lodgings at the palace). The 3/4 mile Long Water Canal was dug for the king and, as a gift to his new bride, Charles planted an avenue of lime trees to flank it – a historic vista that was restored in 2004, with a new planting of 544 lime trees alongside the canal.

But it was the arrival of a new dynasty that really ushered in the biggest changes at HCP. William III and Mary II enthusiastically developed the palace when they came to the throne in 1689, commissioning Christopher Wren to add a fashionable baroque palace to the existing Tudor one and creating new gardens quite literally left, right and centre. The Great Fountain Garden was laid out along the East Front of their new palace – in their day it consisted of a 13-fountain parterre. Today it retains its original 'patte d'oie' (goose's foot) shape and radiating spokes of topiarised yews, although over the years these have grown into giant mushrooms. Presumably retained for historical rather than aesthetic interest, the rather incongruous formal flower beds dotted around the perimeter are a remnant of the garden in Victorian times. The one remaining fountain punctuates the central avenue, its plume of water drifting on breezy days to sprinkle unwary visitors. Even the Broad Walk herbaceous border along the East Front is on a palatial scale – in the summer a majestic sweep of phlox, delphiniums, dahlias, sweet peas and sedums.

Over on the south side of the Baroque palace, the new monarchs installed a new private garden featuring the latest in continental garden design. Thanks to a major restoration in 1995, William and Mary's Privy Garden today appears as it did in 1702 – a three-acre essay in full-blown formal gardening. Key design elements are the four plats of gazon coupé (turf cut with intricate patterns picked out in fine sand) and the carefully orchestrated topiary that adorn them. Control freaks will love this style of horticulture, others may find its regimented approach disturbing. The approach is certainly a labour-intensive one, with a team of gardeners continually at work trimming edges, tweaking weeds and grooming the gigantic hornbeam bower. A nifty remote-control mower keeps the grassy banks velvety smooth (much easier than the previous hover-mower-on-a-rope arrangement). Seasonally changing – and historically accurate – bedding displays inject colour, warmth and scent into the glacial layout. Between June and September the Lower Orangery terrace hosts a display of tender plants such as aloes, agaves, lantanas and citrus trees – as they would have done in the 18th century. An ardent plantswoman, Queen Mary housed her collection of tender exotic plants from around the world at Hampton Court, overwintering them in specially constructed 'stove houses'. An unashamed demonstration of wealth and power, Mary's vast collection included 1,000 orange trees – a none-too-subtle reference to the House of Orange, the Protestant dynasty to which her husband belonged.

Continuing along the southern side of the palace, two 'pond gardens' take the form of sunken flower gardens, with pretty displays of spring and summer bedding – in spring a colourful confection of hyacinths, tulips, bellis and primulas, giving way in summer to tagetes, fuchsias, pelargoniums and nicotiana. Their water features are a reminder of the gardens' origins

as Henry VIII's fishponds. The nearby 'Tudor' knot garden looks the part, but is in fact a 20th-century design – its recent restoration to Ernest Law's original 1924 plan perfectly illustrates Hampton Court's multi-layered history. The Great Vine has witnessed many of the changes since being planted by Capability Brown in 1768. It is now the oldest and largest vine in the world. Housed in a specially built glass house, this gargantuan plant still produces up to 320 kgs of sweet black grapes a year, its remarkable vigour assisted by generous dressings of manure.

Of course, most people come to HCP to get lost in the famous maze. Originally planted in 1690 as part of the Wilderness garden, the maze survived Capability Brown's tenure as Royal Gardener to become Hampton Court's most visited attraction. Every year some 330,000 visitors navigate its green corridors, taking an average of 20 minutes to reach the centre. Like its namesake at Ham House (see p.121), the Wilderness is anything but wild. It was designed as a place to wander in private, with tall hornbeam hedges, secluded benches and winding paths – the ideal place for romantic encounters. In spring the Wilderness is an enchanting vision of massed daffodils and narcissi and clouds of cherry blossom and magnolia flowers. Although there is a separate charge for the maze, this part of the garden has free entry and is a perfect destination for a relaxed stroll, and a picnic.

The formal gardens (to which there is an entrance charge during British summer time) cover some 60 acres – horse drawn carriage rides are available if the legwork gets too much. Even at Hampton Court time doesn't stand still and in addition to the historic gardens, there's also a 20th-century garden, which is used as a training ground for apprentice gardeners. It's a little more rough-and-ready than the immaculately tended main gardens but is a good place for a quiet picnic on a crowded day.

Hampton Court Palace Gardens
www.hrp.org.uk
See website for seasonally changing opening times and prices

The Pond Gardens

This page and opposite: Pergola, Hampstead Heath

The Hill Garden and Pergola

H

It's not every back garden that can accommodate an 800ft (244 metres) long pergola, but then the Hill Garden is not your usual kind of back garden. Commissioned by soap magnate Lord Leverhulme and designed by Thomas Mawson, this impressive brick, stone and timber structure was to be the defining feature of the gardens laid out behind The Hill, Lord Leverhulme's capacious Hampstead home. Today the Hill Garden and Pergola is managed by the City of London Corporation. It has been open to the public since the 1960s, but still retains the aura of a private, somewhat melancholy, secret garden.

Built between 1905 and 1925, the Pergola exudes the confidence and opulence of the Edwardian era with its Italianate styling, spectacular scale and commanding position overlooking Hampstead's West Heath. Thousands of wagon-loads of earth contributed to the Pergola's domineering height (over 15ft above the natural lie of the land), provided from the Northern line extension, which by happy coincidence was being built at the same time. Canny businessman Lord Leverhulme even received a fee for taking the soil he needed to build his project. After the war the elaborate, zig-zagging structure fell into disrepair but it was restored in the mid-1990s.

Mawson was a prolific garden designer and a leading exponent of the Arts and Crafts garden (the style took its name from his influential 1900 book *The Art and Craft of Garden Making*). Calling himself a 'landscape architect', Mawson took his lead from Humphrey Repton and stressed the importance of linking the garden to the wider landscape with gradually lessening degrees of formality. It's an approach that can be seen at the Hill Garden where the untamed heath and wailing sirens of the city lie beyond the garden's encircling iron railings and chestnut palings.

Resting atop its red brick plinth (which prosaically housed garden stores and the like), the Pergola consists of a majestic avenue of classical stone columns supporting wooden beams, punctuated by timber 'domes' and 'tents', as well as a stone belvedere. Assorted wisteria, clematis, roses, hops and vines wind their way tenaciously around the columns, providing colour, scent and interest for much of the year. Tucked into the angular folds at the base of the Pergola is a Mediterranean-style garden featuring wall-trained fruit trees, magnolias, drifts of euphorbia and sage, gravel paths and giant terracotta pots, an aromatic herb garden, and a box parterre. At the western extremity of the pergola lies a pleasant expanse of gently sloping lawns, plantations of mature trees and shrubs, and an orderly lily pond (built in 1963 on the site of a tennis court). Generously provisioned with benches, this little known Hill Garden is the perfect spot for a romantic picnic or quiet afternoon away from it all. With no dogs allowed, it's a perfect place to enjoy one of life's most sensual pleasures – running barefoot on newly-mown grass.

The Hill Garden and Pergola
Inverforth Close, off North End Way, NW3 7EX
www.cityoflondon.gov.uk
Open: Daily 08.30 until dusk
Admission free

H Horniman Museum and Gardens

A South London institution for over 100 years, the Horniman Museum was founded by Victorian tea tycoon Frederick Horniman with the intention of 'bringing the world to Forest Hill'. This popular local museum continues to do just that in the 21st century with Horniman's extraordinary collections of anthropological artefacts, musical instruments and natural history specimens still firmly at its core.

The museum's gardens have always been a popular part of its family friendly identity and boast an original 1903 bandstand, fine views of the South Downs, a small animal enclosure and London's first wildlife trail, which follows a ½ mile stretch of the original Crystal Palace Railway line. A valuable local green space, the gardens also form part of the Green Chain, a wider network of green spaces across SE London.

A recent £2.3 million refurbishment programme has linked the gardens more closely to the museum collections, creating imaginative new display gardens which showcase medicinal and food plants, and flora whose fibres are used to make textiles and musical instruments. As part of the new scheme, the Arts and Crafts-style Sunken Garden has been replanted with a colour-coordinated display of dye plants and a Sound Garden has been added to the bandstand terrace. The improvements to the garden combined with the charm of the museum, make the Horniman a great place for the avid gardener to bring the family while also getting a crafty horticultural fix...

Horniman Museum and Gardens
100 London Road, Forest Hill, SE23 3PQ
www.horniman.ac.uk   T: 020 8699 1872
Museum open: Daily 10.30-17.30
Garden open: Mon-Sat 7.30-sunset, Sun 8.00-sunset
Admission free (except for the Aquarium)
www.greenchain.com

Opposite, clockwise from top left: Bandstand, The insect Conservatory. This page: Art Nouveau clocktower by architect C. H. Townsend

133

I Inner Temple Garden

London's legal heartland might not be the most obvious location for horticultural thrills, but it is that very unexpectedness which makes Inner Temple Garden all the more delicious.

This three-acre site, overlooking the Thames, could hardly be more historic, having been in cultivation since at least the start of the 14th century and with its first recorded Head Gardener having been appointed as far back as 1546. Over the centuries the garden has taken many forms, from productive medieval orchard to Tudor 'knott' garden to formal parterre. In its time it has weathered all kinds of threats from the great storm of 1703 to the 1987 hurricane. The current garden consists of an unfussy sweep of lawn studded with specimen trees, and a double avenue of 19th-century plane trees running parallel with the river along the 'Broad Walk'.

Glorious as its historic 'bones' are, it is the garden's magnificent mixed borders that attract attention today. The High Border, which flanks the elegant iron railings to the north of the garden, has been transformed by Head Gardener Andrea Brunsendorf into a flamboyant mixed border using shrubs, perennials, annuals, climbers and bulbs to create year-round interest. At its radiant climax in late summer, the border pulsates with strong, contrasting colours that are able to stand up to the uncompromising red brick backdrop of Crown Office Row. Bold planting combinations here might include dahlias such as 'Emory Paul', 'Wigo Super' and 'Hillcrest Royal' and mid to later flowering perennials such as *Phlox* 'Franz Schubert' or *Aster pyrenaeus* 'Lutetia', with fiery highlights of *Canna musifolia* 'Grande' and *Tithonia* 'Torch', woven through with clumps of various ornamental grasses such as *Miscanthus* 'Rotsilber' or *Calamagrostis* × *acutiflora* 'Karl Foerster'. The large flower spikes of the *Aralia californica* are a magnet for bees as well as providing a majestic bookend to the border, while the *Dahlia imperialis* (tree dahlia) is Andrea's pride and joy, and quite possibly the only outdoor flowering specimen in the country. Preparation for the next year's High Border display starts even as the herbaceous plants are being cut down in the autumn, with Andrea's meticulous planning and artistry ensuring a seamless succession of colour and interest, with spring bulbs

Andrea Brunsendorf

yielding to tulips and alliums underplanted with aquilegias, followed by tender bedding. Self-sown poppies, verbena and Scotch thistles (*Onopordum acanthium*) grow where they will, ensuring things don't look too regimented. In winter stately grasses, cardoons and pretty early flowering *Rosa banksiae* 'Lutea' lend seasonal elegance to the border.

The Mediterranean beds, on either side of the steps down to the lawn, have also been spiced up. In June they are in full swing, their predominantly silvery grey palette studded by strategic dabs of colour. The scope of the planting here in fact extends well beyond the actual Med, with exotics like *Arbutus menziesii* from NW United States, *Berkheya purpurea* from South Africa and *Dasylirion quadrangulatum* from Mexico. Pink and white roses are the ostensible mainstay of the War of the Roses Border (according to Shakespeare, hostilities began in 'Temple Garden'). In spring, however, it is massed ranks of daffodils, sweet rockets and foxgloves that make a pre-emptive bid for glory in this bed. And when the spring bedding fades, it is replaced with vibrant annual summer bedding beneath the warring roses.

Tucked away on the other side of Paper Buildings, the Peony Garden is a tranquil space, slightly separate from the rest of the garden. Here the colour scheme is pastel hued, with a ghostly *Wisteria sinensis* twining around the railings and blowsy herbaceous and tree peonies putting on a brief display in early summer. Seasonally changing displays of pots brighten the steps of Kings Bench Walk and the circular pond, the latter providing a shady spot to show off aquatic and marginal plants like gunneras, irises and sedge. It is here also that Andrea is able to indulge in her unexpected newfound passion for plectranthus, developing an extensive collection of specimens such as purple-leaved *Pletranthus ciliatus*.

Since her appointment in 2007 – and she is the first woman to hold the post as Head Gardener – Andrea has set about reinvigorating the 'Great Garden' with some élan. As well as revamping the borders, and steering the garden away from any municipal tendencies, one of her priorities has been to improve the organic content of the garden's free-draining alluvial soil. To this end, 40 or so tons of horse manure are imported each winter – no easy task given the twin challenges of the congestion charge/super cycle highway and the slender dimensions of the service entrance. The garden has too many high-maintenance and mildew prone roses to be completely organic but it is managed with concern for the environment – propagation of annual bedding reduces 'plant miles', and a wildlife friendly native hedge has been planted by the work area. Andrea's permanent staff of three and team of enthusiastic volunteers are supplemented by Boris the spaniel and Hunter the cat, both of whom provide chemical-free pest control.

Another innovation has been a mass planting of 14,000 *Liriope muscari* for naturalistic spring colour along the Broad Walk – these pretty 'turf lilies' tolerate the dry shade beneath the plane trees. Other exciting projects have included the creation of a woodland garden underneath the Manchurian walnut tree, and Andrea has also revamped the King's Bench Walk border with an English herbaceous border that addresses all four seasons.

In the 19th century, under dynamic Head Gardener Samuel Broome, the garden became a venue for a series of chrysanthemum shows, as well as being used by the RHS for its Spring Shows until 1911, when the event moved to Chelsea. Appropriately, under Andrea's energetic stewardship, this connection with the RHS has been revived with a September Floral Celebration being held in the Great Garden in 2008. Day-to-day the garden is a private haven enjoyed by the students, barristers and benchers of the Inner Temple, but it is normally open to the public every weekday between 12.30-15.00. In addition, the garden opens for the Chelsea Fringe Festival and Open Garden Squares Weekend and hosts private garden tours.

Inner Temple Garden, EC4Y 7HL
www.innertemple.org.uk

Access to the Garden is via the north gate opposite Crown Office Row. The garden is normally open from 12.30 to 15.00 each weekday. In high winds, it is closed as a precaution.

Japanese Kyoto Garden

An unexpected outpost of Japan in Holland Park, Kyoto Garden was built by the expert gardeners of the Kyoto Garden Association as a gift to Kensington and Chelsea by the Kyoto Chamber of Commerce. This tranquil space opened in 1991, in time to celebrate the Japan Festival held in London the following year, and has been providing a soul-soothing counterpoint to the hyperactive sportiness found elsewhere in the park ever since.

The garden is designed as a traditional *kaiyu-shiki* or 'stroll' garden. Stroll or 'excursion' gardens developed in Japan in the Edo period (1603-1867), when travel inside Japan was restricted and its grounded grandees took to making gardens in which they could take 'excursions' without the need for travel. Such gardens took the form of a symbolic tour through Japan, with features such as rocks, waterfalls, lakes and meadows standing in for aspects of the country's forbidden landscapes.

Although on a more modest scale than most native *kaiyu-shiki*, the Kyoto Garden ticks most of the genre's boxes. Features include a circular path winding its way around the garden, a noisy waterfall cascading down a rugged terrace to represent steep mountain gorges, while the pond with its islands and neatly constructed pebbly shoreline evokes the ocean's mighty expanse. Peacocks – white as well as the usual blue – strut across the grass and sip water from a stone wash basin (*chozubachi*) fed by a bamboo spout while ducks and colourful koi carp patrol the waters of the pond. Other traditional features include picturesque stone lanterns (*toro*) dotted around the garden, a *shishi-odoshi* (bamboo animal scarer) and carefully placed boulders.

Nothing happens by chance in a Japanese garden – be it a dry gravel garden or a ceremonial tea garden – and the Kyoto Garden's planting scheme is as nuanced and considered as its hard landscaping. In its striving to create the essence of

a natural landscape in a garden setting, the *kaiyu-shiki* has some affinities with the classic English landscape garden of the 18th century (see Chiswick House and Garden p.60). As in English landscape gardens, trees play a vital role in creating rhythm and texture within the design and, for a small space, the treescape of the Kyoto garden is particularly satisfying. As you would expect, cherries are well represented, with varieties including 'Ukon', 'Kanzan' and the Tibetan cherry *Prunus serrula*; spring blossom is also provided by the native Japanese magnolia (*Magnolia kobus*). The carefully sculpted conifer collection includes Scots, Weymouth and Bhutan pines, their vertical accents balanced by soft mounds of evergreen shrubs such as choisya and box. In spring rhododendrons, irises and azaleas inject vibrant colour into the tasteful scene, while fiery acers (*Acer palmatum* 'Senkaki' and *Acer rubescens* 'Rosie') maintain the heat in the autumn months. Skillful design and specialist care ensure that the garden looks good whatever the season. Every few years a team of gardeners flies over from Japan to make sure the trees and shrubs are pruned correctly. Comprehensive renovations take place every ten years, the most recent having been completed in the summer of 2011, to celebrate the 20th anniversary of the garden's installation.

Holland Park, Ilchester Place, W8 6LU
Open: Daily from 07.30 until 30 minutes before dusk

Kensington Roof Gardens

The Roof Gardens in Kensington have been a lofty London landmark since they opened in 1938. Over the years they have been known by a number of names; for some, they will always be 'the Derry Gardens' or 'the Derry and Toms Roof Gardens', in reference to the department store for which they were originally designed by landscape architect Ralph Hancock. For many they are simply 'the Kensington Roof Gardens' while for a brief, brilliant moment in the 1970s they were 'the Biba Roof Gardens', when the famous fashion house took over Derry and Tom's sleek Art Deco premises. Today they are glamorous again, in their current incarnation as one of Sir Richard Branson's 'Virgin Limited Edition' retreats, and are open to the public when not closed for private events.

Occupying a 1½ acre expanse that most London gardeners can only dream of, The Roof Gardens were the biggest in Europe when they were built. Although they were designed to outshine the roof garden at rival department store Selfridges, the Derry and Toms' gardens took their cue not from London but from New York, where Ralph Hancock had created a 'Garden of Nations' on the 11th floor of the Rockefeller Centre in the 1930s. Hancock certainly set a high standard, creating eight gardens including examples of the Japanese, Spanish, Dutch and English styles, as well as a bird sanctuary and a 'sky-scraper vegetable garden'.

D&T's chairman, Trevor Bowen, commissioned Hancock to make something similar in Kensington and was rewarded with a garden that comprehensively knocked the one at Selfridges' into a cocked hat. In London Hancock restricted his thematic palette to a Spanish, a Tudor and an English Woodland Garden, but at 100 feet above pavement level, the logistics remained formidable. The roof was waterproofed with a thick bitumastic base, followed by a layer of rubble for drainage and topsoil for planting. Artesian wells were sunk

beneath the neighbouring Barkers department store to provide the copious water supply required and Derry and Tom's service lift was kept busy hauling materials up to the 6th floor.

Hancock made life a little simpler for himself by re-using several elements from his Rockefeller scheme – the barley-twist columns in The Spanish Garden's arcades and the sequence of 'stone' arches in The Tudor Garden were concrete casts of their American forebears. But with more space to play with in London, Hancock was able to go to town in other ways. The D&T's Spanish Garden had not just one loggia but three, as well as a campanile, and a court of fountains, while The English Woodland Garden featured a cascade and a steam running the length of the roof, overlooked by a tea pavilion. A full-on planting scheme complemented the hard-landscaping with over 500 varieties of trees and shrubs, and annual deployments of thousands of bulbs and bedding plants, the latter produced in the gardens' own roof-top nursery.

Today the gardens are protected by Grade II* listing while the trees have been under a preservation order since 1976. A major renovation was undertaken in 2007 and returned the gardens to their 1930s glory; a commemorative plaque to Hancock was unveiled at the gardens in 2012 and was the first of its kind to honour a gardener. Current head gardener Pilar

Medrano-Dell took up post in May 2015 and has spent her first year on a watching brief: "You always need a full year to get to know a garden", she says, but in the last few months has started to make her presence felt, with sustainability and wildlife appeal high on her agenda. "The garden has to look good all the time, so changes are introduced gradually, in little pockets," she explains, and in The Spanish Garden she is slowly adjusting the vividly coloured 1950s-style planting scheme, with its hot-hued dahlias and Mediterranean stalwarts such as olive, juniper, palm trees and yuccas, by adding water-thrifty plants such as salvias, heleniums, coreopsis, verbena bonariensis, agastache and one of her favourite plants, cosmos. As an added bonus, the new plants will extend the season, flowering from late spring through to autumn.

In The Tudor Garden the cool black-and-white scheme harks back to the Biba era, when the shop ran its own gin-fuelled after hours 'gardening club' for the staff – "it's a challenge to find the right plants', says Pilar, "but really good fun!" The Woodland Garden remains true to its 1930s self with recent additions of liquidambar and elm joining the mature pollarded English oak, American red oak, limes and mulberry trees that remain from Hancock's original planting. Pilar plans to introduce a more naturalistic planting scheme here, and she and her team have been busy clearing and renovating shrubs in readiness. A favourite haunt of the resident ducks and famous flamingos, The Woodland Garden is magical in springtime with carpets of snowdrops, anemones and bluebells; further plantings of spring bulbs are in the pipeline.

Hancock probably didn't design them as such, but his gardens have turned out to be eco-friendly before their time, keeping the building below cool, and reducing run off. Pilar and her three part-time gardeners avoid chemicals where possible and opt for biological controls for pests such as vine weevil, while the ducks take care of the slugs. Pilar has incorporated vegetable crops such as courgettes, beetroot, peas, squash and salad leaves into The Spanish Garden, and cleared space for vegetables behind The Woodland Garden. Babylon restaurant, one floor above, makes use of the fresh produce where possible, and Pilar has indulged her love of herbs on the restaurant's terrace with lively planters that brim with ornamental and deliciously aromatic specimens such as chives, tangerine sage and anise hyssop.

In the Biba years, the gardens were known as a hang-out for celebrities such as David Bowie and the Rolling Stones. Today they likewise welcome many well-known faces but are also a haven for wildlife, attracting several varieties of bees, a regular gang of green finches, and a heron, which comes to call whenever the stream is stocked with fish. The flamingos are defiantly exotic residents, but have been a signature feature of the gardens for decades; in the Biba era they were joined briefly by a troupe of penguins.

The gardens keep in touch with the spirit of its past in fun ways such as the quarterly gardening club, which recalls Hancock's 'Horticultural Halls' at the Rockefeller as well as Biba's hedonistic gardening group. Today's equally sociable members enjoy exclusive opening of the gardens, and talks from high-profile speakers such as Nigel Dunnett. The Roof Gardens are also open to the public (with free admission) when The Roof Gardens are not hosting an event.

Designed with an intended lifespan of no more than 10 years, The Roof Gardens will celebrate their 80th anniversary in 2018, a date that Pilar is already working towards. "Watch this space" she says, tantalisingly!

The Roof Gardens
99 Kensington High Street, W8 5SA
www.roofgardens.virgin.com
T: 020 7937 7994
Open: Daily 09.00-17.00, subject to bookings
(phone in advance to check)

Pilar Medrano-Dell

Meet the Gardener

With a background working in period gardens (Moggerhanger Park, Wrest Park, Walpole Park and a variety of English Heritage and National Trust properties), Pilar is used to gardening sensitively within the needs of historic locations. But every garden has its quirks and at the Roof Gardens one of the main challenges is not necessarily horticultural. "The roof gardens are busy all year," says Pilar, "it can be difficult to get into the garden some days!" A flexible approach is vital and Pilar sometimes comes in on a Sunday or in the evenings, and is adept at 'speed gardening' in certain areas when the opportunity arises. "It's a big challenge to work in a place with so many different events and visitors, but it is also one of my favourite things: we have such a fantastic array of guests, and I love to see them enjoying the garden".

Pilar's enthusiastic team of co-gardeners is another plus of the job. "I'm so fortunate, we respect each other and work well together." They certainly cover the ground - although the Roof Gardens is a relatively compact site, Pilar and her team reckon on covering as many as seven miles a day as they go about their work.

One particular aspect of the Roof Gardens seems to have captured Pilar's heart: "I really enjoy feeding the flamingos!" she admits, "They get to know you and they make a particular head movement when they see you. It's by far my favourite way to finish off a busy day in the Gardens!"

143

Kew Gardens in Autumn

With an estimated 14,000 trees to its name, Kew is a tree-hugger's paradise, which in autumn blazes with a bravura display of burnished leaves, brightly coloured berries and fulsome fruit.

Although tree-climbing is strictly off limits at Kew, the Xtrata Treetop Walkway offers legitimate high level fun without risk to life and limb (tree or human). Snaking its way past mature Spanish chestnut and common lime trees, the 262ft (80m) high walkway gives visitors a squirrel's eye view of the tree canopy and the city beyond. The structure was designed by the architects of the London Eye and is based on a Fibonacci sequence, but clever maths hasn't stopped it getting pretty wobbly up there, so you'll need sea legs as well as a head for heights. Back on terra firma, the Rhizotron installation digs deep into the secret world of roots, offering advice on how to plant a tree and celebrating the good work done by mycorrhiza, worms and woodlice.

Incredibly, some trees still survive from Kew's foundation as a botanic garden in 1759 by Princess Augusta, George III's mother. These five 'Old Lions', are a tangible link with Kew's past and include the bizarrely contorted Pagoda Tree whose trunk is supported by an equally odd variety of structures. Not to be outdone, the mighty ginkgo, another Old Lion, has officially been designated a 'Great British Tree', in celebration of the Queen's Golden Jubilee. New arrivals to the arboretum ensure the collection is kept up-to-date, one of the most exciting in recent years being the Wollemi pine, a species which despite being some 90 million years old was only discovered in 1994. With less than 100 mature trees existing in the wild, Kew's specimen is a particular rarity.

Those interested in getting to know Kew's trees more intimately should look out for the Bark Trail, a self-guided tour introducing 25 specimens, whose bark is either beautiful, useful or both. Along the two-hour route you'll encounter the ruby-red stems of the medicinal wonder tree, the Tibetan cherry, and the incense cedar so favoured by pencil makers. Some of these trees have other claims to fame – no.7, the lacebark pine, is a 'Champion Tree', (ie one of the largest of its species growing in this country), while the swirling bark of no.22, the sweet chestnut, inspired the Whomping Willow in the Harry Potter books and films. Other arboreal attractions include the Holly Walk, which contains the largest collection of mature hollies in the world. In November and December these prickly customers bear a mass of red, black and white berries – if you want to see them in flower, June is usually the time to visit.

Also looking good in autumn is the grass garden, tucked away in the south-eastern corner of Kew's grounds. The recently redesigned garden showcases over 500 species, from the stately spires of pampas grass to the jaunty golden feather of *Stipa tenuissima* and the improbably fluffy white seed heads of *Pennisetum villosum*. Beloved by garden designers, grasses aren't just airy-fairy border fillers but are a major player in the global economy with grass family members maize, rice and wheat providing half of the protein consumed by the world's population.

Royal Botanic Gardens
Kew, Richmond, Surrey, TW9
www.kew.org
T: 020 8332 5655 (visitor information)

Xtrata Treetop Walkway

Livery Company Gardens

With a history stretching back to Saxon times, the City of London's livery companies are a remarkably enduring feature of the Square Mile.

These ancient guilds represented all the great trades and crafts of the day from apothecaries to woolmen (and even gardeners, whose own guild was incorporated by Royal Charter in 1605). The guilds acted to enforce standards as well as being educators, running a system of apprenticeships. Today philanthropy is their primary activity, and their ranks have been swelled by modern liveries representing the likes of Information Technologists, Security Professionals and Tax Advisors. Those Livery Halls that survived the Blitz or were rebuilt post-war, have found profitable second lives as upmarket venues for hire, whilst still fulfilling their time-honoured role as a meeting place for their members and governing 'Court'.

Among the 40 existing livery halls in the City, ten lucky ones still have gardens, an asset valued as much in the modern day as in the medieval era when they were used for a variety of activities, from the homely (clothes drying, growing fruit and flowers) to the recreational (strolling and bowling). Today the bowling alleys and greens may be long gone, but the pleasure principle lives on. The livery companies below are happy to shares their precious green space with visitors...

The Salters' Garden

The Salters are one of the twelve oldest Livery Companies in the City but their hall is one of the newest, a crisp white concrete number built in the 1970s to a design by Sir Basil Spence. The garden is newer still, having been designed by David Hicks in 1995, to commemorate the 600th anniversary of the Salters' Company. Bounded on the southern side by a high section of London's Roman wall and to the north by the white walls of the hall itself, this subterranean garden was designed to be seen from above, from the 6th floor balcony of the Salters' Hall. With its hornbeam, box and yew hedged compartments, plashing fountains and elegant arrangement of York paving, gravel paths and lawn, this is a knot garden in the modern style. Clematis scramble up the iron obelisks and roses ramble over the pergolas in the summer, although the restricted light of the canyon-like site mean they are rather leggy specimens. Each cocooned within a leafy hornbeam enclosure, the garden's wooden benches are the perfect spot to enjoy some peace in the heart of the city. The garden is usually open during business hours.

Salters Hall, Fore Street, EC2Y 5DE
Open: Mon-Fri 9.00-17.00

The Goldsmiths' Garden

The Salters' Garden, viewed from St Alphage Highwalk

The Goldsmiths' Garden

The Goldsmiths' Garden

Like the Salters, Goldsmiths are one of the Great Twelve Livery Companies of the City of London, receiving their Royal Charter way back in 1327. Their magnificent hall, on Foster Lane – the third on the present site – was built in 1835 but the first reference to a Goldsmiths' garden dates from 1495. Their current garden is a more recent affair, with its origins in the destruction and turmoil of the Blitz. Situated on the corner of Gresham and Noble Streets, this two-level garden was formerly the site of the church of St John Zachary, which burnt down in the Great Fire. In 1940 incendiary bombs devastated the area once again and the following year fire watchers from Goldsmiths' Hall began to develop the bomb site as a garden. These prototype guerrilla gardeners created such a flourishing space from the rubble that the Goldsmiths' Company set up a competition for the best bomb site garden in the City, which 'their' garden promptly won five years in a row.

In 1957, the garden was redesigned by Peter Shepheard and refurbished in 1994/5, with a further replanting in 2003. A manicured lawn and central fountain form the soothing focal point of the lower garden, with benches stationed at the foot of the perimeter walls. Avian visitors are equally well provided for, with feeders, nesting boxes and natural perches provided by roses, magnolias, climbing hydrangea and Chinese Virginia Creeper. The scarlet bottlebrush blooms of *Callistemon citrinus splendens* add vivid summer colour to this pared-down planting scheme, as do the bedding plants on the cantilevered façade of the Nicholas Grimshaw designed office building that overlooks the garden. On street level the garden is dominated by two London plane trees with a serene, predominantly white-and-green planting scheme featuring hydrangeas, *Anemone blanda*, hart's tongue fern and sweet box (*Sarcococca*). The resulting garden offers a formal but lush green space to escape from the noise and chaos of the City.

Goldsmiths' Garden
at the junction of Gresham Street and
Noble Street, EC2
Open: Daily, all day

The Barber-Surgeons' Garden

Like the Salters' garden, the Barber-Surgeons' garden is situated in the lee of the Roman wall, although with the added glamour of the remains of an early fourth century defensive bastion. Informal lawns studded with specimen trees, including a foxglove tree (*Paulownia tomentosa*), tulip trees (*Liriodendron tulipifera*) and a yellow Magnolia 'Elizabeth' (planted to commemorate the Queen's Golden Jubilee in 2002) make up the bulk of the garden but it is the herb garden that is perhaps of most interest.

Built in 1987, on a derelict bomb site by the Barbers post-war livery hall, this petite physic garden is divided into 45 beds demonstrating the use of plants in medicine from ancient times to the modern day. The selection ranges from aromatic herbs such as meadowsweet and lavender to plants like yew and liquorice with a proven modern pharmaceutical track record. The planting scheme also includes herbs such as parsley, comfrey and spurge that were recommended by John Gerard, the celebrated 16th-century surgeon and author of the eponymous *Herbal*, who became Master of the Barber-Surgeons' Company in 1607. A descriptive list of the all the plants can be found in the garden or alternatively on the Barbers' Company website.

The strange mound behind the curved wall that partly encloses the herb garden is a grisly reminder of the area's history. Buried beneath are thousands of pieces of skeleton from plague pits and churchyards in the area, as well the surgeons' dissecting rooms which once stood on this site. Open to the public but without any benches to rest weary legs, the garden is usually sparsely populated, making it a good choice for quiet picnics.

Barber-Surgeons' Garden
Off London Wall/Wood Street, EC2Y 5BD
Open: Daily, all day

This page: Barber-Surgeons' Garden
Opposite: Goldsmiths' Garden

L | London Plants

Over the centuries London's seemingly unpromising terrain has nurtured a surprising variety of plants and even given its name to a few along the way.

Rosebay Willowherb

A colourful opportunist, this once scarce upland plant owes at least some of its current ubiquity to the two world wars of the last century. Its tall, purple-pink flower spikes flourished on forestry sites newly cleared for the war effort of WWI, but it was the Blitz that turned rosebay willowherb into an urban phenomenon. With the disturbed and burnt ground of London's bomb sites providing ideal germination conditions for its wind-borne seeds, rosebay willowherb appeared there in sudden, purple profusion during the summer of 1941. Its Latin name is *Chamerion angustifolium* but to many Londoners it is simply 'fireweed' or 'bombweed'.

Rosebay Willowherb

London Rocket

An immigrant species, despite its misleading common name, *Sisymbrium irio* hails from the Mediterranean. It was known to be flourishing in London by the mid 17th century, but the plant's fortunes waned from the early 19th century until 1945, when it was rediscovered growing near the Tower of London. Specimens of this yellow-flowered annual can still be spotted on the London Wall at Tower Gateway but urban botanists will need to be alert to the presence of the similar looking Eastern Rocket (*S. orientale*), which grows on the Wall at Noble Street, and its hairier relation, the helpfully named False London Rocket (*S. loeselii*), which has naturalised in a few sites in the city.

London Rocket

London Plane

London Plane

Synonymous with the capital's parks, garden squares and tree-lined streets, this is another 'London' plant that botanically speaking is nothing of the kind. Its precise lineage is debatable but it is probably a cross between the eastern and western species of plane, originating in Spain sometime in the 17th century – hence its Latin name *Platanus x hispanica* (although it is also sometimes referred to as *Platanus x acerifolia*). Recognisable by its leathery palmate leaves, its flaking bark, and its furry seed heads, London's signature tree is also remarkably long-lived and can grow up to nearly 50 metres high.

Berkeley Square is home to some venerable London planes, which are among the oldest in London having been planted in 1789 by Edward Bouvier, a resident of the square. They include one tree whose amenity value has been calculated at £750,000, making it Britain's most valuable tree – and a canny investment by Mr Bouvier, had he lived to see it. Other notable specimens are 'Barney', a 17th-century London plane on Barnes Common whose girth measures 8 metres, and the Richmond Riverside Plane, which is thought to be London's tallest London plane. Planted in 1931, the London plane outside the Dorchester Hotel is a newcomer by comparison but, elegantly illuminated at night, it has become a much-loved landmark on Park Lane, and it too has been designated a 'Great Tree of London'.

Resistant to drought, pollution, pruning (expert or otherwise), compacted soil and high winds, the London plane is often regarded as the perfect urban tree. But after some 300 years at the heart of city life, it is facing a worrying new threat from Europe – Massaria, a fungal infection that seems to target plane trees. By 2010 around 200 trees in London's Royal Parks had been affected and in March 2011 a branch from a tree in Highbury Fields provided the first formal ID of the disease in Britain. Massaria attacks the upper side of individual branches, making them susceptible to sudden breakage – a bitter irony for a tree that is revered for its reluctance to shed branches (hence its popularity as a street tree). The disease poses a real challenge to cash-strapped councils as trees will need to be inspected frequently and close-up, with the additional expense of platforms or tree climbers. But the good news is that the disease doesn't seem to affect the health of the tree as a whole and can be contained by early identification and bough removal.

Deptford Pink

This now rare wild flower, *Dianthus armeria,* owes its name to John Gerard, who in his 1597 *Herball* described it growing in 'the great field next to Detford' (sic). At the risk of ruining a lovely story, it's possible he may have actually meant a different plant, *Dianthus deltoides,* but Gerard's mistake has been Deptford's gain. If you want to grow your own Deptford Pinks, seeds are available from specialist wildflower nurseries.

Deptford Pink

London Pride

A cheerful cottage garden plant, *Saxifraga x urbium* is tolerant of both shady and dry conditions. It flourished on London's bomb sites after the Blitz and was immortalized by Noel Coward's patriotic wartime song of the same name, penned in the summer of 1941. Coward's lyrics picked up on the plant's ability to thrive almost on thin air:
There's a little city flower every spring unfailing
Growing in the crevices by some London railing' .

London Pride

Haringey Knotweed

This is a 'new to science' hybrid of two notoriously thuggish plants – Japanese Knotweed (*Fallopia japonica*) and Russian Vine (*F. baldschuanica*). It was discovered in 1987 growing on Railway Fields Nature Reserve, off Green Lanes, by botanist David Bevan. Haringey is still the only place in the UK to harbour a wild population of its eponymous knotweed, more formally identified as *Fallopia x conollyana*.

Haringey Knotweed

London Fruit and Veg

Gone are the days when 'Battersea bundles' meant freshly cut asparagus from the fields of Wandsworth, or the herbalist-surgeon John Gerard could praise the quality of Hackney's turnips, but remnants of London's market gardening past live on. Short's Gardens (WC2) remembers the Mr Short who once rented a market garden there, while 'Cellini', the aniseed-flavoured dessert apple raised in Vauxhall in 1828 by nurseryman Leonard Phillips, can still be found growing in the area today, at Lambeth Walk Open Space Community Garden, next to Roots and Shoots (see p.194). An even older variety, the scarlet dessert apple Fearn's Pippin, was raised sometime before 1780 in the Fulham garden of one Mr Bagley. Popular in Victorian times, this apple has recently been planted in a number of London school orchards as part of the Fruit-full Schools project.

In the 20th century the John Innes Institute, based in south London from 1910 to 1967, developed several new fruit varieties as part of its research into plant breeding and genetics. Easily recognisable by their 'Merton' prefix, the apples include Merton Charm and Merton Beauty, as well as the Award of Garden Merit-winning Merton Worcester (released c 1950) and Merton Knave (released 1975) – the latter two can be seen in the orchard of Fenton House (p.94). Other, quite literal, fruits of their labour include the Merton Gage, the Merton Pride pear and the Merton Bigareau cherry. The Institute's decades-long research into apple breeding also resulted in the 'Malling-Merton' (MM) rootstocks, a joint venture with the East Malling Research Station to develop rootstocks with resistance to woolly aphids. Two of these, the MM106 and the more vigourous MM111, are still widely used today.

Orchard at Fenton House

L Lost Gardens of London

Gardening's ephemeral nature is nowhere more evident than in London, where even the most acclaimed of gardens are not immune to the city's insatiable appetite for development. The roll call of London's lost gardens includes historically significant ones such as John Evelyn's garden at Sayes Court, the Vauxhall Pleasure Gardens and Loddiges Nursery in Hackney. Street names mark their once vibrant presence: Evelyn Street in SE8, Jonathan and Tyers Streets in SE11 (which commemorate the canny proprietor of the Vauxhall gardens), while in E9, Loddiges Road remembers the nursery that was once home to the world's largest hothouse.

Deptford's surprising horticultural hinterland includes not just its eponymous Pink (see p.152) but also the garden created by the 17th-century diarist John Evelyn. Along with his friend Samuel Pepys, Evelyn was one of the foremost chroniclers of his age, as well as an ardent horticulturalist. As a young man, sitting out the Civil War on the Continent, he was a keen garden goer, visiting Villa d'Este and Monte Cavallo in Italy, the Tuileries and Luxembourg Gardens in Paris. On return to England in 1652 he lost no time putting his enthusiasm for modern gardening into practice at Sayes Court, his wife's 100-acre estate in Deptford.

For over 40 years Evelyn painstakingly created a garden out of what had been farmland, introducing elegant features such as a long terrace, a parterre and a 'fountain garden' as well as working areas including a physic garden, a kitchen garden, orchards and beehives. Although Sayes Court is long gone (and the site about to be further submerged beneath a new development), Evelyn's 1653 plan gives us a good idea of its scope, from its epicurean moated island (planted with asparagus and raspberries), to Evelyn's own Private Garden, planted with 'choice flowers and simples'. We even know how it was managed, thanks to the *Directions for the Gardiner at Says-Court* that Evelyn wrote

for his garden staff, a document brimming with practical tips on frost protection, manuring and pruning. It also listed the numerous fruit varieties he grew and gardening tools he owned. Further advice was dispensed in Evelyn's *Kalendarium Hortense*, published in 1664, the world's first month-by-month gardening guide, whose 'to do' lists included pest control and cider making.

In 1661 Evelyn, ever the keen garden visitor, went to the recently opened New Spring Gardens in Vauxhall, beating Pepys to it by a year. Post-Restoration, Vauxhall's 12 acres of tree-lined gravel walks were a place to enjoy simple, al fresco pastimes such as fruit-picking, picnicking and promenading. In the following century they developed into full-blown pleasure gardens under the proprietorship of Jonathan Tyers. The entrepreneurial Tyers took over the lease in 1728, relaunching the Spring Gardens as *the* place to see and be seen, frequented by all strata of society from the Prince of Wales downwards, and even enticing Casanova over from Venice.

Under Tyers ownership Vauxhall became a cultural destination, showcasing contemporary artworks by Hayman, Hogarth and Roubiliac, music by Handel and Arne, and specially commissioned 'Vauxhall songs' performed by popular artistes. Roubiliac's informal life-size sculpture of Handel greeted visitors as they entered, ushering them into Vauxhall's enchanted, somewhat racy, nocturnal world, illuminated by thousands of lights attached to the trees. Here the normal codes of behaviour were suspended, and the sexes could mingle freely amongst its shady groves and 'dark walks'.

Vauxhall captured the collective imagination, and its attractions were recorded for posterity in literature, as well as in paintings and engravings. An ever-changing menu of attractions kept the punters coming through the reigns of ten monarchs, from fireworks and balloon ascents to a recreation of the Battle of Waterloo. Even Vauxhall's exorbitant refreshments – its wafer-thin ham became the stuff of legend – couldn't dent its appeal. Rival gardens such as Ranelagh and Marylebone came and went, but Vauxhall outlived them all. The end finally came in 1859, when rising land prices and competition from seaside resorts newly accessible by rail, made residential redevelopment inevitable. By 1870 the site had been completely built over, and stayed thus until a century later when a park was created on the site. The palest of shadows of its namesake, Spring Gardens has recently received a £200,000 architect-led makeover, with the aim of reviving its fortunes.

Upwardly mobile land values and London's ever-expanding girth also sounded the death knell for Loddiges Nursery Garden, which also closed in the 1850s. From small 18th-century beginnings in rural Hackney, Loddiges became one of Europe's most notable nurseries. It was also one of the best-connected, cultivating new species delivered by the top plant hunters and supplying royal gardens, stately homes and botanic gardens around the world. A trailblazing commercial outfit with exacting horticultural standards, Loddiges was responsible for popularising the Wardian case, the revolutionary glass box used to transport live plant specimens at sea, and for introducing many new species, including the thuggish mauve *Rhododendron ponticum*.

The Loddiges weren't afraid to think big and their pioneering collection of centrally heated glass houses included the Grand Palm House – the largest of its kind in the world. These were populated with exotic palms, ferns and orchids, while their on-site arboretum gave Kew a run for its money with over 2,500 species. The neatly labelled trees were arranged on one side of a spiral path, in alphabetical order from *Acer* to *Quercus*; on the other side of the path unfurled Lodigges' enormous collection of roses which were admired by Charles Darwin when he visited in 1838. Nothing of these achievements remain on the site in Stoke Newington, the arboretum at nearby Abney Park Cemetary is the last surviving testament to the genius of George Loddiges.

South Walk Vauxhall Gardens by J S Muller c1751

M Market Gardens

'Fresh', 'local' and 'sustainable' may seem like contemporary consumer buzzwords but when it comes to ticking eco-friendly boxes, 17th-century Londoners beat their modern-day counterparts hands down. Back in the day, a swathe of market gardens in outlying riverside villages such as Chelsea, Battersea, Wandsworth and Bermonsdey, as well as eastern suburbs like Hoxton and Hackney, kept the hungry city daily supplied with a seasonally changing menu of fruit and vegetables.

Market gardening took off in England in the 1600s, galvanised by Dutch and Flemish immigrants who were escaping religious persecution. These green-fingered, commercially savvy newcomers bought with them improved vegetable varieties and a talent for optimising the soil's productivity, using techniques such as hot beds to defy the vagaries of the British climate. Proving the adage that where there's muck there is indeed brass, intensive manuring was the key to their success and a neat reciprocal trade evolved with Thames barges carrying fresh produce towards city markets such as Newgate Street, Leadenhall and Spitalfields, and those travelling in the opposite direction piled with horse manure and human 'night soil'. With around 725,000 inhabitants in 1760, London's population must have kept the appositely named Dung Wharf, near Puddle Dock (as shown in John Rocque's 1767 map of the city), busy.

Poor grain harvests in the late 1500's and the newly fashionable trend for eating vegetables meant that market gardening, although by definition a small-scale enterprise (cultivation by the hoe as opposed to the plough), could be a nice little earner. In 1605 the Worshipful Company of Gardeners (see p.265) was founded as an (ultimately unsuccessful) attempt to regulate the burgeoning trade. In 1670 a charter formalised the fruit and veg trade that had grown up by the Duke of Bedford's house in Covent Garden, paving the way for it to become the capital's main produce market in the 19th century. Different areas became famed for particular crops – according to the 18th-century author Daniel Lysons' *General View of the Former and Present State of Market Gardens*, Battersea was synonymous with fine asparagus, Twickenham with strawberries, while Deptford was a notable producer of onion seed. Evidently veg plots were considered as attractive then as they are today. The Neat House Gardens beside Millbank also doubled up as a kind of pleasure garden, where city dwellers like Samuel Pepys (who recorded several visits), might stop and buy a melon, or simply enjoy a wander.

London's rapid growth throughout the 18th and 19th centuries pushed market gardening further out of town. Today, the trade continues in pockets of Surrey, Kent and Essex, with some producers selling their wares at London Farmers' Markets, where stallholders are kept as local as possible, typically within a radius of 100 miles.

Market gardening itself has, however, made a surprise re-appearance in Hackney courtesy of Growing Communities, a not-for-profit social enterprise dedicated to creating a more sustainable and resilient food system. As well as having an organic vegetable farm in Dagenham and

organising a weekly organic Farmers' Market in Stoke Newington, the group runs three organically certified urban market gardens at Clissold Park, Springfield Park and Allens Gardens, which are open to visitors. Volunteers help grow the crops, guided by a full-time grower, and at Allens Gardens visitors can follow a self-guided tour on days when work takes place on the plots. Volunteering is a hands-on way of learning about urban, organic growing but even a site visit is educational, with display boards explaining the niceties of crop rotation and interesting compost heaps and propagation techniques to explore. With productive space at a premium, Growing Communities is also harnessing the potential of small, previously neglected patches of land in Hackney through their Patchwork Farm scheme, in which trained apprentices raise food for the box scheme on micro-sites such as churchyards and back gardens.

Of course, compared to the thousands of acres of local market gardens that once kept Londoners' supplied with their five-a-day, this initiative is small fry, but Hackney's soil clearly still has what it takes: the GC gardens produce over a tonne of salad a year, and their salad leaves are clearly a cut above, having won 'Best London Leaves' in the Urban Food Awards 2015.

www.growingcommunities.org

The Growing Communities Farmers' Market
St Paul's Church,
Stoke Newington High Street, N16 7UY
Open: every Sat 10.00-14.30

Medicinal Garden (RCP)

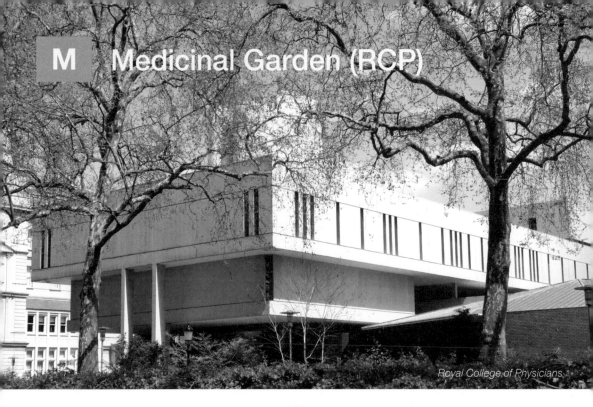

Royal College of Physicians

With its origins stretching back to the reign of Henry VIII, the Royal College of Physicians is the oldest medical college in England. Housed in suitably distinguished quarters – an elegant, Grade I-listed Modernist slab by Sir Denys Lasdun and a collection of adjacent white stucco Regency houses – this venerable institution also has a well-endowed garden.

Although a garden has been in place here since 1965, it was replanted with a medicinal theme in 2005. Its seven distinct zones offer a fascinating rummage through the global medicine cabinet, from the 'muthi' plants of traditional South African medicine to the herbal remedies used by native North Americans, as well as modern plant-derived drugs like Tamiflu and Taxol (the former from the star anise shrub, the latter from yew).

Laid out primarily as an ornamental garden, rather than the beds in the geometric order you might

expect from a traditional physic garden, the College garden nevertheless packs in the medically relevant specimens and contains over 1,000 different plants, all clearly labelled. The Arid Zone beds feature medicinal plants from dry climates such as yellow flowered *Senna corymbosa* (the source of the purgative Senakot) and the architectural *Aloe vera*, whose soothing juice can be used as a treatment for burns. In the Far Eastern bed the Chinese fan palm, *Livistona chinensis* is another elegant plant that is used as herbal medicine by the Chinese and valued in western medicine as a tumour inhibitor.

At the front of the college, the World Medicine beds feature a selection of medically valued plants from around the globe, including apparently humble specimens like *Vinca major*, the blue-flowered greater periwinkle, which turns out to have a medical application reducing blood pressure. Over in the European and Mediterranean beds one can find the blues-beating *Hypericum perforatum* (known

to many as St John's Wort), and plants from the Classical world such as the sedative Mandrake (*Mandragora officinarum*), and the pomegranate (*Punica granata)*. The pomegranate tree is frequently featured in classical mythology and widely revered for its medicinal properties; its fruit appears on the College's coat of arms. Not all the plants are entirely beneficial to human health – the leaves of the cycads in the Arid Zone beds cause Parkinson's and dementia if eaten, while the toxic alkaloid derived from Monkshood (*Aconitum carmichaelii*) has a deadly application when used as an arrow poison.

As well as showcasing medical plants, the garden is also liberally stocked with plants whose names honour famous physicians, including mythological ones such as Paeon, doctor to the ancient Greek gods, whose name lives on in the peony. Pedanius Dioscorides, the first century Greek author of *De Materia Medica*, a medical encyclopedia that was used as a reference until the middle ages, is immortalised in *Acanthus dioscoridis*. Appropriately, many of the illustrious doctors memorialised in plant names were also pioneering botanists: the *Lobelia* is named for the botanist Mathias de L'Obel, who was also James I's physician while Nicholas Monardes, the Sevillian physician-cum-botanist, gave his name to *Monarda*, or bergamot. Hippocrates, the father of Western medicine, is honoured here by a magnificent plane tree, *Platanus orientalis subsp. Insularis* which dominates the main lawn. This

flourishing specimen is supposedly a descendant of the very plane tree under which Hippocrates taught his students on the island of Cos.

The eight parterre gardens in front of the Regency terraced houses of St Andrew's Place take their cue from the *Pharmacopoeia Londonensis*, a medical book published by the RCP in 1618. The *Pharmacopoeia* laid the foundations for the Culpeper's famous *Herbal* of 1652 (originally published as *The English Physician*) and cemented London's role as the centre of plant-based medicine. Each of the gardens contains plants authorised for use by the *Pharmacopoeia* – some, like roses and marigolds, were valued for the medicinal properties of their flowers, others for their bark, seeds, roots or fruit. The gardens are planted accordingly, thus House 5 (the Pepys Garden) contains plants such as sedum and yarrow whose leaves were used medically, while House 3 contains plants like peony, marshmallow and angelica whose roots had a medical application. This appealing octet of gardens shows that charm and utility can be achieved in the urban front garden, as well as harking back to the College's Tudor days, when it rented a garden by its premises in the City for the purpose of growing medical herbs.

Royal College of Physicians
St Andrew's Place, NW1 4LE
www.rcplondon.ac.uk

Myddelton House Gardens

It's been a long time coming, but after years of decline and almost as many of restoration, Myddelton House Gardens are finally back on the horticultural map. Something of a shrine in horticultural circles, the gardens – the life's work of revered plantsman E A Bowles – re-launched in spring 2011, following a major Heritage Lottery funded restoration project.

Edward Augustus ('Gussie') Bowles died in 1954 but his presence is still tangible in the garden he created. Many of the rare and unusual plants he raised here are still in situ, such as the enormous *Wisteria floribunda* grown from seed by Bowles and planted in 1903. The primary restoration and infrastructure of the garden having been completed, the current team of gardeners and garden volunteers, led by Head Gardener James Hall, are concentrating on the planting and history of the garden, tackling overgrown and weedy areas, and instigating new planting such as the succulent bed by the visitor centre and the recently cleared and excavated Rock Garden.

Born in 1865, Bowles was destined for a church career but the deaths of two siblings curtailed his studies and bought him home to Myddelton where he spent the rest of his life collecting and breeding plants and developing the gardens. Although self-taught, Bowles led a distinguished horticultural career and was awarded the Royal Horticultural Society (RHS) Victoria Medal of Honour in 1916, and served as an RHS Vice-President from 1926 until his death. His clout in the gardening world can be gauged by the huge number of plants bearing his name – *Erysimum* 'Bowles's Mauve' and *Carex elata* 'Aurea' (Bowles's golden sedge) being among the most well known. Bowles in turn named plants after his friends and neighbours, and he was responsible for numerous plant introductions including the still widely available *Crocus* 'Snow Bunting'. After his death, Bowles's famous two-pronged gardening fork and plants from the garden were taken to Wisley to create a living memorial, 'Bowles' Corner' (see p.259). Myddelton's reciprocal 'Wisley Corner' contains plants with Wisley in their name, since Mr Bowles devoted much of his time to RHS Wisley and its development. Bowles's influence spread through his writings and his trilogy about Myddelton, starting with *My Garden in Spring*, remain classics, while his handbook on his passion, *A Handbook of Crocus and Colchicum for Gardeners*, became the standard reference book on the species.

Extending to some eight acres in total, the gardens follow the layout created by Bowles and while there are visitor maps and interpretation boards available to help with navigation, this is really a garden for exploring at will. Although known as the 'Crocus King', Bowles was skilled at raising all sorts of plants in the scant, dry soil at Myddelton and he created a garden with year-round appeal. In early spring there are snowdrops, hellebores and daffodils to enjoy, followed later in the season by a National Collection of Dykes Medal-winning Iris. The lavender colour flowers of the *Pawlonia tomentosa* (Foxglove trees) are another spring feature. The Tulip Terrace was traditionally planted with tulips to coincide with the celebration of Gussie's birthday on 14th May, an occasion he dubbed 'the tulip tea'; this sunny terrace still features tulips in season and these are followed each year by a different summer planting scheme.

Dykes Medal Winning Irises

The sloping alpine meadow – inspired by Bowles's plant hunting holidays in the Pyrenees – is carpeted in spring with snowdrops, snowflakes and crocus, which give way in summer to a blue haze of wild geraniums. It's a Mecca for wildlife too, and a haven for the garden's resident grass snakes. The sheer diversity of Bowles's horticultural interests means there is a world of variety in the garden – visitors in June can admire the glowing red lantern flowers of the *Crinodendron hookerianum* from Chile, inhale the heady scent of *Philadelphus coronarius 'Variegatus'* (AKA 'Bowles's Variety'), or recoil from the carrion-scented, flowers of *Dracunculus vulgaris*, a pungent British native. In July Cape fuchsias and a variety of bottle brush plants burst into vibrant flower, showcasing the readiness of flora from hot countries like South Africa and Australia to settle in Britain. The national flower of Chile, *Lapageria rosea*, grows up the clinker wall of the old conservatory and other exotics include *Bauhinia corymbosa* (the orchard vine) and the Taiwanese *Tetrapanax papyrifera* (also known as the 'Rice Paper Plant').

The garden's mature trees, many of them planted by Bowles, generate microclimates invaluable for the tender specimens but the garden is also packed with less rarefied, self-sown plants like aquilegia, hedge garlic and *Smyrnium perfoliatum*. However, Bowles's open-minded approach to plant choices sometimes backfired and the Japanese Knotweed he admired for its architectural qualities is now feared and reviled as an invasive alien species. Two towering clumps of knotweed have been retained as a gardener's cautionary tale, their stems supported within sturdy metal frames.

Foliage interested Bowles as much as flowers, a line of enquiry that resulted in the area known as 'Tom Tiddler's Ground', which showcases variegated plants. The gold-and-silver colour scheme reminded Bowles of a children's game whereby a 'Tom Tiddler' protects his 'ground' from those who would steal his 'gold'. This area is poised for a revamp, as part of a project being researched by a student on the Historic and Botanic Garden Training Programme. Another strangely named part of the garden is 'The Irishman's Shirt', which turns out to be a diamond shaped brick pillar attached to a wall. Bowles acquired the pillar from nearby Gough Park and had a wall and summerhouse built to keep it company – like the Irishman who asked for a shirt to be added to his solitary button. The 'Lunatic Asylum' also requires explanation, being Bowles's name for the bed where he kept his 'demented' plants – those exhibiting unusual variations such as the corkscrew hazel, yellow-berried yew and Hedgehog holly.

Surprises abound at Myddelton. At the centre of that most English of garden features – a rose garden – stands a romantic centrepiece, the old stone market cross from Enfield Town, rescued from demolition by Bowles and recently conserved. It's just one of several pieces of architectural salvage that Bowles enjoyed collecting for his garden. The adjacent 'Pergola Garden' comes into its own in late summer and autumn with its swags of grape vines and autumnal hues. A classic year-round feature is the carp lake developed by Bowles as he wasn't allowed to grow aquatic plants in the New River, which at that time ran through the garden. Visitors keep the lake's present-day carp population happy thanks to a special fish food dispenser on the lakeside terrace (judging by their size, the fish do very nicely out of the arrangement). Giant rhubarb still grows by the margins of the lake as it did in Bowles's day, but this section of the river was closed and filled-in after Bowles's death in the 1960s, its course is now traced by an arching green ribbon of lawn.

Refreshingly, Myddelton still feels like a living garden – since Bowles gardened here for many decades the garden can't be returned to a particular moment in time; there are more plant choices available to today's gardeners, and ever-evolving challenges of plant diseases and pests have to be addressed. The current team always ask themselves 'what would Mr Bowles have done?' but are able to move things forward without offending the soul of the garden. Once derelict, the Kitchen Garden is a powerhouse of productivity again, generating cut flowers, fruit and vegetables in abundance, with the fresh produce being sold from a cart in the garden. With box blight a worry these days, the kitchen garden paths have been edged with evergreen *Teucrium x lucidrys* (hedge germander), whose pink flowers are appreciated by the Myddelton House bees (elsewhere in the garden Japanese holly has successfully been used as a box substitute). Tender stone fruits such as peaches and nectarines bask in the warmth of the rebuilt Peach House, while tender exotics (including a sinister looking *Aristolochia*) enjoy the temperate and hot zones in the smart new Alitex glasshouse that was built on the footprint of Bowles's former greenhouse. The original wooden cold frames where Bowles kept his crocus collection have been restored and house a current National Collection of Crocuses.

Preserving the ethos and ambience of Myddelton House Gardens was central to the restoration project and even the visitor facilities in the old stable block were developed with 'Gussie' in mind. The tea room recalls Bowles's fondness for afternoon refreshment in the English tradition while the sympathetically stocked plant sales area ensures that, as in Bowles's day, visitors won't go away empty handed. The small museum tells the Bowles story, puts the garden into context and includes a fabulous pair of newly restored 18th-century lead ostriches, which used to grace the garden as ornaments. Its wilderness years now a fading memory, and with a dedicated and enthusiastic team at its helm, Myddelton House Gardens is once again a must-see on any garden lover's 'to do' list.

Myddelton House Gardens
Bulls Cross, Enfield, Middlesex, EN2 9HG
www.visitleevalley.org.uk
T: 03000 030 610

Newly planted hosta bed in the Rock Garden

The Alitex glasshouse

Crocus Collection

Enfield Market Cross

James Hall

The choice of plants available to gardeners today might appear seemingly limitless but whilst there's certainly no shortage of companies wanting to sell us plants, the range is not in fact as abundant as it once was. The whims of horticultural fashion plus the demise of many small-scale plant breeders has spelled the disappearance of many once readily available cultivated varieties. It's a loss not just for gardeners, but also for garden historians, pharmaceutical botanists and plant breeders themselves, since a large gene pool is vital for breeding the drought, pest and disease-resistant plants required in the climate-changed future.

National Plant Collections are one response to this plight. Set up by the conservation charity Plant Heritage, there are now over 650 such collections across the country, each one a 'living library' dedicated to a particular group of plants. Anyone can be a collection holder, from botanic garden to local authority, from commoner to Queen (and just to prove it, the Royal Household in London has the national collection of Morus, or mulberries).

The capital is home to several other collections – West Ham Park holds two, Liquidamber and Trachelospermum, while Regent's Park's

This page: Eccleston Square, SW1

collection of *Delphinium elatum* hybrids with the RHS AGM can be seen near the Jubilee Gates. Myddelton House (see p.160) holds another very specific group of plants – the Iris Dykes Medal Winners. The superb soil and microclimate of Eccleston Square supports the national collection of Ceanothus, with some 60 different varieties, including Ceanothus 'Marie Simon' and C. 'Snow Flurries'. This award-winning garden square opens for the NGS (see p.270) and for the Open Garden Squares Weekend (see p.170) and is well worth a visit. Although its openings don't coincide with the Ceanothus blossom in April, the garden,

which is managed by renowned horticultural photographer and author Roger Phillips and tended by Kiwi contractor Neville Capil, boasts an exciting collection of rare and tender plants. Other attractions include southern hemisphere plants such as *Metrosideros excelsa* (New Zealand Christmas Tree) and *Clianthus puniceus* (Kaka Beak), as well as an extensive holding of Camellias and climbing, shrub and tender Tea Roses.

www.nccpg.com
www.ngs.org.uk
www.opensquares.org

O Ockendon Road Tree Gardens

Lovingly created and tended by residents, the Ockendon Road tree gardens have become something of an Islington landmark. As a certain guidebook might put it, they are 'worth the detour' and taxi drivers and local walkers do exactly that to admire these charming mini gardens, flourishing in the 'pits' of the trees that line the road. The gardens' modest proportions belie their clout, as they are regular 'Islington in Bloom' prize winners and their kerb appeal has even been known to sway prospective house buyers.

Inspired by similar gardens in Holland, the first Ockendon Road tree garden was planted in 1993; by 2004 nearly all 35 tree-pits had been similarly transformed, thanks to the hard work of newly-retired Ockie Road residents, Tony Campbell and Julie Davies who decided to extend the concept to the whole street. Salvaged Victorian edging tiles were used to define the new beds and create a better planting depth, with a wooden alternative devised by Tony's wife, Tessa, being used where traditional edging wasn't possible. Keeping the project as sustainable as possible, the 'tree-pitters' preferred planting medium is a home-produced soil-compost mix, with plants being funded by Ockie Road residents (and subsidised by the gardens' prize winnings).

The prime movers behind the tree gardens are Aida Trabucco, Julie Davies, Janet Payne, and Tessa and Tony Campbell, with ad hoc assistance from others in the road. Each garden they create is different – by design and by necessity, as the road's east-west orientation produces one sunny and one shady side. Surprisingly, given the opposition to tree-pit gardening in neighbouring boroughs such as Hackney, the gardeners have the support of Islington Council, who have even allowed them to extend some of the smaller tree-pits. The council retains responsibility for the street's trees, the majority of which are elderly crab apples, although these are steadily being replaced with a more diverse selection, including ginkgo, liquidamber, maple, cut-leaf alder, and a tulip tree. New tree pits cannot have permanent planting for three years, a restriction the Ockie Road gardeners get around with wildflower seeds, annuals and bulbs.

The tree gardeners' year starts in May with a buying spree and intensive planting activity; recently they introduced a 'Street Planting Party' to galvanise the street, and attract new volunteers. July is the focus of their endeavours as this is when Islington in Bloom is judged, while in October the gardens are tidied and bulbs put in for the spring. With the street trees acting as giant umbrellas deflecting rainfall from the gardens below, watering keeps the four main gardeners busy – it's an intensive job involving buckets, wheelbarrows and external taps made available by residents along the street – and extra help is always welcome for this routine but essential task.

Tony, Tessa, Aida and Julie are always striving for variety and colour, and their tree gardens can feature anything from rambling nasturtiums and Californian poppies to hebes, dwarf gorse and rustic hollyhocks and one bed is devoted to herbs. Aconite, vinca and cyclamen have proved successful in the shady beds, while the tree gardeners – ever keen to inject a bit of height into their creations – also deploy an array of climbers such as passion flower, honeysuckle, trumpet vine and clematis, as well as an irrepressible perennial sweet pea which fills the main trunk of one tree. Shrubs and perennials are favoured, and feature some unusual choices such as *Oenothera* and *Mimulus cardinalis*. Easy to pinch annuals are too tempting for thieves and other problems have included vandalism, dogs, litter and basal growth from the trees.

By Tony and Tessa's own admission between May and August their own garden might take a back seat while they concentrate on the tree gardens. But despite the work involved, the rewards are great, the tree gardens have injected real personality to the street while also creating an informal focal point for the community. Keen to promote the concept, Tony and Julie happily offer advice for would-be tree-pitters, from plant choices to hard-won practical tips on materials, planting techniques and aftercare.

Ockendon Road, Islington, N1 3NL
www.orra.org.uk

Ockendon Road's Tree-Pit Tips

1) Materials:
   Earth and compost can be sourced for free from neighbours, or skips.

2) Edging:
   Edging tiles are cheap to buy, but often thrown out when gardens are revamped. You might need 15-30 for a tree-pit. Bricks – need fewer than tiles and require less depth.

   Tiles, bricks or stones can be tamped down (with a hammer and strip of wood). Drop in small stones behind or under them to make the fixing stronger. If faced with the spreading base or roots of an established tree it may be impossible to edge all the way round. An alternative is to make a rectangular box using strips of wood, placed level with the surface. These can, if necessary, be anchored into the earth with vertical wooden posts (placed to avoid the roots).

   Allow for the earth level to fall. Keep well below the height of the surround and leave a groove for the water. Remember that new planting raises the earth level.

3) Waterproofing:
   To stop water running out through the gaps in the edging, plastic strips (lawn edging) can be cut and pushed down.

4) Prepare the bed:
   It is likely that the existing 'soil' will be of poor quality, with sand, rubble, bricks and concrete to contend with. Taking great care not to damage the tree roots, and ensuring that they remain moist, you may want to dig out the existing materials to a depth of six inches (15cm) where possible and replace with earth and compost. Suckers coming up from the base of the tree or its roots can be cut back. This should be done cleanly and close to the base.

5) Watering:
   This will be the biggest single commitment. In the case of a mature tree – the tree's leaves stop most of the rain reaching the pit, and the tree roots take what they can. For this reason try to achieve a critical mass of plants so that little earth is exposed to the sun. In summer it will probably be necessary to water once a week; in a heatwave, this can be as frequently as every other day.

6) Organisation:
   In any street, much of the effective work is likely to be done by a small handful of people. If a whole street is to be tackled, the hard-core helpers will probably have to take on a number of the 'orphan' beds. Co-operation (e.g. over sharing equipment) and good co-ordination (for example about any watering rota) is essential.

7) Funding:
   If a group of beds, or even an entire street, is involved, and if no other source of funds is available, it is probably necessary to have a whip-round. In Ockendon Road we found a number of people happy to offer – indeed most would rather pay than do the work!

8) Problems:
   Expect and accept a few minor set-backs, e.g. dog mess, careless individuals and occasional vandals. There may be plant theft too. If so, see what they take and avoid those plants. In general, best not to put in expensive and unusually attractive plants (and remove the price label!)

Tree gardens can feature anything from rambling nasturtiums and Californian poppies to hebes, dwarf gorse and rustic hollyhocks...

This page: Nomura Rooftop Garden
Opposite top: Postman Park
Opposite below: Nomura Rooftop Garden

170

Paris may have its boulevards and New York its gridiron, but luckily for garden lovers, London discovered years ago that when it comes to town planning, it's hip to be square.

The first residential London square to be developed around a central garden was Soho Square in 1681, following on from the first, gardenless 'piazza' of Covent Garden (1631). With their light, airy properties grouped around a pleasant open space, squares were popular with house-buyers and over the next two centuries dozens were built throughout London, from St Andrew's Square in Kingston to Albion Square in Hackney.

The fashionable garden designers of the day were often called into landscape these desirable new developments, with luminaries such as Charles Bridgeman and John Nash working at St James' Square, Humphrey Repton designing Russell Square, and Thomas Cubitt responsible for the planting of Belgrave Square. As on the great country estates, rustic landscapes were all the rage in 18th-century London, with Portman Square and Grosvenor Square being laid out as 'wildernesses', while Cavendish Square even had sheep grazing on it to conjure a rural idyll. By the mid 18th-century most squares had been enclosed for ease of security and maintenance and today many remain tantalisingly out of public reach, their leafy interiors glimpsed behind railings and shrubberies and open only to key holders.

One weekend every June, however, something magical happens, when private squares and gardens across the capital open their gates to the public as part of Open Garden Squares Weekend. The event is run by the London Parks & Gardens Trust and has grown from a one-day event with 43 participating garden squares in 1998 to a city-wide extravaganza of over 200 gardens in 2016. Gardens now taking part include well-groomed private squares such as Earl's Court Square and Eaton Square, but also more contemporary creations such as prison gardens, community gardens, therapeutic gardens, allotments, as well as gardens belonging to shops, hotels, hospitals, schools, religious and legal organisations. The atmosphere is festive, with picnicking opportunities aplenty, and some gardens also lay on food, music, children's activities and plant sales. Following hot on the heels of the fantasy gardens of Chelsea Flower Show (see p.46), the Open Garden Squares Weekend shows off some of London's most private and special 'real' gardens, as well as some of its most historic green spaces.

Open Garden Squares Weekend
www.opensquares.org

London Parks & Gardens Trust
www.londongardenstrust.org

O Osterley Park

The skies above may echo to the relentless roar of airborne traffic from nearby Heathrow, but on the ground, walking through Osterley's gardens, all is serene.

With over 350 acres of grounds to its name, Osterley Park exudes the air of a country estate, complete with a perfectly choreographed Arcadian landscape contained within simple black park railings and, at the centre of it all, a gracious stately home. The house and its environs assumed their current form in the latter half of the 18th century, when the wealthy Child family began remodelling the existing Tudor mansion into 'the palace of palaces'. With top Georgian architect Robert Adam at the helm, the house was dressed to impress with its statement corner towers, swanky pedimented entrance portico and glacially elegant neo-classical interiors. The grounds too were revamped to complement the house, a task that involved creating a pleasure garden, a series of lakes, and tree planting on a grand scale. Today Osterley's treescape includes a fine collection of oaks, featuring North American red oaks, as well as cork oak, holm oak, and a Japanese Daimyo oak.

Although it's not known who reshaped the grounds, Sarah Child took a keen interest in the garden and Mrs Child's Flower Garden was the first part of the garden to be restored to its 18th century splendour by the National Trust. This part of the garden was strategically placed so that it could be seen from Mrs Child's dressing room and in her day it was laid out with the most fashionable plants. The garden is focused around a pretty, semi-circular Garden House designed by Adam, which was used for entertaining and to overwinter orange and lemon trees. Flower beds stud the lawn, and are at their brilliant best from June to September but with attractive shows of tulips, daffodils and forget-me-nots in spring. Mature trees add a sense of scale and history to the garden, and include a redoubtable Cedar of Lebanon, planted here in 1760 and one of the oldest trees in the garden.

Entertaining and showing off was very much at the core of Osterley's raison d'être and the pleasure garden reflected these concerns. In the same way that the house flaunted the fashionable design and architecture of the day, the garden showcased the latest plants. As its name implies, Osterley's American Garden featured recently discovered plants from the New World, which began to reach Britain in the second half of the 18th century thanks to American plant hunters such as John Bartram. The discovery of a list of plants ordered for the garden by Mrs Child in 1788 has paved the way, in 2010, for an ongoing restoration of this part of the garden. Named after a gardener at Osterley in the 1940s, 'Dickie's Border' illustrates the 18th century style of planting in 'height order', whereby tall plants such as *Ilex aquifolium* were placed at the back of the border, while the shortest such as *Armeria maritima* (thrift) were deployed at the front.

The old Tudor walled garden houses a cutting garden and a vegetable plot. Marigolds, being the symbol of the Child family (as well as excellent companion plants), are well represented here. The Temple of Pan hails from a slightly earlier phase of Osterley's re-development and is the start point for the Outer Pleasure Ground Walk. Its classical portico looks out over the Great Meadow, which having never been ploughed or fertilised, is a vision of wildflowers and grasses in the summer. In April and May, blossom and bluebells are twin attractions at Osterley. But, regardless of season, the parkland as a whole offers lovely walks and picnicking opportunities – proof that the pleasure principle still holds strong at Osterley.

Osterley Park and House
Jersey Road, Isleworth, Middlesex TW7 4RB
www.nationaltrust.org.uk
T: 020 8232 5050
See website for opening times and
admission prices.

Petersham Nurseries

Petersham Nurseries

Stepping into Petersham Nurseries is like entering a parallel universe – it's light years away from the aesthetically challenged supermarket approach of many garden centres. This aspirational world is one where everything – from humble garden twine to antique wrought iron benches – is carefully selected and beautifully displayed.

Plants are inspirationally arranged in old wine crates, on wooden barrows or battered zinc-topped tables while inside the vintage greenhouses the relaxed, bohemian vibe continues with colonial-style ceiling fans whirring above and expensively distressed furniture, planters in all materials from zinc to vintage terracotta, luxurious bath products and tender exotics like orchids and stephanotis. The hands-on gardener hasn't been neglected either with practical gardening kit including gloves for all situations and good quality, traditionally crafted tools. For those who like to grow their own from scratch the nursery stocks their own branded seeds.

The well-edited plant list aims to provide gardens with year-round colour and structure and includes seasonal bedding and bulbs, unusual herbaceous perennials and a gorgeously scented collection of old fashioned roses. Trees – ornamental and fruit – are chosen with the smaller urban garden in mind and there is an enticing choice of pots for container plants.

Petersham is also home to a café and a Teahouse, which serves delicious cakes, ethically sourced coffees and teas, as well as light lunches in a more relaxed, garden shed ambience.

The current incarnation of Petersham Nurseries owes its existence to Gael and Francesco Boglione, who live in neighbouring Petersham House and who bought and renovated the nursery, reopening it in 2004. Petersham House itself has a glorious garden (occasionally open to the public – see website), whose 'hedgerow gone mad' 150ft (46m) double herbaceous border inspires the stock in the nursery and whose kitchen garden supplies the restaurant with salad, herbs and edible flowers. Petersham House is set within a historic Thames landscape, known as Arcadia, which runs along the Thames from Teddington to Kew. It's a beautiful but sensitive site and visitors are strongly advised to avoid coming by car but instead to visit on foot, bicycle or public transport. The website has details of all the permutations as well as delivery options for purchases.

Petersham Nurseries
Church Lane, Off Petersham Rd,
Richmond, TW10 7AB
www.petershamnurseries.com
T: 020 8940 5230

Nursery & shop open:
Mon-Sat 9.00-17.00, Sun 11.00-17.00

Teahouse open:
Mon-Sat 9.00-17.00, Sun 11.00-17.00
(due to planning restrictions on Mondays visitors are only able to purchase tea, coffee or soft drinks).

Café open for lunch Tues-Fri 12.00-14.00,
Sat & Sun 12.00-15.30

P Phoenix Garden

Oasis is an overused word in the context of urban gardens, but it perfectly describes the Phoenix Garden, an unexpected green space hidden away behind the Phoenix Theatre, off busy Charing Cross Road. Surrounded on all sides by buildings, and overlooked by Centre Point, the Phoenix is like a modern-day version of a London garden square, albeit with significant differences from its historic cousins.

Run as a communal garden by volunteers, the Phoenix is open to the public 365 days of the year, so it's worlds away from the exclusive key holder-only access of some London garden squares. The garden's laidback atmosphere makes it a popular lunchtime retreat for local workers and residents alike, with its handsome wooden benches (some carved with pithy epigrams), and grassy areas offering sanctuary for the world-weary.

Unlike typical London garden squares, which were a carefully planned element of the city's expansion in the 18th and 19th centuries, the Phoenix sprang into life on the site of a car park, which itself was a former bomb site. From these unpromising origins, the garden has developed over the past thirty years into a flourishing green space, and collected numerous Camden in Bloom awards in the process.

Sustainability is at the heart of the garden's ethos, with plants being chosen for their drought-tolerant qualities and wildlife friendliness. It's a strategy that seems to have paid off – in summer visitors walk amidst groves of foxgloves, drifts of valerian, daisies, euphorbia and geraniums, with the sound of bird song and the thrum of busy bees and hoverflies all around. A couple of ponds provide a suitably moist habitat for urban frogs and fish, while some areas of the garden are left deliberately unkempt to benefit wildlife – brambles, nettles, thistle and teasel all have a place in this garden. The garden's bird population make the most of the collection of nicely maturing trees which form the backbone of the space and which include chestnut, ginkgo, birch and cherry.

Lovingly tended by its teams of volunteers, the Phoenix is filled with quirky details and informal planting, which gives it a lively, distinctive personality so often lacking in municipally run gardens. Here, plants thrive in all manner of containers, from concrete tubs to an old wheelbarrow, while the hard landscaping uses all kinds of material from old kerb stones and paving to brick-filled gabions. Sinuous paths make the small space seem bigger and in summer blowsy roses in cheery shades of red, yellow and pink punctuate the greenery while bananas and echiums strike a more tropical note.

Hard work underpins the apparent informality of the garden with volunteers giving their time and muscle power to maintain its green and pleasant appearance; the twice monthly Sunday workshop group tackles heavy-duty projects like paving and gabion construction. The garden has a community gardener and hosts planting workshops, parties and an 'agricultural show' with traditional rural attractions like morris dancing, falconry and farm animals. At the time of writing the garden is closed while a smart new garden building is constructed, with reopening scheduled for later in 2016.

The Phoenix Garden, 21 Stacey Street, WC2H 8DG
www.phoenixgarden.org
Open: Daily 08.30-Dusk

Oasis is an overused word in the context of urban gardens, but it perfectly describes the Phoenix Garden...

P Phytology

Based within the Bethnal Green Nature Reserve, Phytology brings a multi-disciplinary approach to the whole business of plant medicine, having been instigated by arts organisation group Nomad Projects in association with the Teesdale & Hollybush Tenants and Residents Association. The project invites artists and botanists to reappraise the medicinal properties of over 30 varieties of native wild plants commonly found on the streets of London and usually regarded as weeds, such as dandelion, nettle, cleavers, and ribwort plantain.

The Nature Reserve, on the bombed-out site of St Jude's Church, already had a rich biodiversity thanks to having been enclosed as an anti-fly-tipping measure in the 1980's, but its medicinal meadow, devised by Kew ethno-botanist Dr Peter Giovannini, aims to engage the wider human community. Visitors are encouraged to harvest herbs (with advice and support from the project's gardeners), brew themselves a healing tisane in the 'plant hide', and invited to adopt an indigenous 'street plant' to take home and nurture. Numerous arts events are embedded in the project, ranging from botanical illustrations by Talya Baldwin to sculpture (in the woodland area) by Lucy McLauchlan, site-specific sculpture by graffiti artist Vhils, music and story-telling, and talks by experts such as Monique Simmonds from the Kew Innovation Unit and herbalist Melissa Ronaldson.

Michael Smythe, the Creative Director of Nomad Projects, explains how interest in the contemporary physic garden has come about:

"As society becomes more urbanised we must re-imagine, occupy and sustain ourselves in alternative ways within these urban landscapes. The resurgence of medicinal gardens is part of this wider conversation. I believe contemporary society is becoming more aware of the limitations of conventional medicine, such as antibiotics; simultaneously we are becoming more attuned to the ongoing value of traditional plant-based remedies. Medicinal gardens provide an important bridge to accessing this information."

Bethnal Green Nature Reserve
Middleton Street, E2 9RR
Open: May-Sept

www.phytology.org.uk
info@nomad.org.uk
www.nomad.org.uk

Where once only guerrilla gardeners dared to tread, now local councils, business improvement districts and City Hall are getting in on the action, finding the ways and means to turn forgotten corners and dingy cut-throughs into life-enhancing green spaces. The Mayor of London's Pocket Parks programme was launched in 2012 and its £2 million budget helped to create 100 new parks in 26 boroughs before the project wrapped up in 2015, converting over 25 hectares of underperforming community land into pleasant places for city dwellers and visitors to use and enjoy.

Crossbones Garden

Redcross Way, Southwark SE1 1TA

A graveyard turned garden, Crossbones Memorial Garden is a poignant place. The site is a historically sensitive one, an unconsecrated post-medieval burial ground for single women and pauper's children, with many of the interred being the 'geese' or prostitutes who worked under license granted by the Bishop of Winchester (the remains of whose palace is located nearby). Festooned with votive offerings placed in remembrance of the some 15,000 souls buried here, the site's railings now enclose a new public garden, created by Bankside Open Spaces Trust with the Friends of Crossbones, on top of the rubble and tarmac that cap the burials.

Visitors enter the garden via a sheltering 'goosewing' entrance way, designed by Arthur de Mowbray. Raised beds, attractively enclosed within Cotswold limestone dry walls, ensure that the below ground archaeology is not disturbed and along with features such as a wildflower meadow and pond help to strike a rustic note in this ultra-urban location, overlooked by the Shard. Designed by Helen John, with input from the local community, the pastel planting palette reflects the feminine history of this unique site.

Edible Bus Stop

Landor Road, SW9 9NU

The first of the London Mayor's 100 pocket parks to be completed, the Edible Bus Stop on Landor Road officially 'opened' in 2013, but started life as a guerrilla garden, instigated and tended by volunteers since 2011.

With funding from the Mayor's Pocket Park programme and Lambeth Council's Neighbourhood Enhancement Programme, the original EBS was redesigned and formalised into an officially sanctioned kerbside edible garden that is both productive and practical, providing somewhere lovely to sit while waiting for the 322 bus to arrive. Upended recycled granite kerbstones, set at a rakish slant, boldly define the edges of the raised beds, which are planted with bee-friendly plants and a selection of fruit trees, vegetables, herbs and sunflowers. Volunteers keep the garden in shape, with regular gardening sessions providing a good excuse for a get-together.

This page: Edible Bus Stop
Opposite page: Crossbones Garden

Fresh Air Square

104 Tooley Street, SE1 2TH

With on-street parking at a premium in inner city London, Team London Bridge (TLB) are to be congratulated on relinquishing, if only temporarily, some of the area's precious parking spaces in favour of 'Fresh Air Squares'. TLB (the area's Business Improvement District) aims to make all of London Bridge a low air-pollution zone and these portable parklets provide a literal 'breathing space' in the busy streetscape, while also monitoring the air quality around it.

The first Fresh Air Square popped up on Tooley Street in 2015. WMB Studio's ingenious design, 'The Parked Bench', incorporates simple modular and flexible features such as natty red, slatted seating made from scaffolding boards, with galvanised planters tucked in neatly behind and, of course, a hard-working air quality monitor. Crococsmia, cornus, persicaria, *festuca glauca* and heuchera complement the vibrant red of the benches.

Although only destined to be in place for a year (can't someone start a petition?), the 'Parked Bench' will be followed by further Fresh Air Squares, all being rolled out as part of TfL's 'Future Streets Incubator Fund', to improve London's streets.

Greenwood Theatre Pocket Park

55 Weston Street, SE1 3RA

Set against the ochre and pink walls of the theatre, this linear pocket park is impossible to miss. But it's not just its zany backdrop that makes it stand out; this cross-disciplinary collaboration between fashion designer Zandra Rhodes and garden designer Joe Swift is characterised by thoughtful planting choices which have transformed a bleak corner site into a beacon of biodiversity.

Stripey orange and red tulips set the scene in spring, and while mounds of Mexican fleabane tumble over the boundaries, the bees can get stuck into the purple flowers offered up by the robust evergreen bergenia 'Overture'. Other cottage garden favourites pick up the purple theme, and include the trusty perennial wallflower *Erysimum* 'Bowles Mauve', ladies' mantle (*Alchemilla mollis*), *Geranium* 'Ann Folkard'; all complemented with stands of purple herb fennel and *Clematis* 'Etoile Violette' scrambling up the walls. Evergreen Christmas box, *Sarcococca hookeriana var. digyna,* ensures this is a fragrant spot even in the depths of winter, with accompanying colour supplied by the aptly named *Cornus sanguinea* 'Midwinter Fire'.

Opened in 2015, the garden has made an immediate impact, scooping a Society of Garden Designers People's Choice Award in the same year. A properly collaborative project, involving not just the designers but Cityscapes, Team London Bridge, King's College London, Network Rail, Southwark Council and the Mayor's Pocket Parks Programme, the garden is cared for by Putting Down Roots, the gardening initiative run by homeless charity St Mungo (see p.184).

Leake Street Garden

Waterloo, SE1 7NN

Emerging from the gritty, grafittied lair that is the Leake Street tunnel, it's rather wonderful to be welcomed by a garden. Opened in autumn 2015, the Leake Street garden was designed by (uncommon) landscape consultants, funded by the Mayor's Pocket Park Programme, and is now cared for by We Are Waterloo (the area's Business Improvement District). This urban gap, hard by Waterloo station had become a problem patch, a magnet for anti-social behaviour and an unloved eyesore. No longer. The space has been reborn as a restful garden that retains a distinctly urban aesthetic, with Corten steel planters that brim with cheery red tulips in spring, and tough but tactile rustling grasses, airy achillea, and evergreen hebe, punctuated by the russet tones of heuchera and multi-stem purple hazels. Evergreen clematis are being trained along wires over the mouth of the tunnel to form a green transition between tunnel and street. The two honey locust trees (*Gleditsia triacanthos* 'Sunburst') add elegant height to the scheme, their golden yellow summer foliage brightening even the most overcast day. Concrete and steel cubes offer a no-nonsense seating solution, perfect for perching while sampling street food from the nearby Lower Marsh market.

*Clockwise from top left: Leake Street Garden,
Greenwood Theatre Pocket Park, Fresh Air Square,
Crossbones Garden, Greenwood Theatre Pocket Park*

P Putting Down Roots

Gardeners come in many unexpected guises, and the volunteer gardeners of Putting Down Roots are no exception, belonging as they do to one of London's most marginalised and excluded communities: the homeless.

The programme is one of the 'Skills and Employment Services' offered by the homeless charity St Mungo's and aims to help clients gain skills and qualifications which will lead to paid or voluntary work. The scheme provides accredited training to NVQ level as well as encouraging participants to get stuck into real gardening jobs at sites across London for clients such as Bankside Open Spaces Trust and Team London Bridge. Working in public spaces also gives the gardeners opportunities to make a tangible contribution to the community and have positive encounters with the public – something they may not have experienced when they were homeless.

The fruits of Putting Down Roots' labour can be seen at Gibbons Rent community garden in Bermondsey, at Greenwood Theatre (also SE1, see p.182) and at St John's Church, hard by the busy transport hub of Waterloo, where St Mungo's gardeners have transformed a run-down formal garden into an award-winning space, with a pretty parterre, smart new paths and cheery mosaic decorations. Over in Bermondsey, food production is at the heart of the vibrant Melior Street community garden, with grown-to-order vegetables being sold to the Table Café restaurant in Southwark to generate funds.

www.stmungos.org

Jeff Morgan and Victoria O'Dwyer

Q Queen's Wood Organic Garden

A rare remnant of ancient woodland, Queen's Wood is a much-loved local nature reserve in north London and a site of considerable ecological importance. Its bosky charms are enhanced by the lively community café (run as a not-for-profit organisation) housed in the old Lodge, and by the organic garden tucked away in what was once the Lodge Keeper's garden.

A team of community volunteers from the Friends of Queen's Wood, co-ordinated by the aptly named Lucy Roots, tends the garden twice weekly in the summer, keeping the café supplied with freshly gathered seasonal herbs, fruits and vegetables and taking home the excess. All manner of veg and fruit fill the raised beds, from Jerusalem artichokes to runner beans and white currants, while the productive areas are complemented by a small shrubbery, a physic bed stocked with medicinal herbs, and a wildflower area.

The produce may be abundant but gardening organically in a woodland glade calls for a firmly defensive approach. Fringed by wildlife-friendly ground cover such as ivy, bluebells and herb robert, the garden is a magnet for slugs and snails, pigeons and squirrels – all keen to partake in the harvest. As a result plants are netted to within an inch of their lives with old net curtains being utilised as low-tech but effective fruit cages. Not all wildlife is made to feel unwelcome though, as the bee hives, hedgehog house and mini-beast log pile make clear. Other eco initiatives include a tidy sequence of compost bins, a leaf pile and solar panels on one of the sheds.

Queen's Wood Organic Garden
(behind Queen's Wood Lodge Café)
42 Muswell Hill Road, N10 3JP
www.queenswoodgarden.org

R Red Cross Garden

Octavia Hill was quite a lady. A co-founder of the National Trust, she was also a pioneering campaigner on behalf of the urban poor, and funded several social housing projects. One of her lasting legacies is this charming garden in Southwark, set out in front of the pretty terrace of Tudorbethan style cottages she built in the 1880s.

With her emphasis on attractive, good quality homes and community space, Octavia Hill's approach to social housing was enlightened, whilst remaining thoroughly domestic in scope. Red Cross Cottages' residents had a community hall – envisioned by Hill as a 'parish parlour' – as well as the garden, which was designed as an 'open air sitting room'. Today, the cottages still provide social housing while the garden has been given a new lease of life as a vibrant community garden, managed by Bankside Open Spaces Trust (BOST). Thanks to the efforts of BOST and local volunteers

the garden's postwar decline has been reversed and it has been restored to its Victorian splendour. Serpentine paths, well-stocked borders, a pond and neatly mown lawns testify to a well-loved space and there are plenty of benches on which to sit back and enjoy the tranquil atmosphere. Even on a bleak February day the garden is worth a visit with winter-flowering jasmine, hellebores and *Iris sibirica* to cheer the spirits. Visits later in the year are rewarded with colourful tulips, and swathes of billowing ornamental grasses and lavender.

Red Cross Garden
50 Redcross Way, SE1 1HA
www.bost.org.uk
T: 020 7403 3393
Garden Open: Daily
Admission free

R RHS Horticultural Halls

Chelsea and Hampton Court Flower Shows may be the RHS's headline events in London but the smaller, seasonally themed shows – held at the Horticultural Halls on Vincent Square – have a particular charm of their own. Perhaps it's the indoor setting: instead of parading through the vast marquees of Chelsea and Hampton Court, visitors admire the floral displays and trade stands in the august surroundings of the Horticultural Halls. Hard by the RHS's Vincent Square headquarters, the Halls provide a weather proof venue with a sense of history – Lindley Hall, with its barrel vaulted glass ceiling, was opened in 1904 by King Edward VII, while the sleek Art Deco styling of the adjacent Lawrence Hall dates from 1928.

Once held every month, there are now around eight shows a year at the Horticultural Hall, starting with the Early Spring Plant Fair in February. The same month hosts the Botanical Art Show, followed by the Spring Plant Extravaganza and Orchid Show in April and, a recent addition to the calendar, the Rose Show in June. The London Harvest Festival and the Shades of Autumn shows both take place in October, the latter being an art and design show celebrating the beauty of autumn colour. Two new shows added in 2016 bring the year to a close, The Urban Garden Show focuses on tropical and subtropical plants for home and garden in November, while the Christmas Show in December is full of gift ideas for the gardener in your life (even if

that gardener is you). Visitor numbers are smaller at these shows – around 5,500 per show (compared to the 157,000 who attend Chelsea) – which makes for a low-key and laidback atmosphere, far removed from the fashionable crush at Chelsea.

The Harvest Festival show in particular feels like a village hall event that has been miraculously transported to London from the sticks, with plates of expertly grown giant vegetables laid out for inspection with pin-point precision. A closer look at these disconcertingly perfect specimens reveals an eclectic range of entrants, from Dukes to humble commoners, all fighting it out for a coveted RHS medal. But it's not all elephantine parsnips and obscure heirloom apples, 'pretties' get a look in too with dazzling displays of late-flowering plants such as dahlias, chrysanthemums and nerines providing colourful inspiration as summer fades.

Thanks to the shows' small scale and friendly ambience it's easy to meet (and buy from) exhibiting nurserymen and women. This might mean a chance to chat to no-dig guru Charles Dowding about winter lettuce production, get some hot tips (as it were) from chilli expert Michael Michaud or glean advice about different rose varieties from specialist rosarians such as Peter Beales Roses. Perfectly timed to coincide with the start of the growing season, the Spring Plant Extravaganza is an obvious port of call for those wishing to stock up on bulbs, plants and seeds and get tips from the plantsmen and women who have raised them. RHS Advisors are on hand at all the shows to answer gardeners' questions from pruning dilemmas to pest problems, so there's no excuse for an under-performing garden. Visitors will find it hard to leave empty-handed with the cream of UK nurseries and garden traders also plying their wares here.

RHS Horticultural Halls
Greycoat Street and Vincent Square, SW1P 2PE
www.rhs.org.uk

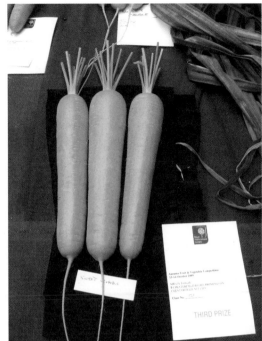

The optimistically entitled 'Sun Deck' on the architects' original plans for the roof of the Queen Elizabeth Hall had for years been a no-go area for the public because of access problems. But in 2011 something wonderful happened – the arid concrete rooftop was transformed into a garden, commissioned as part of the Southbank's 60th anniversary celebrations of the Festival of Britain.

The pop-up plot featured raised beds overflowing with vegetables, an orchard and a lawn as well as naturalistically planted native trees and wildflowers. The project paid homage to the British love of gardening and the countryside, and regenerated not just the QEH roof, but also the lives of the people who helped install and plant it. Created in partnership with the Eden Project, the garden was built from scratch by volunteers from homeless charities St Mungo's and the Providence Row Housing Association.

With its own café-bar, mellow vibe and panoramic views over the Thames, the Roof Garden was an instant hit and visitors clamoured for an encore. Their wish was granted and now the roof garden re-opens each spring and summer, thanks to the skill and dedication of volunteers from Grounded EcoTherapy (part of Providence Row Housing Association) who continue to maintain and develop the garden. The features that went down so well when it first opened are flourishing: a wildflower meadow with over 150 native species, picnic-perfect lawn, fecund fruit trees, productive vegetable plots, perfume pergola, olive grove, and a shady birch woodland (this latter area is closed while the Hayward Gallery is being renovated). In true Field of Dreams 'Build it and they will come' style, the garden has become a magnet for wildlife with nesting wrens and robins and sightings of several species of butterflies, including the rare Painted Lady.

The Roof Garden is more than just a leisure venue; thanks to its collaboration with Grounded EcoTherapy it is also a place of healing (helping those who have experienced homelessness, mental health and addiction problems through gardening), and learning – hosting a range of schools workshops to support outdoor learning.

Queen Elizabeth Hall
Southbank Centre,
Belvedere Road, SE1 8XX
www.southbankcentre.co.uk
www.providencerow.org.uk
www.stmungo.org
www.groundedproject.org

This one-acre site in Lambeth is productive in more ways than one: a place where people are nurtured as much as plants. Half the site is given over to the teaching facilities, greenhouses and raised beds of the vocational educational charity, Roots and Shoots, the remaining half-acre is a flourishing wildlife garden. Even the wooden-clad learning centre is eco-friendly with a trio of biodiversity-boosting roofs – a large solar one, a green one planted with sedums and thrift and a brown one designed to attract miner bees and digger wasps.

Set up as a charity in 1982 by Linda Phillips, Roots and Shoots offers disadvantaged young people aged 16-21 training in horticulture and retail, as well as offering environmental education for the wider community. Trainees stay for a year and learn a range of life skills to prepare them for the world of work. The approach is holistic – for example working in the on-site shop improves numeracy and imparts retail and social skills. Placements in high-profile gardens such as Buckingham Palace and the Royal Hospital provide quality work experience. The Roots and Shoots shop sells wonderful plants (raised on site by the trainees) which are acclimatised, sturdy specimens and reasonably priced.

Young people thrive here, as does the wildlife garden. Although a garden had been in place since 1984, it didn't really take off as a wildlife one until 1999 and the arrival of David Perkins, the Wildlife Outreach worker. Under David's care the garden has become a beacon of biodiversity, and is a popular venue for local school groups. Visitors enter through the 'Secret Gate' – beautifully crafted by the handy David from curvy oak planks and reclaimed hinges – and step into another world. In midsummer such is the garden's abundance that it is sometimes difficult to spot the different habitats it contains, but there is still space for a magnificent horse chestnut and oak trees. The summer meadow is rich with native plants and is only cut once a year – a regime that ensures a healthy population of moths such as little skipper, common blue and six-spot burnet, multiple species of hoverfly, crickets

Linda Phillips

and grasshoppers. Hard-working honey bees live in an apiary tucked discretely behind a hedge of espaliered Discovery and Egremont Russet apples and there are hand-crafted insect boxes all around, including a bee friendly 'Trellick Tower', populated by several species of bees. A new apiary with more space for the bees is planned, and a log hive to show honey bees working as they do in the wild.

The large pond with reed bed and dipping platform is home to frogs and newts while the romantically named 'William Blake's Paradise Corner' contains two further small ponds surrounded by exotic South American planting. Throughout the garden plants have been chosen to appeal to gardeners as much as the wildlife, and in amongst the self seeded verbascum, fennel and euphorbia are well-established 'Fantin Latour' and 'Graham Thomas'

roses and *Hypericum* 'Hidcote'. But although clearly well-loved, it's far from being a manicured space and (tidy-minded gardeners look away now) insect-friendly weeds like dead-nettles and brambles are often left in situ. Beloved by bumble bees, echiums are a particular feature and their lofty stature reflects how much they enjoy the mild microclimate of this sheltered site. Both *E. pininana* and *E. candicans* are now rarities in their native habitats.

Enveloped in greenery and surround-sound insect and bird noise, the garden utterly belies its earlier history as a former industrial site, with oil-contaminated soil and strewn with engine debris. A new Wildlife Garden Centre has recently been finished, replacing the last of the site's post-war pre-fabs. Part-funded by the charity's gold-medal

winning garden at Chelsea Flower Show in 2015, the new building will host the Natural Roots Programme, the charity's new environmental education programme, and will house a wildlife library and exhibition space, as well as being a place where volunteers can relax over a cuppa.

The gardens are generally open on weekdays between 10am and 4pm but you need to be aware that there may be school groups booked into the garden, as well as trainees using the garden. Contact Roots and Shoots first if you want to visit as a private individual, or with children. Alternatively, a great way to experience this inspirational set-up is at one of its regular public events, such as its monthly dining pop-up Magpie Kitchen, or on Apple Day every October.

Walnut Tree Walk (off Kennington Rd), SE11 6DN
www.rootsandshoots.org.uk   T: 020 7587 1131

" Young people thrive here, as does the wildlife garden."

St Mary's Secret Garden

a cluster of bee hives. The bees are managed by the Golden Company – a social enterprise teaching beekeeping skills to young people. A children's bug trail winds through the woodland, and the branches of the trees above reverberate with bird song – a real tonic in this built-up part of London. Other senses are stimulated in the herb and sensory garden, whose raised areas and level paths have been constructed with accessibility in mind, and which bring delicious herbal aromas within sniffing distance. The garden's bees make full use of the flowers here and in the herbaceous and shrub borders, in return producing honey that is sold at the Golden Company stall at Borough Market and is highly sought after.

Raised beds are also a feature of the veg growing area where neat metre square beds ensure easy access to crops for those with mobility difficulties. A new well-being zone is currently being developed; funded by Ecominds, the garden is being built with the participation of people with direct experience of mental distress, and will create a garden for the whole community to enjoy.

The large, fully accessibly greenhouse is the propagation hub of the garden, generating plants for the garden and supplying St Mary's thriving plant sales area. This is a great place to source reasonably priced organically grown produce such as salads, tomatoes and beans as well as herbs (either freshly cut or in a pot), seasonal bedding plants and house plants. The shop also sells seeds gathered from the garden, own-made compost and comfrey plant food. The home-made preserves are also really popular and make it almost impossible to leave this place empty handed.

Tucked away behind the Geffrye Museum (see p.108), this aptly named garden is a hive of activity. A community garden-cum-horticultural project, St Mary's takes a truly inclusive approach to gardening, aiming to provide a resource for the whole community. This includes the running of accredited horticultural courses for local residents, youth training and therapeutic gardening sessions for those with physical disabilities, terminal illness or mental health issues. Clients, students and volunteers all help to maintain the garden, which local key holders can use at weekends.

A series of interlinking garden areas have been created on the tardis-like 0.7 acre site and, as the whole space is managed on organic principles, it's also something of a wildlife sanctuary as well. Birds, newts and hairy-footed flower bees have all made a home here. The woodland garden features wildlife-friendly drifts of cow parsley and jack-in-the-hedge, wood piles for mini-beasts, as well as

St Mary's Secret Garden
50 Pearson Street, E2 8EL
www.stmaryssecretgarden.org.uk
T: 020 7739 2965
Open: Monday-Friday 09.00-17.00

S Seeds of Italy

Ladies selecting and grading seeds, Franchi warehouse, Bergamo, early 1900s

If you enjoy eating Italian food, why not grow the ingredients yourself? This is the question that north London based 'Seeds of Italy' has helped to answer for many years.

Founder Paolo Arrigo is passionate about growing and cooking fresh regional Italian vegetables and he's keen to convert us Brits to the cause. For some he's pushing against an open door but, sceptics take note, his proposition is not as outlandish as it might sound. With the Alps, Dolomites and Apennine mountains within its borders, Italy has a climate that is more Alpine than Mediterranean and consequently many of its vegetable varieties are easily hardy enough to withstand the British weather (whatever that is these days). The Seeds of Italy catalogue is filled with cold-loving veggies like *Radicchio Orchidea Rossa*, Alpine Fennel Montebianco, Savoy Cabbage of Mantova, and Snow Pea Taccola Gigante, all of which thrive on these chilly shores.

Seeds of Italy import from 'Franchi Seeds', who are seventh-generation seedsmen based in Bergamo. Using a traditional 'commissioning' system, Franchi (pronounced to rhyme with 'chianti') sources over 90% of its seeds from local growers in Italy, rigorously maintaining regional provenance and quality – if the seeds aren't up to scratch, the whole crop is destroyed. It's a traditional approach that has stood Franchi in good stead since 1783, fostering long-standing relationships (some of their growers have been with them for three generations) and making their products a byword for reliability and authenticity. Franchi produce dozens of regional varieties such as Cavolo Nero di Toscana which, Paolo reveals, actually sells better in the UK than in its native land.

Food is at the heart of everything that London-born, Italian-bred Paolo does: the Seeds of Italy story started in the family deli when customers kept asking him to bring back seeds from Italy. Paolo thought it would be fun to have a seed stand at the deli and once he had found a partner in Franchi, the business took off, selling to other delis before expanding to include garden centres and mail order (Paolo makes the interesting point that in Italy seeds are sold where food is sold, not in garden centres). Sixteen years on and the Seeds of Italy catalogue offers rich pickings, featuring staples like tomatoes, lettuce, courgettes and pumpkins, as well as flowers and green manures, Italian truffle trees, and fruit such as grapevines and pomegranates. Fig-lovers will be thrilled to discover that there are some delicious Italian alternatives to the ubiquitous 'Brown Turkey' fig, such as the purple-black Brogiotto from northern Italy – perfect for serving with Parma ham.

With the trend for grow-your-own, business is brisk, selling not just seeds but their logical extension – specialist Italian preserving equipment to convert gluts into long-lasting supplies for the larder. Reinforcing the link between growing, cooking and eating, Paolo's cookbook *From Seed to Plate* shows not just how to cook Italian produce but how to grow it too. Italians, Paolo notes, are 'just so' about their food, and this means particular dishes demand exactly the right ingredients: San Marzano tomatoes for passata, Borlotti 'Lamon' for the Venetian speciality 'Pasta e Fagioli', Tonda courgettes from Piacenza for stuffing with the cheese and ham of that region. Even herb varieties know their place in Italian cuisine, with no self-respecting cook using Bolloso Napoletano basil to make pesto – for that you would, of course, use Basilico Classico Italiano from Genova, while the enormous leaves of its Neapolitan cousin are far more suited to wrapping buffalo mozzarella.

Paolo Arrigo

So, with the pick of his warehouse at his disposal, what does Paolo grow in his own garden? Like any retailer he tends to use up unsold stock – broken seed packets and short date seeds and so on – but his veg patch essentials include Pea Piccolo Provenzale, Chicory Rossa di Treviso, yellow French bean Meraviglia di Venezia and Tomato Principe Borghese (traditionally used for sun-drying and known as the 'eternal tomato' for its storing qualities). Paolo shares his enthusiasm and knowledge of cooking and growing Italian-style at regular masterclass events and the Seeds of Italy warehouse in Harrow is open to the public throughout the week, allowing gardeners to buy direct and get expert advice at the same time. With row upon row of tempting Franchi seed packets to choose from, it's the horticultural equivalent of being let loose in a sweet shop. Seedaholics, you have been warned…

Seeds of Italy
D2 Phoenix Business Centre Park,
Rosslyn Crescent, Harrow, Middx, HA1 2SP
www.seedsofitaly.com
T: 020 8427 5020

S | Sheds

If gardens are a refuge from the world, then sheds are the ultimate inner sanctum; a calm haven where gardeners can shelter from the elements, store tools, pot up seeds, ponder the meaning of life or simply have a quiet brew up. Modestly sized, and of haphazard construction, sheds exert a charm that is inversely proportionate to their architectural status. Even off the peg editions can inspire affection, though only after their brassy orange shiplap planks have mellowed, or been tempered with a lick of paint – the natural state of the shed is picturesque decay. Home away from home for allotmenteers, sheds – be they ramshackle or regimented, practical or playful – unerringly reflect their inhabitants. They are one of gardening's most perfect forms of self-expression.

S Skip Garden

" *I love London – I don't have a dream of going to the country, I have a dream of escaping into a green London.*" *Paul Richens*

Paul Richens

Portability is not usually a requirement when starting up a veg garden but when your 'patch' happens to be in the middle of Europe's biggest construction site it's essential.

Currently residing in the heart of the King's Cross development, the Skip Garden is an innovative project run by Global Generation, an organisation that supports young people to increase their awareness of self, community and the environment. Working with the developers, GG have negotiated temporary leases on sites where building is yet to start, but with the proviso that the garden can, in the words of Garden Manager Paul Richens, "up sticks and move at the drop of a hat" when the site needs to be developed. Created out of seven old rubbish skips (the ultimate large-scale portable growing container), the garden has already moved twice, a process that was accomplished in a matter of days.

The garden's skips have been ingeniously adapted to provide a variety of growing spaces, including polytunnels and even a mini orchard, using the materials commonly found on building sites: pallets, scaffolding planks, water pipes, and monoflex sheeting. Soil is the imported ingredient here, because of the polluted on-site soil, but it will never need to be replaced as it is replenished courtesy of the garden's arsenal of composters, wormeries and comfrey plants, as Paul proudly states "that's very cosseted soil in there!"

The seven original skips have recently been joined by a collection of quirky but practical buildings designed by students from the Bartlett School of Architecture at UCL. In keeping with Global Generation's focus on sustainability, the designs include a greenhouse created out of old sash windows, and a cool store made from reclaimed timber and recycled coffee sacks. And one of the new structures, Charlie Redman's kinetic 'Welcome Shelter', has already picked up an architecture award.

As well as being used by local businesses for corporate training and volunteering, the garden is a resource where local schoolchildren acquire hands-on gardening and plot-to-plate cooking skills, as well as encountering – often for the first time – bees, worms and other garden wildlife. Older students take the Business and Sustainability BTECH, which involves them sharpening their entrepreneurial reflexes by setting up their own micro-enterprises. The organic produce grown in the garden makes its way to the Skip Garden's onsite café, which transforms them into healthy fare such as super salads.

For Paul, born to a long line of food-growing Londoners, getting young people to connect with the natural world around them is his reward. For him gardening touches every aspect of being human, "it's craft, it's science, it's art and it's spirituality – it's a wonderful thing".

Global Generation
www.globalgeneration.org.uk

S Spring Fever in Kew

Go down to Kew in lilac-time, in lilac-time, in lilac-time;
Go down to Kew in lilac-time (it isn't far from London!)
And you shall wander hand in hand with love in summer's wonderland;
Go down to Kew in lilac-time (it isn't far from London!)

Alfred Noyes wrote these celebrated lines over a century ago, but his recommendation to visit Kew when the lilacs are in flower is still a good one. The current lilac garden was renovated in 1993 and contains over 100 hardy lilac specimens – from early flowering 'Hyacinthiflora' hybrids to the later Series Villosae cultivars. Flowering dates vary each year but an advance telephone call or email will help you ascertain when the fragrant blooms are strutting their stuff.

Of course by the time the lilac gets going, spring is already well under way and from late winter right through to May visitors can saunter through a sequence of massed bulb displays (achieved by lifting large areas of turf, throwing the bulbs on the ground and replacing the turf). Cheerful yellow aconites light up the Holly Walk, signalling the end of winter, and are followed in March and April by a blue mist of *Scilla siberica* along the Cherry Walk. A carpet of *Crocus vernus* cuts a purple and white swathe between Victoria Gate and King William's temple in March, while the Broad Walk is planted with two Narcissus cultivars to ensure a good show of daffs from February through to May – the aptly named 'February Gold' giving way to fragrant 'Pheasant Eye'. In May the Conservation area around Queen Charlotte's Cottage transforms itself into a bluebell wood, giving visitors a chance to see why our native *Hyacinthoides non-scripta* are superior to their Spanish cousins.

For more showy late-spring displays head for the Azalea Garden and Rhododendron Dell. Kew's first Azalea Garden was laid out in 1882 but this current incarnation dates from 1995 and traces the development of deciduous Azalea hybrids from the 1820s to the present day. Its beds are a riot of hot pink, yellow and orange flowers – the perfect way to lift the spirits on a less than kind spring day. Another popular destination at this time of year, the Rhododendron Dell showcases over 700 species, including scented varieties like *R. Kewense* 'King George' and *R. loderi*. It is located in a part of the gardens landscaped by Capability Brown in the 1770s. Unfortunately on my visit this area was out of bounds due to spraying against Oak Processionary Moth – an unwelcome spring and summer visitor to Kew, whose hairy caterpillars seriously damage trees and can cause an allergic reaction in humans and animals. It's a reminder that Kew is not a botanical theme park but a complex entity that, as home to the world's largest collection of plants, requires constant nurturing. A major research and conservation hub, Kew in fact contains one in every eight of the world's plant species, making TW9 the most plant bio-diverse postcode in the world.

Spring and summer is the best time to pop into the Waterlily House – the hottest of Kew's glasshouses. Built like a tiny glass Greek temple, albeit one whose shrine is a circular pond, this is the humid home of giant *Victoria cruziana* waterlilies, whose leaves can grow to 2 metres in diameter. On a larger scale the semi-subterranean Princess of Wales Conservatory also has a pond and ten computer-controlled climatic zones. It showcases animal as well as plant life with resident piranhas, terrapins, and jazzy yellow and black poison dart frogs (safely behind glass). In the Dry Tropics section the cactus collection sports a gratifyingly high quota of rude shapes, whose spines however emphatically signal 'look but don't

Syringa vulgaris 'Sensation'

Hanami (Cherry blossom viewing)

touch'. More user-friendly plants inhabit the moist tropics and these include banana, pineapple and ginger. The Prince of Wales Conservatory is also big on orchids – Kew's huge collection is the oldest in existence and encompasses specimens that flourish in sub-arctic conditions as well as those that enjoy basking in the warm fug of a tropical rainforest.

Alpine plants get a glasshouse to themselves, in the award-winning Davies Alpine House, which opened to great fanfare in 2006. The arched design of this wacky-looking building, coupled with some computer wizardry, creates the cool, dry and windy conditions favoured by alpines (defined as plants growing above the tree line). Displays change frequently and, depending on the time of year, may feature campanulas, dianthus, primulas, saxifrages and thymes or even the rare Chilean Blue Crocus. The nearby Rock Garden is packed with a permanent display of plants with altitude – this 'Pyrenean mountain valley' was built in 1882 and is planted with mountain and Mediterranean flora. Its rugged terrain takes you across six continents in the space of half a hectare, including British natives like Cheddar Pink (*Dianthus gratianopolitanus*) and Cuckoo Pint (*Arum maculatum*). Cascading 'mountain streams' are also a feature of this area.

Spring also sees Kew Palace awakening from its winter hibernation. This 17th-century red brick house was used by King George III and his family and today it is run by Historic Royal Palaces. There's an additional charge to visit the palace, which is open roughly April-September (see www.hrp.org.uk for exact dates), but it's well worth it. The palace has two gardens of its own to explore: a formal parterre with manicured box-edged beds and the adjacent 'nosegay garden', which is framed by a magnificent laburnum tunnel.

Royal Botanic Gardens
Kew, Richmond, Surrey, TW9 3AB
www.kew.org
T: 020 8332 5655 (visitor information)

S South London Botanical Institute

The SLBI is an organisation in the best British tradition: altruistic, egalitarian and just a little eccentric. Founded over 100 years ago by A O Hume, a retired Indian Civil Servant, the SLBI is dedicated to encouraging and enabling local people to study botany.

The Institute's rather formal nomenclature, with its whiff of worthy Edwardian self-improvement, is misleading. The organisation is in fact notably inclusive and friendly, and is open to professional and amateur botanists, or indeed anyone with an interest in learning about plants. The well-used education room brims with specimens which are regularly scrutinised by after school science clubs. Annual membership currently stands at £18, for which members get the run of the institute's facilities, including its well-stocked library and microscope room, a varied programme of lectures by distinguished botanists, social events and field trips (excluding travel costs and entrance fees). Members can also get involved with research projects such as the long-running survey of St Leonard's churchyard in Streatham – the findings of which will feed into the *London Flora* currently being prepared. Courses in botanical illustration are run twice yearly and there is often a plant-themed art exhibition to admire in the upstairs meeting room. At the heart of the Institute's resources is the Herbarium, a historic collection of over 100,000 dried plant, lichen, algae and fungi specimens, diligently mounted on card, annotated, and stored in the original black iron cabinets designed by A O Hume. Many specimens are over 100 years old and are an invaluable resource for botanists today. Consisting of several herbaria, the collection, with typical SLBI idiosyncrasy, contains a particularly strong record of Shetland Isles flora. A Heritage Lottery Fund funded project has recently got underway to conserve the herbarium and bring it into the digital age, making it accessible to all; the project should be completed in 2018.

The SLBI is still based in its original home in Tulse Hill, the magnificent mature *Ginkgo biloba* in the front drive perhaps the first hint to the unsuspecting passerby that this is no ordinary Victorian house on Norwood Road. For, in addition to its other resources, the SLBI has the perfect aid to plant study in the shape of its own botanic back garden. Measuring just 79 x 53 feet (24 x 16 metres), it is billed as 'London's smallest botanic garden' but size appears to be no object to its ambition and its neatly labelled beds contain over 500 species. The garden was a feature of the SLBI from its inception, when it was described at a 'living museum of strange visitors'. Today, although none of the original 'strangers' have survived, the garden is packed with interesting specimens from home and abroad, exploring a lively selection of botanic themes.

Visits to the garden get off to a bloodthirsty start in the greenhouse, whose collection of carnivorous plants provides a grisly source of fascination, particularly for younger visitors. The Australasian bed showcases the extraordinary range of plant life from down under, including 18th-century introductions by the plant hunter Joseph Banks such as *Sophora tetraptera* (New Zealand Kowhai), and *Callistemon citrinus* (bottlebrush). Closer to home the 'weed garden' flies the flag for British native plants – its label is ironic since these plants used to be regarded as weeds. Over in the Dry Border, Mediterranean plants take centre stage with grey leaved toughies like *Stachys byzantina* (lamb's ears) and *Phlomis italica* specially adapted to reduce evaporation, and succulents such as *Sedum populifolium* which have their own in-house water supply in their fleshy stems. Fragrant plants like rosemary, lavender and sage are also drought resistant but other scented plants are given their own border. This includes *Iris* 'Florentina' – whose violet-scented roots are used in the perfume trade – and its foul smelling relative, *Iris foetidissima*.

Medicinal plants strut their stuff in two borders, one of which is themed around Gerard's Herball of 1596, the other exploring pharmaceutical and medicinal plant remedies. By way of counterpoint, poisonous plants in the garden include deadly nightshade, aconite and poison ivy. Over by the pond there's a bed dedicated to monocots, an important division of the plant kingdom whose subjects are defined as having only one seed leaf (cotyledon). Monocots include grasses, bamboos and palms, sedges and architectural plants such as *Cordyline australis*, as well as native flowers like *Iris pseudacorus* (yellow flag iris) and later-summer flowering South African plants like *Eucomis bicolor*. The garden is also home to London's first moss trail, a collection of twelve different mosses and liverworts whose common names alone make you want to track them down: Bird's-claw beard moss (*Barbula unguiculata*) and Swan's neck thyme moss (*Mnium hornum*).

Formally laid out and packing a lot of plants into its modest urban footprint, the garden is tended by part-time gardener Sarah Davey, and an assistant, together with volunteer help from members. This verdant plot is a popular venue for plant sales and events such as the Open Garden Squares Weekend and the Chelsea Fringe. SLBI events are famous for the excellence of their cakes; members can also enjoy the garden with a glass of wine on summer 'twilight' openings.

Having celebrated its centenary in 2010, the SLBI has embarked on its second century with renewed vigour; its mission to inspire interest in plants and to reconnect Londoners to the natural world. Current president, (former Natural History Museum botanist) Roy Vickery, dismisses the idea that you have to go far out of London to discover plants; his mantra is "rediscover the local" and according to him, cosmopolitan London is just the place to do that. Enthusiastic about the future of the SLBI, Roy sums up its charms by describing it as a place where "you can be yourself and you don't have to pretend to be cleverer than you are". It is nothing short of a south London treasure.

South London Botanical Institute
323 Norwood Road, SE24 9AQ
T: 020 8674 5787
www.slbi.org.uk
Open: Thurs 10.00-16.00,
other times by appointment

S Summer in Kew

On a broiling July day, you may prefer to give the famous glasshouses a miss, but Kew's outdoor attractions are at their most enticing during the summer months, filled with fragrance and flowers, and shady woodland paths to explore.

Even if you don't want to sweat it out inside the Palm House, its environs are still an attraction at the height of summer. The parterre in front of the iconic building is planted with a different theme every year – celebrating suitable events such as Charles Darwin's bicentenary, or the Year of Biodiversity. At the rear of the Palm House, everything's coming up roses with the recently replanted Rose Garden, a reinstatement of William Nesfield's original 1848 plan. With over 1,400

plants (and more in the pipeline), deadheading the rose garden is no small task over the summer, but it's an important weekly chore, ensuring this quintessentially English feature remains a swooningly fragrant seasonal showstopper.

New for 2016, Kew's 984 feet (300 metre) Broad Walk (which runs from the Orangery to the Palm House Pond) has been completely redesigned to create the longest double herbaceous borders in the UK. This promises to be a powerhouse of summer flowering perennials, grasses and bulbs, but one that also finds space for a little light instruction too, with plants educationally arranged in family groups, and illustrating topics such as pollination and seed dispersal.

From the rose garden take a stroll up the Syon Vista, the broad avenue flanked by holm oaks, which leads up to the Thames and a view of Syon House on the far bank. On a hot day the shade of these stately old trees makes a welcome place for a picnic – if you don't mind being under the Heathrow flight path. Keeping the lake on your left, hang a right to find the Bamboo Garden. This was planted in 1891 with numerous varieties of these most talkative of whispering grasses. The centrepiece of the garden is a recycled *minka* – a traditional thatched Japanese house, rescued from its native land, where they are under threat, and brought to England in 2001. Built from wood and bamboo, without the use of any nails, this house would have once resounded to the sound of thousands of silk worms munching on white mulberry leaves. Referencing this aspect of its history, Kew's minka has a mulberry tree planted among its bamboos, ginkgos and acers while its simple interior houses a small display about bamboo in Japanese culture.

Tucked away at the southern end of the garden is another thatched building – Queen Charlotte's Cottage. This chocolate-box version of an English county cottage was installed in the mid 18th-century as a picturesque backdrop for royal picnics and in spring floats in a sea of native bluebells (*Hyacinthoides non-scripta*). The 40 acres of wooded grounds surrounding the cottage are run as a conservation area and are noticeably wilder than the rest of the gardens, with a stag beetle loggery, bird and bat boxes, and swathes of nettles, rosebay willowherb and brambles. A charcoal burner can sometimes be seen at work, tending his kiln in this traditionally managed woodland.

If you're longing to see a more manicured garden, the Duke's Garden might be just the ticket. The borders of this walled garden look fabulous in high summer, with bold drifts of *Achillea filipendulina* 'Gold Plate', *Romneya coulteri* and *Helenium* 'Moerheim Beauty'. Greedy bees flock to dine on the garden's richly scented lavender trail, which offers a great opportunity to compare the merits of the different species of lavender – angustifolias,

x intermedias and *stoechas*. There's also a gravel garden here, populated with drought-loving plants like *Aeonium* 'Zwartkop' and *Crambe maritima*.

High summer is a great time to visit the Kew Guild Student Vegetable Plots, near the Davies Alpine House. Students are each given a bed to cultivate and grow the same selection of plants, all of which must be grown from seed. For many students it's the first time that they've attempted veg growing and it's fascinating to see the different planting layouts and the ingenious supports and protective coverings devised by the fledgling gardeners. Surplus produce is sold to raise funds for study trips abroad.

Museum No.1 makes a good refuge from summer sun or sudden cloudburst. Its interactive Plants + People exhibition explores the essential role of plants in our daily lives and displays all manner of plant-based artefacts from hunting implements to musical instruments. Refreshment and a chance to sit and relax is provided by Kew's numerous cafés. Recently overhauled, they provide a good variety of pit stops serving freshly prepared food, from the child-friendly White Peaks Café to the more sophisticated Pavilion and Orangery restaurants.

Royal Botanic Gardens
Kew, Richmond, Surrey, TW9 3AB
www.kew.org
T: 020 8332 5655 (visitor information)

T Thames Barrier Park

Not a garden per se, but included here for its dramatic and modern planting, the work of French landscape architect Alain Provost. The park was carved out of a 22 acre, de-contaminated, brownfield site on the north bank of the Thames. It was opened in 2000 and affords incredible views of the flood defences of the same name and was the first riverside park to be opened in London in 50 years.

The park's most photographed feature is the Green Dock, a 16 foot (4.87 metres) deep sunken garden that runs diagonally across the rectangular site. Referencing the area's industrial maritime past, the canal-like Green Dock ripples with undulating topiarised yew hedges. These evergreen tramlines enclose ribbon-like paths and a 'rainbow garden' planted with colourful blocks of single species such as iris, perovskia, sedum and lavender. The Dock is topped and tailed by a fountain-filled plaza at its entrance and a Pavilion of Remembrance beside the river. It is the park's pièce de résistance, although its impact does depend on the yew hedges being kept in trim and indeed surviving – some are looking a little unwell. Up on ground level, the park's open spaces are divided up by single-species stands of silver birch, oak and pine planted in grid formations, with swathes of wild meadow contrasting with crisply mown lawn. Design interest aside, the park's other attractions include a ringside view of the Barrier, a children's play area, basket ball court and a reasonable café.

Thames Barrier Park,
North Woolwich Road, E16 2HP
www.thamesbarrierpark.org.uk   T: 020 7476 3741
Open: Daily from 07.00
(closing time varies according to season)

T Thrive in Battersea

Long proven as a means of improving physical and mental health, gardening is a remarkably potent and supple therapeutic tool. National charity Thrive harnesses the power of gardening to improve the lives of disabled people and their inspirational work can be seen in action at their project in Battersea Park, where the charity runs three gardens.

Thrive's services are tailored to the needs of the individual clients (or 'gardeners', as they are known), and include programmes for those recovering from strokes or heart attacks, for dementia sufferers, and a transition programme for mental health patients moving back into the community. Young people with special educational needs are also catered for and Thrive run gardening courses leading to vocational qualifications. With the emphasis firmly on ability rather than disability, everyone at Thrive wears the charity's signature purple shirts, an egalitarian policy that makes it difficult to tell therapists and volunteers from gardeners.

Thrive's main Battersea garden can be tracked down on East Carriage Drive, near the tennis courts. Its smart new timber eco-building opened in 2014 and contains an office, and training rooms as well as practical details for hands-on gardeners, such as tool and boot storage and shower facilities. The orangery that curves along the front of the building also serves as an impromptu greenhouse when required, sheltering delicate seedlings and tender plants. Outside the surrounding garden is still being developed but already includes a multi-textured path designed to help stroke victims and a plant sales area where members of the public can buy keenly priced plants raised in Battersea by Thrive's green-fingered client-gardeners.

The best place to see Thrive's work is the Herb Garden. This magical plot enjoys a slightly less high-profile location, being hidden away in Battersea's staff yard, but it feels pleasantly like a secret garden, and is worth seeking out. Created in 2000, like Thrive's other gardens it's a socially inclusive showcase for the charity. Visitors are welcome to come and soak up the relaxed, happy atmosphere, see the gardeners at work and interact with them. An elegant Alitex greenhouse overlooks the well-ordered, abundant herb beds, which are divided into distinct zones, exploring different aspects of these versatile plants, from culinary and dye uses to medicinal herbs. Although the garden is not officially organic, it is managed without chemicals and the plants positively burst with health and their vigorous growth, vibrant blooms and enticing scents make them perfect ambassadors for Thrive.

Thrive's gardening skills can also be seen at the Old English Garden in Battersea Park, where Thrive works as a contractor. With a formal pond at its centre, a wisteria-clad pergola, box parterres and herringbone brick paths, this enclosed Arts & Crafts style garden has recently been regenerated thanks to funding from Jo Malone Ltd. The pretty new planting scheme by Sarah Price includes evocative fragrant plants such as jasmine, violets, mint and roses to reflect this association, and some specimens are accompanied by labels that explain each plant's use in the perfumes that they inspire.

Thrive
Battersea Park, SW11 4NJ
www.thrive.org.uk

T Topiary

After centuries of falling in and out of fashion, the ancient art of topiary is staging a 21st-century comeback. The practice of clipping evergreen shrubs and trees such as yew, box and privet into interesting shapes goes back to the Roman era and in one of his many letters Pliny the Younger proudly describes the box hedges and topiary sculptures at his villa in Tuscany.

The Tudors were very keen on topiary too with a fondness for intricate knot gardens and fantastical beasts sculpted from living trees. The form went into steep decline, however, in the 18th century; mocked by Alexander Pope and ruthlessly swept aside by the 'naturalistic' vistas of landscape gardeners like Capability Brown. Revived by the Victorians and the 'English Garden Movement' of the early 20th century (Christopher Lloyd's father wrote a book on the subject), topiary became a quirky feature in many a British garden.

In London topiary can most famously be seen at Hampton Court (see p.126), which condenses several centuries of topiary styles into one garden – from the 17th-century yew maze (which, on the express orders of the King, escaped Capability Brown's attentions) to its ancient umbrella-like yews and the recreated Privy Garden. But for all its ancient pedigree, topiary is perfectly suited to the modern small urban garden, providing year-round interest and structure with an often humourous twist – animals, trains and even baked goods are all fair game for the topiarist's shears. And there's no need to make like Edward Scissorhands either – established topiary is surprisingly low-maintenance, requiring a trim once or twice a year.

www.topiaryhouse.co.uk
www.topiaryarts.co.uk
www.paramountplants.co.uk

 # Meet the Topiarist

Architect Tim Bushe has put his talent for topiary to good use, creating a portfolio of quirky green sculptures in return for donations to Hft, a charity that supports people with learning difficulties. His parallel career (which now consumes entire weekends and evenings during the summer months) started when he repurposed the privet hedge in his front garden into a steam train. As the train grew ever more ambitious, Tim's hedge trimming expertise became correspondingly in demand with friends and neighbours in Highbury, for whom he has conjured a menagerie of cats, foxes, squirrels

Tim's best known topiary is the troupe of elephants on the corner of Ambler Road and Romilly Road in Finsbury Park, created in response to concerns about the anti-social behaviour being encouraged by a high, over-grown hedge. "After I did the elephants, I was swamped with requests and decided to do it to raise money for charity", says Tim, whose work is created freehand, with no armatures or preliminary drawings. Clients pay for an initial design and for the follow up trims, with a topiary usually taking around three years to become fully established.

"it's nice to do something that is appreciated by the general public"

Five years on he has become a self-confessed addict, going on topiary tours around the country and unable to pass a hedge without mentally converting it into topiary. Tim's early training as a sculptor perhaps accounts for his facility with three-dimensional forms; he advises aspiring topiarists to start with simple, curving geometric shapes, adding reassuringly "the great thing is if you go wrong it will grow again". Tim uses a lightweight electric hedge trimmer for most of his work but has a heavier, petrol-powered one for going through thicker wood. "You do have to be reasonably athletic to do this job," he notes, "and not worried about using ladders".

Although Tim modestly describes his topiary sculptures as cartoons ("they are not meant to be serious, they are meant to be fun"), their transformative power should not be underestimated. "They make people feel better about their area," says Tim, and such is the positive response to his creations that passers-by have been known to spontaneously donate to his Justgiving page.

Tim only accepts commissions for front gardens, ensuring that the community benefits from his labours as much as the householder – "it's nice to do something that is appreciated by the general public".

U Underground in Bloom

For an activity whose therapeutic benefits are widely acclaimed, gardening can be a surprisingly adversarial pastime. London's gardeners are no exception, with a long tradition of competitive horticulture – from the 'best bombsite garden' competitions of the 1940s to the annual inter-borough floral combat of London in Bloom (see p. 268).

In recent years London Underground has got in on the act, with around 70 stations across the capital vying every summer to see which one has the best hanging baskets, tubs or cultivated garden. Gardens are judged on additional criteria such as sustainability, or 'greenness', as well as interpretation of a theme, which in 2013 was 'Tube150', to mark the 150th anniversary of the London Underground.

With space at a premium the Underground gardeners tend to go for planting schemes that pack a punch, with bright, cheerful colours and interesting foliage deployed for maximum impact. The positive effect of these gardens is tangible, turning hard-working transport hubs into transports of delight and lifting the spirits of customers and staff alike.

TfL staff tend the gardens in their spare time but some stations present more challenges than others. Hampstead, for example, is the capital's deepest tube station and therefore not the obvious location for a vegetable patch. But – as part of the Capital Growth programme – it has developed a well-stocked, above ground 'behind the scenes' potager that has been a first prizewinner in the competition's productive garden category. Hampstead's street level garden has also caught the judges' eyes, and in 2013 the station scooped the Best Overall Award in the Underground in Bloom competition. Other station gardens to look out for are South Kensington (whose Circle and District Line platform garden is beautifully tended), Morden, Epping, Kensal Green and Bromley-by-Bow.

Prizes are awarded in September at City Hall.

V Vertical Garden – Athenaeum

Land. They're not making any more of it, or so we're told, and in cities even less so – which can make finding a decent garden a challenging proposition. A small, shaded backyard, a long thin strip or a balcony are the most that many would-be urban gardeners can hope for and such unyielding sites often demand a radical approach in order to succeed. A vertical garden could well be the answer, according to garden designer Daniel Bell. He should know, since he is the man responsible for the magnificent 'living wall' at the Athenaeum Hotel on Piccadilly, as well as numerous others across London, Europe and further afield.

The Athneaeum's vertical garden has been delighting hotel guests and passers-by since 2009, when Daniel and his team installed the Patrick Blanc design, and they return four times a year to keep the ten-storey high wallscape in trim. Routine maintenance jobs include weeding out excess volunteers – "we allow wild flowers to stay for a while as we don't want it to look too manicured", Daniel explains. Pollution from the busy roadside is another issue, requiring occasional replacements of plants such as choisya which die off after a couple of years or so, while on the other end of the scale less sensitive souls like solanum need to be kept in check.

Pruning follows the same seasonal patterns as in horizontal horticulture but other routine tasks like mulching are irrelevant, as are many of the usual tools – "secateurs, kitchen scissors and a staple gun are pretty much all we need up here", says Daniel, "it's a low-maintenance garden really, if you consider how much time a comparably sized flower border would require."

Gardening ten-storeys above pavement level in central London however requires a bit of forward

planning – and a head for heights. The former is simply a matter of logistics and making sure new plants arrive at the same time as the cherry picker; the latter is more of problem for Daniel, who suffers from vertigo. Luckily his passion for plants trumps any misgivings he may have about aerial gardening – "provided I just keep looking at the plants, I'm OK. I get by!"

For Daniel, plants are one of the main attractions of gardening vertically. "It's such an interesting way of working," he enthuses, "It's really opened me up to plants I hadn't used before as a designer. Things like *Stephanandra incisa*, and *Iris confusa*. Plus you can put a garden absolutely anywhere and that's really fun!" Daniel proves that last point both at his previous home in Sweden, where he installed a vertical garden inside the dining room walls, and in his latest commissions, which include an underground car park in north London, and a roof garden on the 25th floor of the new Trump Towers in Baku, the capital of Azerbaijan.

It's the versatility of vertical gardening that makes it so relevant to urban sites – low light levels aren't a problem since there are many shade-loving plants to choose from (Daniel mentions ferns and pachysandra as just two examples), and lack of cultivatable land isn't an issue since plants are grown hydroponically. London's warm microclimate opens

up the choice of plants even further: "it's practically tropical compared to Sweden!" notes Daniel, who likes to use as many different plants as he can. One of his favourite subjects for vertical planting are fuschias: "they are fabulous. In London gardens they can start flowering in April, May and they will go right through with only a short dormant period. And you can eat the flowers as well!"

For those wanting to have a go at vertical gardening, Daniel suggests starting with a small project, planting lavender. He recommends using a simple double-layered felt, made into pockets (this is where the staple gun comes in handy). Carefully pick off all the compost from the plant and make sure the roots touch the felt at all times. "Don't be tempted to use any soil at all", warns Daniel, "keep the felt moist and the plant will root into the felt, no problem." Feed with a liquid food every so often. It is also easy to raise seeds and strike cuttings in the felt, so developing a vertical garden need not be an expensive proposition. For inspiration, simply hop on a number 38, 22, 19 or 14 bus between Hyde Park Corner and Piccadilly Circus, nip up to the top deck and hope that you get stuck in traffic just outside number 116 … you'll have a ringside view of the finest vertical garden in London.

The Athenaeum, 116 Piccadilly, W1J 6BJ
www.athenaeumhotel.com   T: 020 799 3464

www.danielbell.se

V Volunteers

It's always surprising where plants are able to put themselves. In London self-seeded 'volunteers' can be spotted growing in all manner of improbable and apparently inhospitable locations: protruding out of chimney stacks or sallying forth from minute cracks in the pavement.

London's railway lines are enlivened by spontaneous colonies of the irrepressible butterfly bush, *Buddleia davidii*, which was recently voted 'the plant that best represents London' by visitors to the Museum of London. Buddleias are a London staple, but their aggressive tendencies don't endear them to everyone. Less domineering plants about town include Mugwort (*Artemisia vulgaris*) and Rosebay Willowherb, while cheery cottage-garden opportunists like hollyhocks and opium poppies always raise a smile.

London's horticultural landscape also benefits from human volunteers. For those whose gardening ambitions cannot be satisfied at home, volunteering provides a range of outlets for green-fingered activity around the city. There are roles ranging from stewarding in the Conservatory at Chiswick House (see p.60) to administrative posts at the RHS and a raft of hands-on helping opportunities at charities like Thrive (see p.218) and community-based enterprises such as St Mary's Secret Garden (see p.198) and Brockwell Park Greenhouses (see p.234).

This page: Hollyhocks in Hackney
Opposite top: Rowan Vuglar,
Harleyford Road Community Garden

The garden is maintained by a group of Volunteers.

W Walled Gardens

Brockwell Park, see page 234

Ravenscourt Park

Ravenscourt Park

With its rose-clad pergola, herbaceous borders, rose beds and crazy paving, the Walled Garden in Ravenscourt Park is very much a period piece. Visitors see a genteel Edwardian 'English' garden that's worlds away from today's informal prairie planting and wildflower meadows.

Originally part of the kitchen garden for Ravenscourt House, the walled garden was re-designed by Lt Col JJ Sexby, the LCC's Superintendant of Parks and Gardens, when the grounds of Ravencourt House became a public park in 1888. Its labour-intensive requirements proved incompatible with the dwindling council resources of the modern era, and this once cosy corner became increasingly unkempt.

The garden's current well-groomed appearance is thanks to a group of loyal volunteer 'friends', set up by local resident Angela Clarke in 2002. They work alongside the Park's head gardener on the first Saturday of every month. Between ten and 15 people turn up for each session, with ages ranging from 'oldies' to parents with young children – one youngster has been coming to help in the garden since before he was born! Having been granted council permission to work in the garden, the enthusiastic volunteers embarked on a war of attrition against the all-pervasive bindweed. As Angela recalls, "Our first task was weeding, weeding, weeding. All very soul-destroying as each month we thought we had made progress, only to be met with just as awful a situation when we returned for our next morning in the garden." Fifteen years on, the garden is in good shape and the volunteers' work is now largely maintenance – although they are poised to give the herbaceous beds a thorough overhaul, a process that will get underway soon thanks to a grant from Tesco Bags for Life. A much-loved sanctuary amid the buzz of the park, the garden looks its best in high summer when the roses and herbaceous beds are in full flower.

www.ravenscourtgarden.btck.co.uk

Brockwell Park

In Brockwell Park, the fortunes of another Sexby-designed walled garden have also been revived, as part of an ongoing multi-million pound restoration project.

Like its counterpart in Ravenscourt, the Brockwell Park Walled Garden was created from the former kitchen garden of a grand house – the Regency mansion Brockwell Hall, whose landscaped grounds became a public park in 1892. Sheltering within old brick walls is a popular 'secret' garden, designed like Ravenscourt as a summer garden, replete with colourful roses, fragrant peonies, herbaceous perennials, yew topiary, and a wisteria-covered pergola. A fairly recent restoration has seen the York stone crazy paving and 'rope' edging re-laid, the timber Arts and Crafts style garden shelters replaced, and over-dominant shrubs and trees thinned out to restore the original sight lines. Volunteers from the Brockwell Park Friends group and the adjacent Brockwell Park Community Greenhouses (BPCG) help tend this generously stocked garden. Like its cousin in Hammersmith, Brockwell's walled garden is a Green Flag Award-winning space.

www.brockwellpark.com
www.brockwellgreenhouses.org.uk

This page and opposite: Brockwell Park Walled Garden

The lovely thing is that everyone really enjoys their morning in the garden and by working all together we can really see the results of our efforts."
Angela, Ravenscourt Park

The Rose Garden

Westminster College Garden

Clocking in at over 900 years old, WCG is what you might call a historic garden. In the Abbey's past it was a hardworking monastic garden, home to an orchard, fishponds and the all important medicinal herb garden. Today this ancient precinct is cherished as a tranquil oasis in the hubbub of modern Westminster.

The modern knot garden – recently redesigned – references the monk's infirmary garden and has been planted with culinary and medicinal herbs as well as a selection of dye plants. A neat little rose garden, enclosed in a double hedge of hornbeam and box and planted with Rosa 'Gertrude Jekyll' and 'Sceptr'd Isle', commemorates the Queen's Golden Jubilee and recalls that Westminster Abbey has been the coronation church for British monarchs since 1066. Two lofty London plane trees stand guard beside the central path that bisects the expanse of neatly mown lawn – these venerable trees are the oldest in the garden, having been planted in the 1850s. Other trees worth seeking out are the lovely old fig at the far end of the garden (sadly its fruits, although copious, are not worth scrumping), a white mulberry and a 'Kanzan' cherry.

En route to the garden (which is accessed via an entrance in Dean's Yard), you will pass two other gardens original to the monastery. The first is The Great Cloister Garth, a dazzlingly minimalist square of immaculately striped lawn where the monk's could recharge their batteries – green being the symbolic colour of rebirth. A little further along is the Little Cloister, a perfectly formed courtyard garden which once served as the Infirmary Garden. This was a therapeutic garden, designed to aid recuperation after illness. It could easily serve this purpose today with its restful colour scheme of silver-leafed plants and evergreen topiary and the soothing sound of the water playing in its central fountain.

The Little Cloister

Westminster College Garden
Westminster Abbey
www.westminster-abbey.org
Open: Tues, Wed, Thurs throughout the year:
Winter 10.00-16.00
Summer: 10.00-18.00

What Will The Harvest Be?

Gardens can flourish in unexpected places and this community 'harvest' garden is no exception. Slap bang next to the recently opened Abbey Road DLR station in West Ham, and overlooked by modern industrial buildings, the location is hardly bucolic. In this inauspicious environment the garden was established in the summer of 2009 and has gone on to answer the question it poses with abundant yields of cut flowers, fruit and veg.

Before its makeover the site was a magnet for fly-tippers but its origins are more romantic as it was once part of the 12th-century Abbey of St Mary, Stratford Langthorne. Its current good looks are down to the Friends of Abbey Gardens, who successfully lobbied Newham Council to improve the site. The community garden design is the work of commissioned artists Nina Pope and Karen Guthrie. Contaminated soil presented an immediate problem but safe growing conditions were created by placing raised beds on top of a 8" (20cm) layer of soil buffered by a water permeable membrane. The 34 narrow oak and steel beds, arranged in flag-like strips, were themselves filled with top soil, and in 2009 volunteers set about raising hundreds of seedlings to plant in them.

With its jazzy contemporary styling and emphasis on organic food production and community involvement, *What Will The Harvest Be?* is very much a 21st century creation. But, contemporary as it is, the garden's design and ethos are also steeped in the area's history, with Karen and Nina drawing particular inspiration from the Plaistow Landgrabbers of the early 20th century. The Landgrabbers were a group of unemployed men who in 1906 squatted a disused patch of land in Plaistow, to grow vegetables and show that the unemployed were willing to work. Although their defiant stand against authority was doomed, the Landgrabbers are honoured in Abbey Gardens, where the triangular arrangement of the raised vegetable beds recalls their ill-fated 'Triangle Camp'. The scheme's name derives from a slogan daubed by the Landgrabbers on the wall of their camp.

What Will The Harvest Be? is run on egalitarian lines, as a shared resource with no one plot being 'owned' or ' managed' by an individual. The garden is open daily and the Friends of Abbey Gardens run free gardening sessions three times a week between March and October. The produce is shared among regular gardeners and the surplus sold via an honesty stall at the garden gate.

What Will The Harvest Be?
Abbey Gardens, Opposite Bakers Row, E15 3NF
www.whatwilltheharvestbe.com
www.abbeygardens.org

A wildlife garden in the congested centre of London might sound a quixotic enterprise but since its opening in 1995 the Wildlife Garden at the Natural History Museum has flourished. What was formerly the museum's unprepossessing west garden was transformed into an evocation of nine semi-natural habitats, typical of Southern England.

The initial installation in 1994 involved a planting list of some 950 trees and 3,800 shrubs, plus huge quantities of herbaceous plants – a seemingly enormous specification for a one-acre site. But the saturation tactic paid off, two decades on most of the habitats are successfully established, pulsating with wildlife and feeling surprisingly plausible, despite the proximity of the Cromwell Road.

A gently meandering path leads visitors on a mini safari through fen and reedbed to hedgerow, heathland and woodland. The free-draining chalk downland is studded with classic downland plants like common toadflax, quaking grass, thyme, oxeye daisies, yarrow and cucumber scented salad burnet. The garden has even attracted the six-belted clearwing moth, *Bembecia ichneumoniformis*, a rare sighting in central London.

The meadow is a tiny souvenir of England's agricultural past, luxuriant with grasses (and grasshoppers), clover and cranesbill, common sorrel, meadow vetchling and burdock. Orchids – common spotted and pyramidal – feature in both the chalk downland and meadow habitats. Once the meadow flowers have set seed (usually by the end of August), a small flock of grey-faced Dartmoor sheep are bought in to graze in traditional fashion – a popular, if surreal, garden attraction.

The garden's watery habitats are rich in wildlife as well, with bejewelled damsel and dragonflies that flit above the ponds in the summer, and newts, frogs, moorhens and mallards with whom they share the water. Nature being red in tooth and claw, this abundance of aquatic protein attracts the occasional attention of a visiting grey heron. The moorhens at least have their own offshore nesting box on an island in the main pond to protect them from the garden's resident foxes.

In spring the woodland habitat is carpeted with wood anemones, bluebells and fragrant wild garlic – through which scuttle mice, toads, spiders, several varieties of woodlice and numerous beetle species including the gloriously named 'Devil's Coach Horse'. Generously planted with native trees such as sessile and pedunculate oak, beech and hawthorn, the garden supports several bee colonies. The cover provided by the trees and hedgerows makes the garden an attractive proposition for city birds such as blackbirds, blue and long-tailed tits, greenfinches, robins, and Eurasian jays. Other airborne visitors include well over 400 species of butterflies and moths as well as nocturnal visitors such as pipistrelle bats.

An amazing creation, this 'wild' garden is a deceptive one, for its *rus in urbe* idyll is in fact very carefully maintained. Dr Caroline Ware is the wildlife gardener and ecologist who manages the garden, and under her supervision slow-to-rot plane leaves are raked up, woodland coppiced, unsuitable plant species removed, blanket weed in the pond cleared away, and fragile eco systems balanced. And all the while the garden is monitored by NHM scientists and a team of volunteers, who keep tabs on everything from algae and lichens upwards.

Established for over 20 years, this Green Flag-winning garden is set to undergo a major change from 2017 as part of the transformation of the whole of the NHM's outdoor space. An ambitious re-landscaping scheme devised by Kim Wilkie Associates aims to ease visitor congestion to the museum, and to integrate its outdoor spaces with

its indoor exhibits, creating 'outdoor galleries' that will 'challenge the way people think about nature'. The plans have been controversial, not least with the scientists who have painstakingly built up the Wildlife Garden's habitats over the years and who are loath to see them disturbed, but apparently 76% of the vegetation in the wildlife garden will be retained in the new plans, although there will be 'different interpretation'.

See the museum's website for details of the developments as they unfold.

The Wildlife Garden
Natural History Museum,
Cromwell Road, SW7 5BD
www.nhm.ac.uk
T: 020 7942 5000

W Wildlife Gardening

The concrete jungle might seem a hostile environment for wildlife but, given a helping hand, wild plants and creatures of all kinds can thrive in the urban landscape. Public wildlife gardens like that at the Natural History Museum (see p.240) and at the Centre for Wildlife Gardening in Peckham (see p.44) are inspirational templates showing how wildlife can be encouraged into the city, and the benefits of doing so. On a domestic scale there are plenty of ways to make our own gardens more wildlife friendly, in the process helping to boost local biodiversity and combat the effects of climate change. And with over three million gardens in the capital, London's gardeners are well placed to make a significant contribution. Wildlife-friendly gardens help to absorb carbon in the atmosphere, offer food and habitat to wildlife and create green wildlife corridors across the city.

Organic

Whatever the size of your plot, be it capacious back garden, standard 10 rod allotment or tiny balcony, going organic is probably the best starting point for the fledgling wildlife gardener. Natural, non-chemical gardening is beneficial for wildlife and humans alike – for example, hand weeding may seem like a chore but it's usually more effective than chemical weed-killers and is great exercise too. Londoners may not have easy access to the horticultural 'black gold' that is horse manure, but it's easy and economical to make your own fertilisers – comfrey or nettle leaves left to rot down in water transform into a foul smelling but effective liquid manure or can be used to activate a compost heap. Organic gardening encourages natural predators, obviating the need for chemical pesticides; frogs and toads help to reduce slug and snail populations, ladybird and lacewing larvae tuck into aphids and garden birds are also helpful in controlling insect pests. For really persistent slug problems, microscopic nematodes can be used (available from green gardening suppliers).

Sustainable

An approach to gardening and life in general which aims to have a positive impact on the environment, minimising the unsustainable use of resources. Gardeners can do their bit too:

- avoid buying peat-based composts (peat is a non-renewable resource and peat bogs are now one of the UK's most threatened habitats).
- Make your own compost.
- Avoid buying garden furniture made from unsustainably managed tropical hardwoods.
- Harvest your own rain water.
- Recycle and re-use wherever possible – for example return plastic plant pots to point of sale so they can be re-used; broken terracotta pots can be used to improve drainage in other containers.

Gardening for climate change

Flash floods, rising temperatures and drier summers are some of the expected outcomes of climate change in London. Whatever your stance on the climate change debate, there's no denying that this country has experienced some extreme weather events in recent years. Gardeners need to adapt to the changing reality and have an important role to play in reducing London's carbon footprint. Here are a few ideas:

- Plant drought-resistant plants.
- Mulch in the spring to conserve moisture levels in the soil.
- Minimise water use – don't mow the lawn so often, water in the evening or early morning and only where needed.
- Harvest rain water and re-use 'grey' water from your bath or shower.
- Extend the green area of your garden by adding a green roof to your shed.
- Don't pave over your front garden – it increases the risk of flooding and displaces wildlife.
- If you have room, plant a broad-leaved native tree or mixed hedge.

Resources

www.britishbee.org.uk

www.bumblebeeconservation.org.uk

www.lbka.org.uk

www.wildlondon.org.uk

www.rhs.org.uk

www.naturalengland.org.uk

www.rspb.org.uk/wildlife/wildlifegarden

www.gardenersworld.com

www.butterfly-conservation.org

Wildlife Garden at the Natural History Museum, see p.240

Attracting Wildlife

Biodiversity is on the decline worldwide but Londoners can become their own conservationists by adopting a wildlife friendly approach to gardening. Attracting wildlife into the garden helps sustain animals threatened by climate change whilst adding interest and vitality to the urban landscape. The London Wildlife Trust *(www.wildlondon.org.uk)* runs a 'Garden for a Living London' campaign and their 'how to' guides are packed with wildlife friendly gardening advice. The RHS *(www.rhs.org.uk)* is also a fertile source of wildlife gardening tips.

In the meantime here are few simple ideas for wildlife friendly gardening:

- Build a pond – it doesn't have to be big and fancy, it could just be an old basin sunk into the lawn. Use native aquatic and marginal plants and don't forget to build up one end so hedgehogs can exit safely.
- Install insect hotels and bird boxes.
- Don't be too tidy – leave areas of long grass for insects and woodpiles for stag beetles.
- Consider the needs of wildlife when maintaining your garden.

Insect hotel

Long grass

Beetle

Pond and bird box

Woodpile

Insect hotel

Plant a butterfly border

Keep your butterflies in nectar from spring through to autumn with a choice selection of tasty flowers. In spring wallflowers and hyacinths could be on the menu while summer butterfly magnets include buddleia, phlox and lavender with Michaelmas daisies, honeysuckle and verbena providing the autumnal rearguard. If you want to provide food for yourself at the same time you could try runner beans, brambles, oregano, chives and raspberries. Make sure your border is south facing and sheltered from the wind and, if you can bear it, try to include some nettles – this much-maligned plant supports over 40 insect species and is the larval food plant of choice for red admiral, small tortoiseshell and peacock butterflies. If the thought of actively cultivating nettles in your garden dismays you, plant them in containers and remember that young nettles can be put to culinary use as well as making excellent garden manure. See *www.nettles.org.uk* for more pro-nettle propaganda.

London Butterflies

Two butterflies make reference to London in their names; the Wall Brown butterfly was known as the 'London Eye' in the 18th century and today can occasionally be glimpsed in north London gardens. The rather more flamboyant Camberwell Beauty is a rare migrant to these shores, its first recorded appearance being in Coldharbour Lane in 1748. There are only a few sightings of the elusive Beauty every year, but during 2010's 'Big Butterfly Count' one was spotted not far from London – in Cobham, Surrey.

Camberwell Beauty

Verbena

Buddleia

Where would we be without the bee? It has been estimated that bees are responsible for one in every three mouthfuls of the world's food but bee populations are in serious decline. England's bees are vanishing faster than anywhere else in Europe, with loss of habitat, varroa mite and colony collapse disorder among the problems they face. The situation is so bad that the government launched a £10 million project to investigate. In the mean time, gardeners can offer practical help by making their gardens bee friendly and enhancing bee habitats. Aim to provide visiting bees with nectar from March to September with a succession of easy-to-access single flowered blooms – think traditional cottage gardens flowers like aquilegias, foxgloves, penstemons, sedum and snapdragons, as well as native wildflowers. Site your bee border in the sun, out of the way of cold winds, and plant in drifts to help bees navigate. Opt for flowers in the blue, purple, pink, yellow and white ranges of the colour spectrum and don't forget to put out some water – it's thirsty work foraging for nectar!

The yellow blooms of insect friendly Achillea

A seasonal nectar menu

STARTERS (SPRING):
Daffodil
Bluebell
Crab apple

MAINS (SUMMER):
Aquilegia
Stachys
Delphinium
Dog rose

**DESSERTS (LATE SUMMER/
EARLY AUTUMN):**
Aster
Lavender
Scabious
Sunflower

A nectar menu to share:
The flowers of many culinary herbs and plants are also very attractive to bees so it's possible to create a bee border that is also edible: Broad Bean, Rosemary, Fennel, Thyme, Chives, Angelica, Borage, Pot marigold and Globe artichoke.

Field Scabious

Rosa rugosa

Sunflower

Runner Bean

Globe Artichoke

Dahlia

Insect hotel

Insects are an integral part of natural eco-systems and in a garden context they are vital because they eat pests and pollinate plants while providing food for birds and other wildlife. Beneficial insects such as ladybirds can be encouraged into the garden through wildlife friendly management techniques (see p.244), and by making 'hotels' which they can check into over the winter months to hibernate and lay eggs.

When it comes to setting yourself up as an insect hotelier, no great technical prowess is required. Small-scale boutique bug hotels can be made by drilling holes in a block of wood or tying together a bundle of hollow bamboo canes; block up one end to exclude draughts and hang from a tree or place against a sheltered wall. Wooden pallets, stacked on top of each other, are perfect for larger constructions – just fill the gaps with insect friendly material like straw, dry leaf litter, pine cones, wood chippings or corrugated card. If pallets prove too cumbersome, a similar effect can be achieved by making a layered structure using bricks and wooden boards.

Although there are no planning permits or building regulations to worry about it is worth following a few guidelines:

- Keep the rain out by providing a waterproof roof for your hotel. This doesn't have to be fancy - old roof tiles or a board covered with roofing felt or simple plastic sheeting will do. The waterproof membrane can be covered with gravel and soil and planted with sedum to create a green-roofed hostelry with five star wildlife credentials.

- Leave plenty of gaps and holes to give your new guests space to move around and make themselves at home.

- Invertebrates, like students, prefer damp, shady living quarters so site your stack in moist, dappled shade if possible.

- There's something highly satisfying about building a bug home and then watching your garden fill with new insect life. Your guests might not bother to post a review on TripAdvisor but they will reward you in other ways – devouring garden pests like greenfly, pollinating flowers and fruit trees, and making your garden more bio-diverse.

Trellick Bee Tower, Roots & Shoots, see p.194

Bee tree

A colony of honey bees is using this tree trunk as their home. About 15,000 bees live here. The hive houses more than just bees – there are also eggs, young bees and honey.

Bee busy

The bees work together to find and store food and look after the queen and young bees. The queen is the only bee in the hive who lays eggs.

Honey bees eat nectar, which they find in flowers. They use nectar to make honey. They visit 50–100 flowers in one trip and can find nectar up to five kilometres away. If they discover a good source of nectar they tell the other bees back at the hive by moving in different patterns and shakes called a waggle dance.

Bee helpful

When bees collect nectar from flowers, they also collect pollen. As they fly from plant to plant, they transfer the pollen, helping the plants reproduce. Gardens with lots of different plant species support more wildlife and make a healthier habitat. These bees will pollinate flowers up to five kilometres away, helping to keep this area's flowering plants diverse and healthy.

Don't worry, bee happy

Bees can sting, but only if they feel threatened. If a bee flies up to you, it is trying to find out if you are a food source. The best way to make a bee go away is to stay still and it will fly off.

W Winter at Kew

The Pagoda, Kew

Kew's historic glasshouses are the obvious destination on a cold, wet winter's day, a low-carbon way to experience exotic flora without cashing in your Oyster card for a plane ticket.

Rising up out of the earth like an enormous glass submarine, the Palm House is probably Kew's most iconic building. It was built in the mid 1840s (to a design by Decimus Burton) to house the palms collected by Victorian plant hunters. Today it's home to *Encephalartos altensteinii*, a venerable palm which has lived through Kew's entire history, having been collected in Africa by Kew's first plant hunter Francis Masson in the early 1770s. Shy and retiring these plants ain't – some of them, like the fishtail palm from Indonesia, soar metres high up to the roof. Carefully placed signs remind visitors to 'look up' to admire the taller specimens. Many plants are reminders of our indebtedness to the plant world – where would we be without the tamarind tree to provide one of the ingredients in Worcestershire Sauce? More seriously, leukaemia sufferers benefit from the alkaloids found in the sap of the Madagascar periwinkle.

With a cosy minimum year-round temperature of 18°C, the Temperate House is a perfect winter destination for non-hardy human visitors. This mighty glass cathedral measures 4,880 metres square, making it the largest surviving Victorian glasshouse in the world – twice the size of its older sibling, the Palm House. Behind its glass walls lies a lush world of tender plants from the world's mountains, oceanic islands and savannahs. The geographical

planting scheme leads the visitor across continents to encounter plants such as *Dicksonia antarctica* (Australia), the multi-talented date palm (Europe), *Tetrapanax papyfer*, the plant used to make edible rice paper (Asia) and life-saving plants such as anti-malarial quinine (America). If the medicines don't work, there's always *Taiwania cryptomerioides* – the coffin tree (Taiwan). This is also the place to discover the disconcerting fact that, like money, bananas don't grow on trees – bananas being herbaceous plants. Following a top-to-toe refurb in the 1980s, growing conditions in the Temperate House are now so ideal that many residents have flowered, some, like the *Protea cynaroides* (king protea), for the first time since the 19th century.

It's one thing to admire exotic plants in the climate-controlled comfort of a glasshouse, quite another to study them in their, often unforgiving, native habitats. Marianne North, an indefatigable Victorian traveller was one such pioneer. At the age of 41, and without any formal artistic training, she embarked on a 13-year painting odyssey, travelling the world with the aim of painting plants in their habitats. An accomplished and prolific artist, by the end of her travels, Marianne had depicted over 900 plant species in 833 paintings. She created a unique record of the plant world which she donated to Kew together with a purpose built gallery – a curious red-brick amalgam of Greek temple and Indian colonial bungalow (complete with verandah). Memorably described by Wilfred Blunt as a 'botanical stamp album', the collection is arranged geographically

with the vividly coloured landscapes covering every square inch of wall space. First opened in 1882, the gallery has recently been restored, with additions of 21st century interpretive displays – making the Marianne North Gallery a must-see on a visit to Kew.

Adjoining the MNG is the Shirley Sherwood Gallery of Botanical Art, a sleek white gallery space that opened in 2008. It's the first gallery in the world to be devoted to botanical art and shows works from Kew's ever expanding archive of botanical illustrations alongside the Shirley Sherwood collection of contemporary botanical art. Exhibitions change thrice yearly, but in a welcome departure from most galleries' practice, there is always work on display even during changeover periods.

Year-round interest is the holy grail for most gardeners and – as you might expect from this centre of horticultural excellence – it's a feat that Kew pulls off in some style. If you're determined to go outside, head for the Winter Garden. Appropriately, Kew's historic ice house lies at the centre of this seasonal garden, planted to give interest in December and January. Scented plants come into their own at this time and visitors to the Winter Garden can breathe in the delicious fragrance of winter flowering plants such as *Sarcococca humilis*, *Mahonia x media* 'Winter Sun' or the chocolate-scented *Azara microphylla*. Early spring bulbs add further floral appeal – among those braving the cold are anemones, hellebores and crocus. There's no need to limit yourself to the Winter Garden. Swathes of cheerful yellow aconites underpin the Holly Walk – which also looks superb in winter – and pale carpets of snowdrops can be found near the Temple of Aeolus, the Ruined Arch and in the Rock Garden. The conifers and broad-leaved evergreen trees of the arboretum look good whatever the weather, and as winter turns to spring, willow catkins enliven proceedings with a promise of good things to come.

Royal Botanic Gardens
Kew, Richmond, Surrey, TW9 3AB
www.kew.org
T: 020 8332 5655 (visitor information)

W Wisley (RHS Garden)

Just 25 miles from central London, for out-of-town horticultural gratification, Wisley is hard to beat. As its acres of car and coach-parking would suggest, the flagship garden of RHS is something of a shrine, and it attracts over a million green-fingered pilgrims each year.

With 240 acres at its disposal, the garden is enjoyably multi-faceted, allowing visitors to roam around an alpine meadow one minute, and through a tropical rainforest the next. For first-timers a free guided tour is a good way to get your bearings and see features you perhaps wouldn't otherwise notice, such as the naturally grafted oak tree by the ornamental entrance gates or the oldest tree in the rock garden, a bonsai larch tree imported from Japan in 1904.

Wisley's legions of repeat visitors appreciate its subtle seasonal variations and its adventurous approach to gardening. Wisley was gifted to the RHS in 1903 as an experimental garden, a tradition that continues to this day, with Wisley's annual trials of fruit, veg and flowers to determine which varieties should receive the coveted Award of Garden Merit. Even the rambling timber-and-brick Arts & Crafts style 'mansion' overlooking the canal and loggia is in fact a laboratory, teeming with soil scientists, plant pathologists and botanists.

While the RHS scientists, staff and students beaver away, visitors can admire the fruits of their labour in the immaculately tended garden. One of the joys of Wisley is seeing things done properly, the 'RHS way'. In the fruit demonstration garden this means a masterclass in precisely pruning and training apples and pears, while the ambitious Bowes-Lyon Rose Garden features a sea of David Austin roses. The Country Garden designed by Penelope Hobhouse is an essay in understated English style, while the long mixed borders unfold in an epic sweep in high summer. 'Bowles' Corner' commemorates the great horticulturalist E A Bowles, whose name also lives on in many popular garden plants, and whose own garden at Myddelton House has recently been restored (see p.160).

Fuchsia
Rose of

Productive gardening gets plenty of space, with a comprehensive herb garden, vegetable garden, a 16-acre 'fruit field' planted with over 2,000 trees, and a wine-producing vineyard. A cluster of model gardens provides inspirational templates for those wanting to make the most of small gardens. Sometimes described as the 'jewel of Wisley', the alpine display house shines brightly even in the depths of winter with daily changing displays of these tenacious little plants, which may include cyclamen, narcissi, saxifrages and auriculas, according to season. Alpines get an outdoor airing in the 'crevice garden' and in the nearby alpine meadow, with its drifts of crocuses, cyclamen-flowered daffodils and dog's tooth violets. Descending dramatically down the hillside from the alpine department are the cascades and pools of the rock garden, which celebrated its centenary in 2011. If all this alpine activity gets too chilly, the state-of-the-art glasshouse offers warmer territory to explore, in the company of lush tropical and temperate plants, exotic orchids and the odd oversized butterfly.

With its light, acidic soil, Wisley puts on a dazzling late-spring show of rhododendrons, azaleas, magnolias and camellias in the winding woodland paths of Battleston Hill and in the Wild Garden. Its ericaceous soil also makes it a natural location for the national heather collection and a pinetum that boasts several Champion trees.

A million visitors a year can't be wrong – Wisley tends its human visitors as carefully as it does its plants, with an appealing mix of eateries, well-stocked shop and plant sales area, a stimulating programme of events and specialist plant shows and probably the world's best garden bookshop. RHS members enjoy the added benefit of free entry and the possibility of personal gardening advice from Wisley's advisors. With an eye on the future, the RHS has recently unveiled its 'Wisley Master Plan', an ambitious ten-year redevelopment of their flagship garden designed by Christopher Bradley-Hole that proposes several new gardens, a theatrical 'arrival walk' planted with flowering cherries and a new Science and Learning Centre.

RHS Garden Wisley
Woking, Surrey, GU23 6QB
www.rhs.org.uk/wisley
T: 0845 260 9000

W World's End Nurseries

The King's Road has seen more than its fair share of fashion fads over the years, but with over four decades of trading under its belt, this Chelsea nursery is something of a timeless classic. Established by James Lotery in 1972, and now managed by James' son Janson, the nursery occupies an enviable one-acre site, making it one of the largest of its kind in central London (although as a retail nursery none of the stock is actually raised on site).

The ivy-covered entrance archway with its naively painted sign is something of a local landmark and invites visitors to enter a green and pleasant world. Beyond the arch, the ambience is deceptively rustic – in fact the nursery is very much geared to the needs of the city gardener. With year-round interest at a premium in the concrete jungle, hardworking evergreens, in a variety of guises, are a mainstay here. Elegant bay and box lollipops, spirals and pyramids confer instant formal structure to the city garden but, proving that the London gardener can have his cake and eat it, there are also flowering evergreens such as camellias, ceanothus and rhododendrons to provide seasonal splashes of colour. Olive trees are bestsellers here and there's a good show of lavenders for optimistic Londoners hoping to recreate the south of France closer to home. Indoor gardeners are well served too. Sheltering in the warmth of the glass house are tender orchids, fuzzy leaved African violets, gaudy Guzmanias, spiky cactus, and fragrant pelargoniums; Robinson, the nursery cat can often be found snoozing here too.

It's not just the postcode that's chic, the nursery's clientele is as fashionable as the locale – although Janson is far too discreet to name drop. He and his team are down-to-earth and welcoming and their prices reasonable. As well as selling plants, the nursery can plan, plant and maintain your garden and they offer a free consultation and design service, tackling anything from rock stars' herb gardens to council house balconies. Their experienced gardeners are used to negotiating front door access only gardens (and the acres of cream carpet that inevitably lie in between). For clients who insist on getting their hands dirty, the nursery sells a practical range of plant-care materials, from compost to pesticides and fertilisers. Janson's top tip is "anything can grow in a pot – as long as the pot is the right size" and to this end, he stocks a wide selection of containers, including some handsome imported Italian terracotta pots. There are also quirky bits of garden sculpture, trellising and troughs. His other bit of advice ("don't expect the rain to water your plants") can be heeded by simply purchasing a watering can.

World's End Nurseries
441-457 King's Road, SW10 0LR
www.worldsendnurseries.com
T: 020 7351 3343
Open: Mon-Sat 9.00-18.00; Sun 10.00-17.00

A prize-winning City garde

Worshipful Company of Gardeners

Today a thoroughly modern institution, the Gardeners' livery company has its origins in the medieval craft guilds, and was incorporated by Royal Charter in 1605. As a 'living guild' it numbers professional and amateur horticulturalists among its membership and its charitable activities focus on promoting the art and practice of good gardening, particularly in the London area.

The most colourful manifestation of the Company's work is the long-running 'Flowers in the City' competition, organised jointly with the Corporation of London. The aim is to beautify the City by encouraging the display of foliage and flowers by the private sector. Prizes are awarded for summer and winter displays with categories including best floral street, atrium, livery hall, courtyard and the newly instituted Skyline Trophy, which recognises the trends in roof gardens and green walls. The much-coveted plaques are presented to winning displays and adorn window boxes and planters around the City with some perennially successful entrants proudly displaying a swathe of awards.

However, the Company has not forsaken its historic past and every year on Whit Tuesday, the Fairchild Lecture (formerly known as the 'Vegetable Sermon') is delivered at St Giles Cripplegate, in accordance with the will of the 18th-century Hoxton nurseryman, Thomas Fairchild. The author of a popular manual for urban gardens, *The City Gardener* (published in 1722), Fairchild was the first person to create a hybrid plant, a cross between a carnation and a Sweet William that became known as 'Fairchild's Mule'. The God-fearing nurseryman was evidently keen to atone for his presumption at usurping the Creator, since the sermon he endowed either takes as its subject the 'Wonderful Works of God in the Creation,' or the 'Certainty of the Resurrection of the Dead, proved by the certain changes of the animal and vegetable parts of the Creation.'

Thomas Fairchild's grave and memorial stone, can be found in Hackney Road Recreation Ground (formerly Shoreditch Old Burial Ground, E2 8ET), not far from Columbia Road market.

www.gardenerscompany.org.uk
www.flowersinthecity.org.uk

Top right: Thomas Fairchild's grave marker

X | X-Factor

Simon Cowell eat your heart out – show-biz ain't got nothing on horticulture when it comes to the competitive spirit. From the high-stakes drama of Medals' Day at Chelsea Flower Show (p.46) to nail-biting needle matches at the local horticultural show, London's gardeners are spoilt for choice in their quest for gardening glory.

Perhaps it's the essentially solitary, contemplative aspect of gardening that brings out the desire for its practitioners to prove themselves against their peers. Civic pride is at stake too with competitions such as London in Bloom and Flowers in the City encouraging local communities and businesses to go head-to-head in the struggle for floral excellence. Meanwhile, parks and public spaces can compete for one of Keep Britain Tidy's coveted Green Flag Awards, which recognise and reward the best green

RHS Horticultural Halls

spaces in the country. Unsurprisingly, London tends to do rather well at this and in 2015/16 received 359 Green Flag Awards.

Even kids get a look in, thanks to the twice-yearly competitions that are organised by the London Children's Flower Society. Every year some 30,000 children, from around 200 primary and special needs schools in London, take part – growing bulbs for the spring competition and flowers, vegetables and herbs in the summer.

Participants are given simple instructions on how to raise the plants, which they nurture at home, or tend in the school garden, before bringing them back to school for judging. Cups, trophies and gardening goodies are awarded to the winners at a special ceremony held at Guildhall in the autumn.

www.londoninbloom.co.uk
www.lcfs.olaves.net
www.greenflag.keepbritaintidy.org
www.conservationfoundation.co.uk

London in Bloom – Campbell Gordon Way

At Campbell Gordon Way in Dollis Hill, the power of gardening to improve the environment and bring people together is tangible, transforming a multi-cultural estate where residents didn't really know each other into a friendly and floriferous community.

Construction worker Bernard Fitzpatrick is the driving force behind the metamorphosis, despite have only taken up gardening five years ago when the recession hit and he had a couple of spare days a week. "It was either golf or gardening" he says, "and I thought golf sounded boring". Bernard started off in his own garden, but his neighbours liked what he was doing so much they wanted to achieve the same results in their own plots. Bernard helped them out with planting and things snowballed from there – within a year the estate had won a Brent 'Green Zone' award. Since then they have gone from strength to strength, scooping more prestigious awards each year. In 2014 they received a five star Outstanding 'It's your Neighbourhood'

award from the RHS and London in Bloom, an achievement repeated in 2015; Bernard has personally been recognised for his hard work with a Brent Community Champions Award.

Over the summer months, Bernard and his team of 30 or so volunteers are busy organising planting weekends and keeping up with the essential aftercare regime of watering, weeding and feeding. "From the end of May to the end of October, everyone comes out in force," says Bernard, "and when the results of London in Bloom are announced in September, we throw a community party with fireworks."

Plants are sourced from the local Homebase, with colourful choices such as petunias, pansies and marigolds being particular favourites. Residents tend their own numbered veg patches, another innovation introduced by Bernard, whose gardening committee has also instituted its own in-house awards for categories such as best veg patch and best balcony display.

Bernard's great success, though, has been in getting children on the estate involved – "it was easy, they love it!" he says. Sporting their own hi-vis jackets, 'Uncle Bernie's little helpers' enthusiastically get stuck in with all the tidying and gardening tasks, and have been kitted out with suitably scaled-down gardening equipment, sourced from Tesco's. It's not all hard work though, Bernard makes sure there are fun seasonal treats to enjoy too, such as an annual Easter egg hunt and trick-or-treating in October.

The awards keep everyone motivated, but for Bernard the best thing about community gardening is getting to know his neighbours he wouldn't otherwise have met. "We're a very multi-cultural community, with lots of different nationalities and religions, and gardening has brought us together".

The Yellow Book (NGS)

Visiting other people's gardens is a long-standing British pastime (just read Jane Austen) and it's one that the National Gardens Scheme has harnessed to charitable effect. Their annually produced Gardens to Visit guide (known to all as the Yellow Book after its signature cover colour) is the Bible of committed garden visitors. It is a county-by-county cornucopia of the thousands of, mostly private, gardens in England and Wales that throw their gates open to the public for the scheme every year.

Although entrance fees are kept low (for years it was just 'a shilling a head'), since its foundation in 1927, the NGS has raised over £45 million for selected cancer, nursing and gardening charities.

Powered by a small paid staff and an army of volunteers the NGS has become a much-loved institution. In London it is something of a growth industry, with visitors jumping at the chance to explore some of the capital's most remarkable private gardens. London County Organiser (and current NGS Chairman) Penny Snell has seen the number of open gardens in London climb from just 31 when she started in 1980 to a whopping 265 in 2015, attracting an annual audience of around 18,000 visitors and raising over £176,000. Recently there's also been a gratifying widening in the NGS demographic, and what used to be a rather middle-aged pursuit, today attracts younger visitors as well as more youthful garden owners – a reflection of current enthusiasm for the joys of gardening and its benefits to health.

Every year Penny and her treasured team of volunteers search out suitable new gardens to open in the capital. They are often acting on tip-offs from neighbours or contacted directly by owners, keen to share their gardens with others. Always looking to raise standards, Penny's selection criteria are stringent with prospective gardens having to show strong design and horticultural interest as well being immaculately maintained. Practicalities such as parking have to be considered and an extrovert owner is a plus, since they will be bombarded with questions from inquisitive visitors. A long season of interest is another holy grail for the organisers, to avoid a glut of rose-filled June gardens.

Penny's decades of hard work mean that Londoners are truly spoiled with the range of gardens they can find in Gardens to Visit. From newly minted designer plots to well-established walled gardens; from blowsy Arts and Crafts style cottage borders to über-urban roof-terraces and floating barge gardens – they're all here. There are gardens with different soil types and every conceivable aspect and scale from woodland glades to south-facing suntraps, from pocket-handkerchief patios to jam-packed plantsmen's playgrounds. Recent years have seen the increasing appearance of fruit and veg in otherwise decorative private gardens and, adding further to the variety, public-spirited community gardens and allotments now open for the scheme.

Great fun to visit – and often with the added attractions of delicious home-made teas, plant sales and invigorating horticultural chat – open gardens are a brilliant resource. The event shows what can be achieved in real gardens, from clever ideas for the classic rectangular London back garden to tips on making the most of minimal spaces. Group openings are a particularly appealing feature of the NGS in London, much prized for their friendly, festive ambience, and ideal for visitors wishing to see several gardens in one hit. Having given away over £25 million to good causes in the past 15 years, the NGS proves that charity really can begin at home – or at least in the garden.

www.ngs.org.uk

Molly St Hilaire's garden (see page 298)

The Reverend Kemmyo Taira Sato

Z Zen Garden

When it comes to Zen gardens, less is more. This one, behind the suburban villa that houses the Three Wheels Buddhist Centre, is no exception. Although the garden's pared down design is the work of an Englishman, art history professor John White, it has all the elements of an authentic Kyoto Zen garden. Typical features include a carefully considered arrangement of rocks and mosses, meticulously raked gravel, surrounding cob wall, tree-lined perimeter and the thatched meditation hut.

The garden was built from scratch in 1996, a year after the house had been acquired for the Three Wheels Centre as the London outpost of the Shogyoji Temple in Japan. Taking the theme of 'Harmony within Diversity' as its guiding principle, the garden's spiritual purpose came into play even during its construction. Deliberately eschewing mechanical aides, the site was cleared entirely by hand by volunteers from Japan, Britain and elsewhere, who as they worked together were able to gain a deeper understanding of each other, and each other's culture.

Meanwhile, Professor White and the priest at Three Wheels, Reverend Kemmyo Taira Sato, had already set out on a series of journeys to Cumbria to handpick eight of the 12 rocks that form the backbone of the garden's layout. The remaining four came, rather more prosaically, from a specialist company in Drayton. The 12 rocks resonate with meanings, both visible and otherwise, and in keeping with Zen tradition some are deeply embedded, so that only the smallest proportion of the rock can be seen above ground. Their number recalls the 12 chromatic tones of *Gagaku,* an ancient form of classical Japanese music, the Apostles and the 12 types of light that Amida Buddha radiates. Professor White's arrangement of the rocks invokes the system underlying the Fibonacci sequence.

Designed as an aid to meditation, this is a garden for looking at, not walking through. Its immaculate gravel 'sea' is raked and weeded every two weeks by a trained assistant, using specialist tools (a job that takes up to five hours). The L-shaped thatched meditation hut is raised to allow the garden to be seen clearly. Planting is restricted to the trees that run in a one metre (3ft) wide strip behind the cob wall; these pines, laurels, hollies, maples, weeping birch and magnolia represent the *shakkei,* or surrounding scenery. Over time the trees have grown and obscured the garden's actual, urban location; likewise the rocks have taken on a life of their own and, colonised by native mosses and water marks, they have become like mini-mountain islands, anchored in their sea of gravel. With nothing to do but absorb the garden's tranquility, visitors experience this garden in a very different way to the average English plot, as suggested by Professor White's poem, written to be read while viewing the garden (see the following page).

The garden is open to the public on selected days through the NGS.

Three Wheels Buddhist Centre
55 Carbery Avenue, Acton, W3 9AB
www.threewheels.org.uk
www.ngs.org.uk

*You can make of the garden
what you will.*

*But it may, perhaps,
make something of you,
which you were not,*

if you wait and are still;

*if you become one
with the garden
and move beyond thought
or imagination,*

*and are,
as the garden,
is.*

MEET THE GARDENERS

An Award-Winning
Wildlife Garden

When Thierry Suzanne moved in to his house in Forest Gate in 2007, his first priority was to create an al fresco dining area in the back garden, along with a herb garden and veg patch. Soon after though, a more adventurous plan began to seed itself. Nine years down the line, that seed has blossomed into a full-on wildlife garden that is as much a haven for birds, invertebrates and amphibians as it is for its human custodians. And it's not just the local fauna that appreciates Thierry's efforts – the garden won Best Small Residential Garden in the RHS/Wildlife Trust's 2012 Big Wildlife Garden competition.

"When we came here, the garden had a more tropical feel, with several large cordylines and a lawn", Thierry recalls, "but I thought the cordylines were out of context in London and I couldn't be bothered with the lawn so I replaced them with a wild flower meadow". While the ready to roll meadow matting that Thierry installed was agreeably low-maintenance, he found that it grew tall and floppy, and made nearby plants too leggy. After two seasons he scrapped it but not before noticing how much wildlife the meadow had attracted. Thierry started to research the subject and had his eureka moment - "I realised that wildlife would make a really great focus for the garden".

Since then, he has gone all out to tempt the birds and bees into his 48 x 14 foot (15 x 4.3 metres) urban patch. His first major project was a pond. The organic oval shape was marked out in pebbles first before Thierry started the labourious process of hand digging. The centre of the pond was dug deeper to provide a sanctuary for hibernating aquatic creatures while the edges were sculpted with shelves for plants and shallow sloping beaches to allow birds, toads and frogs to enter and exit the water. Thierry then laid down a triple layer of landscape fabric, liner and a further fabric liner before filling the pond with rainwater harvested from his water butt. Carefully arranged boulders and pebbles define the pond's margins, and the water is kept sparklingly clear with barley straw, which releases a chemical that naturally prevents algae.

Wildlife-friendly native plants were sourced from an online aquatic plant specialist with Thierry's choices including Water Crowfoot (*Ranunculus aquatilis*), Flowering Rush (*Butomus umbellatus*), Miniature Waterlily (*Nymphaea pygmaea helvola*) and purple loosestrife (*Lythrum salicaria*). Thierry's local Freecycle group turned up trumps with a Marsh Marigold (*Caltha palustris*) – a water's edge plant that the Forest Gate hoverflies, bees and butterflies just can't get enough of. A few seasons on, the pond is as busy as any watering hole in the Serengeti, although instead of wildebeest and crocodiles, its clientele takes the form of teeming tadpoles, thirsty songbirds and clouds of darting dragon and damselflies.

Elsewhere in the garden, Thierry has also selected plants for their wildlife worthiness. The inappropriately exotic cordylines were replaced with fruit trees – crab apple for the wildlife, cherry and plum for Thierry and his wife Sarah. Fragrant lavender was sourced from a lavender specialist with Thierry opting for hardy varieties such as 'Gros Blue', 'Loddon Blue' and 'Peter Pan' to maximise the flowering season. Buttercups, plantain, silver-leaved rose campion and pink and white valerian - remnants of the ill-fated meadow – still pull their wildlife weight, while the raspberries that bask on the sunny side of the garden, are veg patch survivors, their stay of execution granted as much for their bee-friendly flowers as for their fruit. Boring boundary fences are camouflaged with flower and berry-rich climbers and shrubs, while the kitchen patio doors

are framed by a luxuriant but tender passionflower ("the bees love it!" enthuses Thierry).

Proving that an ecological approach does not have to come at the expense of style, Thierry has built attractive pathways around the pond – pea shingle and sleeper on one side, mellow reclaimed brick paviours on the other – and experimented with colour themed planting. A white border illuminates the shady side of the garden with a tranquil scheme of honeysuckle, variegated ivy, *Pulmonaria* 'Sissinghurst White', aquilegia, saxifrage, white geum and Japanese anemone.

On this side too, inspired by a recent visit to Japan, Thierry has added a stone *chozubachi* water basin, with a surrounding plantscape of lamiums and slug-resistant hosta varieties, such as H. 'Sum and Substance', *H.* 'Love Pat', *H.* 'June' – all AGM holders. Slugs and snails are always a worry with hostas, but regular applications of nematodes and an every-other-day collection in a plastic bag seem to be doing the trick. Thierry also uses biological controls to tackle the aphids that so enjoy his climbing roses and two plum trees, sourcing native British ladybird larvae (*Adalia bipunctata*).

The Japanese-style gazebo at the far end of the garden has been built from recycled timber. Its green roof was inspired by the one installed on Thierry's bike shed by The Grass Roof Company. Using a DIY guide as its template, Thierry's green roof incorporates different soil types and even two 'hills' into its compact dimensions. A 'dry stone wall' made from recycled roofing slates keeps this high-rise habitat in place while offering additional nooks and crannies for wildlife. The plants themselves came, fittingly, from the packet of seeds that was part of Thierry's Big Wildlife Garden prize and include cornflowers, poppy, and corn chamomile (*Anthemis arvensis*).

Seeing habitat opportunities at every turn, Thierry has planted a native hedgerow as the rear boundary. Purchased as bare root plants, the hedge is a tapestry of dog rose, dogwood, *Viburnum tinus*, spindleberry, blackthorn, hawthorn, field maple, wild plum and common elder. At the side of the gazebo, Thierry has stationed fragrant, single-flowering rose varieties 'White Star', 'Frances E. Lester' and 'Mermaid'. Enclosed within a protective gabion, these thorny customers have bee appeal, but will also provide cover for the robins that Thierry hopes will take up residence in the nesting boxes he has installed there. Frankly, they'd be mad not to – this garden is tailor made for them, with Thierry laying on daily supplies of live mealworms, served in a magpie, squirrel and starling-proof feeder improvised from a wire hanging basket.

Thierry researches everything exhaustively – "I'm not an impulse buyer", he says firmly. To earn a place in the garden, plants must not only be the right ones in the right place, they must also have impeccable wildlife credentials too. Eco-gizmos too have to meet Thierry's rigorous standards – the first rain water downpipe insert he installed clogged up quickly, with most of the water bypassing the water butt and heading straight down the drain. He's now sourced one that has a fine mesh insert and is pleased with the results, "The water is very clear, and not much water bypasses it, which means the waterbutt gets fuller quicker."

Thierry's attention to detail has paid dividends, and nine years on, he still relishes his daily sightings of wildlife, from the common mint moth in the herb patch to the sex-mad shield insects on the raspberries. His enviable rosta of avian visitors alone includes goldfinch, fieldfare, great tits, greater woodpecker,

and jays, as well as the less welcome green parakeets and magpies.

With the Wildlife Trust award under his belt, Thierry is well placed to offer advice to wannabe wildlife gardeners but his top three tips are disarmingly straightforward: dig a pond, install a bird feeder ("it's simple but it works!"), and finally do your homework – "you can always find a plant that does what you want it to do aesthetically but that is also wildlife-friendly".

Open by appointment only
thierry@yellownemo.com

Thierry's Wildlife Gardening Address Book

Plant Resources
RHS Perfect for Pollinators downloadable plant lists
www.rhs.org.uk
Bumble Bee Conservation plant list
www.bumblebeeconservation.org

Pond Resources
www.fawcettsliners.co.uk
www.wildaboutgardens.org.uk

Green Roof Resources
www.livingroofs.org
www.greenroofsubstrates.co.uk

Suppliers
The Grass Roof Company
www.grassroofcompany.co.uk

Shade-Loving Plants
Long Acre Nurseries
www.plantsforshade.co.uk

Aquatic Plants
Waterside Nursery
www.watersidenursery.co.uk

Bareroot trees, hedging and roses
Ashridge Trees
www.ashridgetrees.co.uk

Lavender
Downderry Nursery
www.downderry-nursery.co.uk

Biological controls
www.greengardener.co.uk

Water Saving
www.guttermate.co.uk

A Botanical Artist's Garden

and ripe for a rethink. Today 5 Burbage Road elicits plaudits from the likes of Anna Pavord, attracts visitors from home and abroad (by appointment) and is a longtime stalwart of the NGS – complete with teas and a plant stall that always sells out.

Beautiful bones lie at the heart of the garden's success. Rosemary has disguised the length of the garden by dividing it, in time-honoured fashion, into a succession of different spaces. The paved terrace leading from the house gives way to lawn, lawn to a 'dusky perennial' border, this in turn is followed by a gravel garden, which leads into a woodland garden. A key design decision was to divide the rectangular lawn into two, making a pair of squares separated by a border of neatly coiffed box balls and instantly improving the rhythm of the garden. "It's amazing the difference it has made," Rosemary observes. This is a garden that works in the round and, walking around it, the visitor is rewarded with any number of interesting lateral views across, an important consideration for Rosemary, whose earlier training was as an architect. To this end, a bisecting central path was removed, disrupting the view straight down the garden and obliging the visitor to go around the side paths and enter the various 'rooms' from an oblique angle.

The garden is well provisioned with evergreen plants for a strong year-round framework. A nuisance in many people's eyes, ivy is put to good use blanketing one of the boundary fences to provide shelter for birds as well as a permanent backdrop to a sunny border. Ivy has also been carefully trained up the vertical supports of the wooden fence that partially screens the woodland area. Evergreens such as *Phillyrea latifolia*, holly, laurel and boxleaf honeysuckle are shaped into well-behaved sculptural forms and a cloud-pruned escallonia in the woodland area shows how this technique can transform a rather ordinary shrub into a real eye-catcher.

As an award-winning botanical artist, Rosemary Lindsay is used to working up close and personal with plants and she brings the same forensic attention to detail to her garden in Herne Hill. At 150 x 40 ft (46 x 12 metres) it's a bigger canvas than her watercolour drawings but one that equally reflects her design flair and affinity with plants.

Rosemary and her husband Crawford came to this garden in the 1970's and although there were vestiges of what had once been a good garden, it was also, as Rosemary puts it, "very boring",

Sculpture by Nesta Hosoon

Judicious specialist pruning also ensures that the stems of deciduous trees and shrubs are attractively shaped, the better to frame the views created by Rosemary. The trio of apple trees alone offers a masterclass in the pruner's art – their textbook goblet shape immaculately maintained by one of three gardeners who occasionally help in the garden.

South-west facing and sheltered, the garden Rosemary says, "gets a bit of everything". The shady border running down the left hand boundary is replete with epimedium, hellebores and *Geranium sylvaticum*, while its opposite number features sun-worshippers such as cistus, lavender and irises. *Euphorbia robbii* and the blue-flowered *Geranium* 'Bill Wallis' are both Burbage Road stalwarts – self-seeders that Rosemary finds it hard to be tough on but whose presence gives this nuanced garden a spritz of informality. A rogue Babington's Leek – which Rosemary grows for their flowers – has arrived unplanned in one of the beds near the house but she has let it stay, a quirky touch, like the old boneshaker bicycle propped up in the shady border, or the purple clematis that winds its way through a forest pansy.

Fragrant plants are a notable feature, some of them, like daphne and choisya, doing double-duty as evergreen interest. Although most of her plants are hardy ("there's no greenhouse here", notes Rosemary), tender specimens such as the evergreen *Magnolia* (syn. Michelia) thrive; housed in a tub of ericaceous compost near the warmth of the house, its crop of scented cream flowers bears witness to its rude health. A magnificent *Drimys winteri* is another supposedly tender plant enjoying this sheltered garden, its glossy evergreen, aromatic foliage, and fragrant creamy white flowers in fine form for the NGS opening.

Rosemary also loves scented roses and she has tracked down some less-than-usual suspects for her own garden. She points out a *Rosa spinosissima* (Burnet rose), whose white scented flowers are followed by dramatic maroon-black hips. *Rosa* 'Sombreuil' climbs up the wooden screen dividing the gravel and woodland gardens, along with 'Evangeline', a rambler whose pink, single flowers are also scented. Another rambler is the magnificently monikered 'Ghislaine de Féligonde' whose sweet musky-scented flowers are borne on almost thornless stems – "how can you resist a rose with a name like that?" asks Rosemary.

Basking in the sunshine the dry garden radiates Mediterranean informality. Crocosmia, irises and self-sown primroses happily grow in the gravel here, along with a white acanthus and aromatic herbs such as fennel, rosemary, lavender, marjoram, and sage. A smartly topiarised lollipop tree turns out to be narrow-leafed bay, *Laurus nobilis angustifolia,* a purchase from Architectural Plants – "a wonderful place to go shopping" says Rosemary. The assorted zinc tubs and troughs contain specimens that object to the garden's London clay, such as pinks, and an olive tree. After years of cultivation, the soil still yields a regular harvest of pebbles but Rosemary uses them as a decorative mulch for her container-grown plants.

The woodland garden is dominated by a large lime tree ("protected", notes Rosemary rather wistfully), that comes with all the attendant problems of the *Tilia* genus – including aphids – but whose leaves provide the raw material for copious leaf mould. This area is lavishly mantled with hardy 'doers' such as lamium, *Geranium phaeum,* pulmonaria, aquilegia, Solomon's seal, and acid-green Alexanders (*Smyrnium olusatrum*). Tucked discreetly behind a hurdle fence in the far corner, the tripartite composting station is where Rosemary, a keen mulcher, mixes her home-made

compost with John Innes to get the consistency she likes. Nearby, at the foot of an ancient pear tree, the recently installed bespoke insect hotel awaits its first check-ins, while another artwork – a rusted wire fox by Rupert Till – breaks cover from the undergrowth (although this being London, the garden is no stranger to the real thing).

Deliberately keeping the colour scheme harmonious and "not too chaotic", Rosemary has also factored in plenty of areas throughout the garden where visitors can pause to admire the carefully composed views, and almost tangible sense of calm. This being an artist's garden, it's perhaps no surprise to find that some of the seats are also works of art, such as the pebble-smooth ceramic seat by artist Hannah Bennett.

And while Rosemary's artistic way with plants can be admired in her garden between April and June, her botanical watercolours drawings are available year round, through her website and in greeting card form from botanic gardens, galleries and bookshops.

5 Burbage Road, Herne Hill, London SE24 9HJ
www.rosemarylindsay.com

www.architecturalplants.com
www.hannahbennett.co.uk

A Garden Reborn

Taking on someone else's award-winning garden might seem a little daunting but that's exactly the prospect that Ben Nel and Darren Henderson faced when they bought their basement flat in Hackney.

The previous owner had been an enthusiastic actor-cum-gardener who drew on his theatrical background to create a much-fêted garden, which opened for the NGS every year. And just to make life really interesting for the fledgling horticulturalists, their new garden embraced two completely different styles, a formal Italian garden near the house and, at the far end of the garden, a small but fully-fledged Japanese stroll garden, complete with meandering stream, red lacquered 'Shinkyo' bridge and tea house. Inexperienced as they were, Ben and Darren threw themselves into the challenge and within months were being invited to re-open the garden for the NGS.

Unlike most new home owners, Ben and Darren gave priority to the garden over their flat. They lost no time in seeking help about how to care for their unusual and beautiful acquisition. Gardening books were bought and pored over, helpful neighbours (who had watched the garden's evolution over the years) offered advice, and they hired a specialist Japanese gardener to teach them the pruning methods required to keep the box and yew in perfect shape.

Since a lot of specimens in the Japanese garden – their favourite area – had died, some expensive trips to specialist Japanese garden centres were required to hunt down suitable replacement dwarf pines, water lilies, ferns and grasses. But the effort was worth it – in the process Ben and Darren came to understand how the miniature landscapes of a Japanese garden should function to create peace and harmony, and they were

determined to find the right plants for it, instead of simply impulse buying at the local garden store – "so easy to get carried away!"

Replacement plants were also needed to fill the dozens of characterful old terracotta pots that furnish the Italian garden. Ben and Darren chose a white colour scheme to stand out against this area's stately cypress trees and evergreen box and yew topiary and ordered hundreds of lilies, hyacinths and tulips from Crocus for a radiant spring display. John Innes 2 & 3 was found to be the perfect growing medium for the pots but Darren quickly learned to cut in chicken wire to stop the grey squirrels from stealing the bulbs.

Although respectful of the garden they inherited, they are gradually introducing new features, such as Ben's bamboo edging along the freshly laid blue chipped slate path, inspired by the Kyoto Garden in Holland Park (see p.139). They have also created a new secret dining space under the cloud-like canopy

of the ceanothus and have even found time to turn their attentions to the front garden. Ben and Darren are learning all the time but, inspired by positive feedback they got from their NGS visitors, they are determined to carry on developing the garden and make it even more their own.

Navarino Road, Hackney, E8
www.ngs.org.uk
www.crocus.co.uk

A Garden Written in the Stars

Clambering up a stepladder and over the fence is not the most conventional way to enter a garden, but that's how I came to visit Kay Thomson's garden in Muswell Hill. Kay's garden shares a boundary with that belonging to her friends Susan Bennett and Earl Hyde, the irrepressible assistant NGS county organisers for NW London (see p.301), and the stepladder arrangement is a pragmatic one for friends whose gardens adjoin but whose houses don't.

NGS visitors to Kay's garden come in through the street entrance, where Kay has solved the problem of how to make her 'side return' interesting by using hers to house a shed, a small greenhouse, and a glass museum case, showcasing finds from her pond excavation and nearby Alexandra Palace. It's an imaginative use of a space that is the bane of many a London property.

Once an arid desert, the concrete terrace at the back of the house was dug up by Earl (what a neighbour to have!) and re-laid with attractive paviours and is now the setting for a mainly containerised Mediterranean garden, featuring oleander, pine, jasmine and a rampant grape vine that romps the length of the garden fence.

The garden's central section takes an astrological theme, with borders arranged in a circle around a pristine lawn (representing earth) that contain plants chosen for their astrological significance. This novel approach is perfect for a garden that opens its doors to visitors, since it's such a popular talking point and everyone inevitably wants to check out what 'their' plants are. Hollyhocks and rosemary, for example, are two plants that come under the sign of Aries, while Taureans can count foxgloves, lovage and thyme as their botanic mascots. Recently Kay and her gardening collaborator Nick Wood-Glover have added even more herbs to the planting scheme, taking Culpeper as their guide.

A sturdy wooden pergola, planted with red, white and blue wisteria (to mark the Queen's Diamond Jubilee), has been cleverly set at an angle across the width of the garden, nicely framing the view into the final 'room'. An evocation of Kay's native Cornwall, this part of the garden transplants the West Country to North London. Once again, neighbour Earl played his part, volunteering to dig the pond that, reports Kay, has been a catalyst for the whole garden, attracting wildlife and human visitors – "I'm never short of people wanting to come and sit by the pond", she says.

Taking care to keep her plant choices as authentic as possible, Kay has populated this sunny area with Cornish hedgerow favourites such as valerian, echinops, Mexican fleabane, crocosmia, fuschias, tamarisk and thrift. Many of these have happily taken up residence in the nooks and crannies of the dry 'stone' wall, built from the concrete that was hammered out from the terrace. Continuing the coastal vibe, the pond has its own pebble beach and is fringed with water buttercups, bulrushes and arum lilies, as well as a statuesque stand of common dock, which looks surprisingly handsome in this context.

Kay has 'mulched' the borders around the pond with smooth grey pebbles, between which grow stands of equisetum, miscanthus and stipa. Tucked in among the vegetation a wooden rowing boat, an old porthole and coiled ropes strike a suitably nautical note and are a bit of fun. "It's an optimistic garden", says Kay, "a place to get away from it all". Soaking up the sun on the terrace, it's hard not to disagree. Taking Voltaire's *Candide* as her touchstone, Kay has followed its hero's resolution to "cultivate our garden" and in doing so has created a garden that is quite simply a joy.

66 Muswell Avenue, N10 2EL

www.ngs.org.uk

Victorian/Edwardian
plant pot feet
discarded by earlier
gardeners

Abandoned Robin's nest
+ eggs found in the
glasshouse at
5 St. Regis Close

David's Ecohouse

A former car-breaker's yard might not appear the most propitious site for a house, or a garden for that matter. It is on just such unforgiving terrain that David Matzdorf has built his eco-friendly house and created not one but two distinct gardens: an experimental green roof and a 'modern exotic' terrestrial front garden.

Accessible only by ladder, the roof is where David pushes the boundaries of accepted green-roof wisdom. Here the usual ground-hugging sedums are joined by loftier, more adventurous plant choices such as spiky dasylirion from Mexico and fascicularia, a Chilean bromeliad whose spiny foliage turns crimson in the autumn. Brightly flowered drought-resistant plants such as cistus, thrift (*Armeria maritima*), mesembryanthemum and aromatic chives ensure this roofscape doesn't turn brown, as 'green' roofs have a tendency to do. Cranesbills also do well up here and David particularly recommends *Geranium x oxonianum* 'Wargrave Pink' as a resilient London plant.

David's gently sloping 'horticultural green roof' has evolved since the house was completed in 2000. The 90:10 topsoil/sharp sand mix that was delivered in place of the 60:40 mix originally ordered has caused a few headaches along the way, not least in its hospitality to perennial weeds. But in deciding to 'rise above' the weed problem by planting taller plants David has discovered that it is possible to grow a wider range of plants – particularly succulents and xerophytic shrubs – than is usually thought possible in London. Ever experimental, he uses lightweight perlite to make mounds to raise the height of certain specimens and increase the standard 100mm soil depth.

Mesembryanthemum

Thrift (Armeria maritima)

While the roof garden resembles alpine scree, down at ground level it's a different story. Tucked between house and boundary wall, the microclimate here is tropical with planting to match. With the glass façade of the house looking directly onto the garden, David has opted for evergreen, architectural plants to give him year-round interest. The garden is a lushly textured palette of cordyline, bamboo, yucca, banana, acacia, abutilon and David's cosseted brugmansias. The latter are overwintered inside but other plants have to take their chances outdoors. Against expectation the *Phoenix canariensis* (date palm) has grown into a 6m x 4.5m (20 x 15 ft) giant, requiring a once sunny area to become a shady home for rodgersias and ferns. With fathomless London clay to contend with there was no option but to import topsoil; the plants in the lower garden flourish in a 500-600mm (20-24 inches) layer of clayey loam, laid over a mulch of rotted organic material.

A plantsman to his fingertips, David shuns expensive hard landscaping in favour of plants, plants and yet more plants – most of them propagated at home or acquired through plant swaps. As a living experiment, the garden is in an ongoing state of flux and suburban tidiness is not on the agenda. What David most enjoys about gardening is "Changing things. Then watching them change themselves. Gardens are never finished." The garden opens for the NGS and by appointment between May and October.

Hungerford Road, N7
www.ngs.org.uk

Dasilyron

"Take limitless pains preparing your soil and extreme care positioning your plants. Then let them get on with it."

Molly's Urban Oasis

The courtyard behind Molly St Hilaire's terraced house in Hackney is petite but perfectly formed. Taking the lush forest clearings of her native Grenada as her inspiration, Molly has created a cosy, contemplative oasis using masses of foliage plants, including ferns and ivy, with robust climbers such as passion flower, roses, wisteria and honeysuckle to build height and add colour. The bold variegation of croton plants (*Codiaeum variegatum*) and the shimmering bamboo are reminders of 'back home' – in Grenada.

The garden's lush abundance is down to Molly: there was nothing in the garden when she moved in nearly 30 years ago. Over the years she has improved the soil with manure and piled on the plants, many propagated by herself. When it comes to pest control, Molly operates a strict zero-tolerance approach to slugs, and keeps the slimy marauders at bay with early morning patrols and swift dispatch in a container of salt.

Although gardening for many years, Molly took it up seriously about five years ago when she decided she wanted to join the NGS, and has opened her garden for the last three. Her joy in sharing her garden is evident – bunting and chairs welcome visitors on the street, there are plants for sale, teas and a visitors' book for comments. Molly's love of bright colour manifests itself in her small front garden. Where most people just stash their rubbish bins or bikes, Molly has opted for an exuberant display of clashing hot pink and red flowers. When pressed to recommend a good plant for London gardens, she advocates hydrangeas – "I think they're nice – you can't go wrong with them."

Bushberry Road, E9
www.ngs.org.uk

"*I come out here in the morning, about half-past-seven, I sit here and I put my thoughts together... You get ideas, it's stimulating coming here because it's so peaceful.*"

The Enchanted Garden

Entering the garden of 5 St Regis Close is like stepping into Narnia. True, there is no snow and nor are there any fauns, but one minute you are in suburban Muswell Hill, the next an enchanted realm, where creativity, imagination and joie de vivre reign supreme. Instead of Narnia's famous lamp-post, this parallel universe features a municipal road bollard, liveried in blue and gold and pragmatically repurposed as a hose bollard. It's one of several quirky eye-catchers that have helped to make this garden such a hit with NGS visitors, along with the more traditional offerings of delicious homemade teas and a "massive" plant sale.

Overseeing this oasis of originality are artists Susan Bennett and Earl Hyde, who have gardened together here for some three decades. Over the years they have been able to gradually acquire extra chunks of land so the once small suburban garden now covers the area of around three tennis courts. Their expanded territory now comfortably accommodates a collection of architectural features designed and built by Earl, as well as Susan's inclusive planting schemes – "I'm the person who decrees 'Thou shalt to go there'", she says, "and I can't think of a plant that I wouldn't use". The sunny border that follows the long rear boundary showcases this philosophy with a vibrant tapestry of *Achillea millefolium* 'The Beacon', purple alliums, salvias, marguerites, pink hydrangea, and hanging baskets of pretty pansies set against a blowsy backdrop of wisteria and clematis.

The "Folly de Grandeur" encapsulates the couple's playful approach and provides a strong focal point. The small-but-perfectly formed Baroque temple's apparently opulent marble columns are made of plastic gas piping, and painted in trompe l'oeil, while the intricate ceramic capitals that adorn them were painstakingly made by Earl and glazed in precious 22ct gold lustre. The resident deity is Maud, a Carrara marble statue of an Indian dancer and standing sentinel at her shrine are two standard salix, whose frothy pyrotechnics are underscored by mounds of glaucous hostas.

A model of the Winter Palace, another of Earl's ceramic creations, looks out across the pond nearest the house, its golden onion domes glinting amid rustling bamboo, magenta fuschias, and mournful weeping willow. A scaled-down Chinese pagoda glazed in turquoise, red and gold, oversees the second pond which is planted with native waterlilies and fringed with flag irises, a prostrate conifer and the odd Himalayan balsam (beloved by the bees and easily controlled by hand-weeding). The pond is patrolled by a squadron of enormous koi carp, their size in part attributable to their diet of slugs and snails, harvested by Susan as part of her campaign to keep her hostas pristine.

Tucked away in the garden's furthest reaches lies "The Forbidden City", the location for the greenhouse and plant nursery. Boldly painted in Chinese lacquer red, the Hartley Botanic greenhouse matches the colour of the fencing and the plants in the greenhouse obligingly co-ordinate, with noble pelargoniums such as 'Lord Bute', and bunches of *Persicaria* 'Dragon's Blood' rooting in pots of water.

Susan's well-stocked nursery would put many professional outfits to shame and she has a talent for nursing sickly specimens back to health. Her plant stall offers fantastic value and not just for its affordable specimens – visitors are as likely to be served by an actor, artist or a retired British Consul, as they are a gardening expert.

The garden is constantly evolving, ensuring something new for its many repeat visitors. Painted yellow and hung with mirrors and candle sconces, the "Liberace Terrace" is a recent addition; superficially tongue in cheek, it's a practical but a witty disguise for an ordinary boundary fence, the mirrors bouncing back light into the garden. The planting here is suitably flamboyant ("just a hint of the Austro-Hungarian Empire", notes Susan), peppered with fiery orange and red geums, spiky equisetum (which Susan loves for their winter interest), and bolstered by the evergreen foliage of *Fatsia japonica.*

Another new addition, a 'Chinese tea house', has breathed new life into the previously dreary far corner; painted in auspicious turquoise and red, it enjoys views out across the garden. For Susan and Earl even garden fatalities offer creative opportunities – a deceased apple tree has been replaced with a statue of a rearing horse and the clematis that once romped through the apple now romps just as happily through the open metal framework of the sculpture, which even after a month looks entirely at home.

The creative hub of the garden is the studio, where visitors can browse and buy pottery made by the couple. Continuing the ceramic theme, vintage chimney pots are used as planters for massed displays of heucheras, succulents, and hostas. This handful of chimney pots are what survive of a collection that once ran into hundreds; the couple are by their own admission not people who do anything half-heartedly. "We are perfectionists", says Earl, "we don't take ourselves seriously, but we take what we do seriously".

As assistant county organisers for the NGS in NW London, Susan and Earl know a thing or two about what makes a visit-worthy garden and are rightly proud that 5 St Regis Close consistently raises more money for the NGS than any other in the London region. With three openings a year, the couple work hard to ensure the garden looks different each time, and are generous hosts, happily sharing their respective expertise with visitors. "We try to help people be themselves in their garden", says Susan, summing up their creative credo, "your garden should be an expression of yourself".

5 St Regis Close,
Alexandra Park Road, N10 2DE
T: 020 8883 8540

Groups by appointment Feb to Dec
www.ngs.org.uk

"your garden should be an expression of yourself"

...unlike a garden which is experienced from 'within', the roundabout is seen by most people only from the outside.

The Magic Roundabout

Caroline Bousfield Gregory has been gardening the Lauriston Road roundabout for over ten years, transforming it from weedy wasteland to a magical Mediterranean island (albeit one set in a sea of tarmac). She started as a guerrilla gardener but went legit after negotiating a contract – and the usual health and safety hurdles – with the council. It was a shrewd move that has enabled her to tend her prize-winning roundabout with their blessing.

With its drifts of euphorbia, cheery pot marigolds and fragrant lavenders, the garden is a masterclass in the art of low maintenance, low-budget gardening. A busy potter (whose workshop is a former stable overlooking the roundabout), Caroline's gardening input varies from half a day each month, to perhaps twice a fortnight. With this in mind, she chooses undemanding, drought-tolerant plants that give year-round interest, such as pretty-but-tough cistus and grey-leaved aromatic evergreens like santolina, sage and rosemary. Grasses including the giant reed *Arundo donax* 'Versicolor', as well as phormiums and kniphofia, all thrive on the roundabout's savannah like conditions, and add architectural interest. Ease of propagation or a willingness to self seed are also virtues – with excess 'volunteers' being sold to raise funds.

Despite its sunny looks, not everything in the roundabout garden is rosy. Theft and rubbish from passing cars are intermittent problems while the arrival of the rosemary beetle, *Chrysolina americana*, has been a challenge. A voracious green and purple striped pest that devours the leaves of rosemary, lavender and sage, it is the only thing that Caroline sprays against.

Gardening is in Caroline's blood and the wild 'gardens' on the dunes in Cornwall, where her parents lived, have influenced the relaxed feel of the roundabout, where pink and white valerian – a staple of the West Country coastline – flower throughout the summer. The naturalistic look of the roundabout is deceptive, belying the care that Caroline has taken over safety considerations such as the height, density and overhang of plants. Caroline's current planting scheme (instigated in 2004, following disruptive work by the gas board) also acknowledges that, unlike a garden which is experienced from 'within', the roundabout is seen by most people only from the outside. To open up its sightlines, Caroline has installed two gravel paths that bisect the roundabout. These are placed at a diagonal from the road crossings, allowing pedestrians to 'see through' the planting to the shops on the other side.

Caroline's public-spirited labours have not gone unnoticed. She was presented with a Civic Award by the Mayor of Hackney in 2016, while her roundabout garden has won prizes in the Hackney in Bloom competition and is supported by the local traders' association. Lavender bags made from flowers harvested on the roundabout and dried using the heat from Caroline's kilns are sold at the local deli. Caroline likes the idea of selling the garden's produce, "When people buy the lavender bags, its not just a simple purchase, it's a way of supporting the roundabout and, by supporting it, they feel part of it too."

Caroline Bousfield Gregory
Craftsman Potter, 77a Lauriston Road, E9 7HA
www.carolinebousfield.co.uk

The Plantsman

Like the proverbial well-made play, Charles Rutherfoord's Clapham garden unfolds in three acts. The action opens in the front garden, a carefully plotted space that was created five years ago from a rarely-used driveway. A trenchant advocate for the urban front garden, Charles – an architectural designer and one time chairman of the Society of Garden Designers – was determined that this utilitarian space should be reinstated as a garden.

Areas of the concrete drive were duly 'Kangoe'd' into submission and replaced by neat wooden-edged beds. The pathways that remained were laid with pea shingle, Charles' first choice when it comes to that gratifying underfoot crunch, and cost-effective too. A young copper beech hedge separates garden from pavement but, generously, Charles plans to keep this boundary transparent, "I love that this garden is to some extent a shared space – it's wonderful that people want to stop and look at it."

And this is certainly a garden worth looking at. Where concrete once prevailed, soft and romantic planting now welcomes the visitor who, thanks to annual NGS openings (*www.ngs.org.uk*), can enjoy the entire garden without having to peer furtively through the hedge. Two hydrangeas act as floral gatekeepers while ahead a cloud of jasmine and a climbing rose, 'Wedding Day', clothe the gold-framed bay window. The planting of the front garden, as the introduction to the house, is focused on scent throughout the year. Here and there are hints at what lies in store behind the house, such as the American shrub rose 'Golden Wings', a pretty variety with simple flower heads and prominent stamens. There is always a spritz of exotic colour that blazes from pots on the porch balustrade and window boxes outside the first and second floors of the house.

Acts two and three play out behind the house and are partially divided by a sturdy railway sleeper partition, against which is trained a japonica ("wonderful early flowers, and makes a good jelly!"). Lilac 'Sensation' gets spring off to headily fragrant start and this second area of the garden is also packed with unusual specimens such as honey scented (*Euphorbia mellifera*), *Arbutus x andrachnoides* (which bears pretty white flowers and fruit, but whose beautiful, peeling cinnamon-brown bark also adds interest) and an *Acacia pravissima*, a sculptural square-leaved mimosa that is one of Charles's favourite evergreen trees for a London garden.

A plantsman to his fingertips, Charles keeps hard landscaping to a minimum. Soft landscaping, however, is a different story and the garden's final and largest 'act' is characterised by two intriguing manmade hillocks. These mounds, sculpted from builder's rubble and topsoil, create high ground in an otherwise level garden. The side mound is planted with ceanothus, through which ramble roses and clematis, while the bank at the far boundary features architectural acanthus. Like a mini amphitheatre, the earthworks, one of them topped by a steel sculpture of a bull (Hugh Kelly's final degree piece at Central St. Martin's) overlook the garden's centre stage, where every year Charles orchestrates a mass planting of some 1500 spring tulips.

The eye-catching stars of the garden's spring NGS opening, the tulips are planted in November to ensure full vernalisation. Charles orders his tulips every year from the "magnificent and reliable" Bloms Bulbs (*www.blomsbulbs.com*) at the Chelsea Flower Show. Each year he changes the varieties both in form and colour. Blowsy irises and tree peonies add their own chorus of colour, joined slightly later by the coppery hues of *Rosa* 'Just Joey' – a "proper old-fashioned hybrid tea", notes Charles approvingly. The scent of *Holbelia latifolia* pervades.

Unlike some spring gardens, which run out of puff later on, Charles is constantly developing the

garden to have year round interest. Developments to the fundamental plan are evident in the new steps from the back of the house leading to a central path made from railway sleepers. These originally formed a dividing screen. The remaining half of the fence now screens the outside dining table from the house. Fresh arrivals light the back left corner, they include a phalanx of white Japanese anemone (*A. x hybrida* 'Honorine Jobert') partnered by the chameleon-like *Hydrangea paniculata* 'Limelight', whose lime green flowers turn white then pinkish with age, and the distinctive *Echium pininana whose* silhouettes march across the garden.

A spirit of playful experimentation infuses the garden. Charles (together with his partner Rupert Tyler, who raises succulents and tender plants in the futuristic geodetic dome greenhouse) welcomes the influx of NGS visitors – and credits them with helping him to keep the garden fresh. "I really enjoy it, not least because it gives an impetus to get things done! We get lots of repeat visitors and we like to give them new things to see each time." The creation of a circular route is a case in point, installed after Charles noticed that visitors weren't able to navigate the garden very easily.

If Charles is, by his own admission, "quite strict" about what goes into the garden, this plantsman is equally discerning about his suppliers. Favourite nurseries within London include the historic (established 1897) Rassells of Kensington nursery in Earls Court (www. rassells.com), Capital Gardens' Neals Nursery Garden Centre (www.capitalgardens.co.uk) as well as recent start-up, Battersea Flower Station (www. batterseaflowerstation.co.uk, see p.20), founded in 2012 and "good for unusual things", according to Charles. And when it comes to roses, and those fragrant but unfashionable hybrid teas, Charles opts for another long-established company, Harkness Roses (www.roses.co.uk) founded in 1879, and still going strong.

51 The Chase, Clapham, SW4 0NP
www.charlesfurtherfoord.net

"Coronilla glauca is one of the best London plants –
it flowers right through from late winter until May; it's
beautifully scented, and when it's not flowering it's
got very beautiful glaucous foliage."

The Rooftop Vegplot

The Dutch Caribbean island of Saba is a long way from Fitzrovia but its rocky landscape provided fertile inspiration for Wendy Shillam's high-rise vegetable garden in W1. Seeing the way the resourceful Sabans raised veg crops in containers or in the thin soil on their mountain terraces, Wendy realised that lack of cultivatable land need not be an obstacle to growing food on her fifth floor roof terrace.

In 2011 she set about converting the 17 x 19 foot (5 x 6m) space from an under-achieving blank canvas to a fully-fledged potager among the chimney pots. As an architect and urban planner, Wendy's approach was disciplined, and resisting the urge to smother every square inch with plant life, she installed a handful of 2ft (600mm) square raised beds, interspersed with decking panels of the same size. The dimensions of the beds are "easier for reaching over and navigating around" notes Wendy, as well as allowing space for a café table and chairs.

As with any garden, Wendy had to consider the plot's orientation and climate when planning its layout ("that's the hard part – growing things is easy!"). The roof terrace's elevation, combined with London's warm microclimate, offers a light and virtually guaranteed frost-free environment but lack of shade was a problem, leaving plants exposed to sun and wind. Growing climbing crops up trellises was Wendy's solution, generating more growing space as well as shade. Her vertical success stories include 'Courgette Tromboncino Albenga' and the pretty purple French bean 'Cosse Violette' ("my best bean crop ever"). Morning Glory is another favourite – albeit non-edible – climber up on the roof terrace; says Wendy "it's quick to get going, lures insects in and is good for growing among crops." A grapevine is a recent addition, a crafty cutting from a French holiday cottage; its variety is as yet unknown, so Wendy awaits the first harvest with more than usual anticipation.

With only 6" (15cm) planting depth to play with, root crops are not generally part of the Rooftop Vegplot equation but by using deeper containers Wendy can harvest new potatoes as a Christmas treat. Salad crops are a constant however, with 'Salad Bowl' the reliable mainstay, but Wendy is still hunting for the perfect rocket variety. A devotee of raising from seed, Wendy has catholic tastes, recommending King's Seeds for radishes, and the Edible Flower Shop for bee friendly borage. The Morning Glory seeds came from Franchi and Chiltern Seeds is another go-to supplier; Wendy also likes French seeds such as Vilmorin as they work well in hotter climates and "the French care about what they eat!" One plant she would not be without is wild celery (*Apium graveolens*), which willingly self-seeds but "never outgrows its welcome, it smells nice and you can use it to flavour autumn salads and stir-fries". The seeds can be also used to make celery salt.

The Rooftop Vegplot is run organically, with nematodes being unleashed against wine weevils, and the slugs that somehow found their way up to the fifth floor. To show how effective the nematodes have been, Wendy points out the pansies that grow among the lettuce: both are in peak condition, with not a hint of slug damage. Other predators are few: no cats venture up here and the trellising deters pigeons. Even Rosa Bar, Wendy and Mike's lively miniature Schnauzer, knows to keep out of the raised beds.

Without a lift to transport materials up and down five flights of stairs, Wendy operates a closed system, composting all green and brown garden waste in situ in an old school trunk. Coffee grounds make a good soil conditioner while egg shells help regulate the compost's acidity – handy, since Wendy runs a highly acclaimed B&B in her home (*www.bb-london. co.uk*) and therefore has a ready supply of both ingredients. The homemade compost is mixed with vermiculite and coir and Wendy constantly tops up the beds, to keep nutrients levels high.

Even in such a tiny space there are climatic variations that need to be accommodated. Overseen by the iconic silhouette of the BT Tower, the plot is walled on the north and south, but open to the east and west. The raised bed that gets the least sun has however been successfully furnished with a Japanese wineberry (*Rubus phoenicolasius),* whose arching bristly red stems add winter colour to the garden and whose flavoursome raspberry-like fruits go in to Wendy's signature Eton Mess.

This compact garden finds space for both a shed and a 4ft (1.2m) timber greenhouse. Peppers, cucumbers and tomatoes thrive in the greenhouse while the shed is a writer's retreat, from where Wendy blogs about the Rooftop Vegplot at (*www. rooftopvegplot.com*). A spot of pottering in the garden makes the ideal displacement activity to which all writers are prone.

Wendy is passionate about the benefits of rooftop growing, describing herself as a "potagista". If everyone grew something on their roofs, she suggests, it would improve building insulation, cut heating costs and water run off, counteract pollution by absorbing carbon dioxide, and reduce inner city over-heating. On a personal level, the Rooftop Vegplot has encouraged her to become less wasteful, but for Wendy gardening is about more than just fresh, low-carbon produce: "it's relaxing and good for the soul".

An inspirational blueprint for a more ecological way of inner city living, the Rooftop Vegplot is bigger than the sum of its parts and its fame is growing. As well as sharing her rooftop veg experiences on her blog, Wendy opens her garden by appointment, and it can also be seen as part of a stay at her B&B.

Wendy's recommended suppliers:

King's Seeds
www.kingsseeds.com

The Edible Flower Shop
www.theedibleflowershop.co.uk

Chiltern Seeds
www.chilternseeds.co.uk

Franchi Seeds
www.seedsofitaly.com

Vilmorin
A small selection available from www.suttons.co.uk

Blackmoor Nurseries (for fruit plants)
www.blackmoor.co.uk

The Tropical Garden

A major house renovation was the catalyst for the contemporary, tripartite garden that lies behind Paul Thompson's and Gordon McArthur's early Victorian terraced town house in Islington. "Although the existing rear garden was perfectly pleasant it was also very mundane", recalls Gordon, and the sleek new kitchen-diner extension was a not-to-be-missed chance to improve the 'flow' between house and garden and to create a space for outdoor entertaining.

A hefty quantity of soil was excavated to create the cool, travertine paved courtyard that now unfolds onto the basement level. Bi-folding doors open fully across the whole width of the extension, uniting house and garden into one seamless space. From here, a short flight of steps, with potted *Crassula ovata* (money plant) in guard-of-honour formation on each side, rises up to a second 'room', with a silvery wooden deck enclosed by smart raised borders, faced with white render. A single step leads up to the final 'room', a sitting area set against a dramatic red rendered wall, in whose niches a trio of cast concrete heads keep a brooding vigil over the dining table. Walls fashioned from glass bricks make unusual but effective dividers between the three garden 'rooms'.

Although the initial garden layout was entrusted to a landscaper, the planting was down to Paul and Gordon. Columbia Road market, just a short Sunday-morning drive away, was the first port of call for the keen but fledgling gardeners, and ten years on remains a favourite hunting ground for the architectural subtropical plants they love.

A tree fern *(Dicksonia antarctica)* – since joined by two others – was their inaugural purchase (from Columbia Road stalwart Lyndon Osborne). In this sheltered, east-facing plot these and other unusual tender plants thrive without any special cold-weather coddling, and include a *Muehlenbeckia astonii*, a divaricate plant from New Zealand, whose tiny, heart-shaped leaves grow on tough and wiry zigzag branches. A large *Pseudopanax crassifolius* is another architecturally inclined Antipodean that relishes the favourable

microclimate within Paul and Gordon's garden. A member of the Aralia family, this plant features unusual dual foliage, with unappetising spiny lance-like lower juvenile leaves (to dissuade grazing animals), and softer, rounder leaves higher up.

Paul's belief that "you can't just rely on flowers – leaves give you a long season" means there is a particular accent on foliage with dramatic interplay between the likes of *Arisaema consanguinium* (jack-in-the-pulpit), *Thalictrum delavayi* (Hewitts Double), *Ferula communis* (Giant Fennel), American Poke Weed *(Phytolacca Americana)* and *Inula magnifica*. Even after flowering the leaves of the flag iris in the bog garden have plenty of interest to contribute, as does the surrounding stand of *Macleaya cordata* (plume poppy), and rheum. Rampant climbers such as *Solanum crispum* and *Clematis* 'Bill McKenzie' (romping away into neighbours overhanging cherry) reinforce the sense of a verdant woodland garden.

The garden is now so well-stocked that by Paul and Gordon's own admission the planting regime has become "dog eat dog", with only the fittest specimens standing their ground. This Darwinian approach to gardening is brutal but effective, with striking plants and combinations at every turn. Paul in particular likes to mix things up with unexpected juxtapositions, teaming exotic tender specimens like *Echium pininana* with cottagey hardy geraniums or catmint.

A recently assembled collection of potted succulents and cacti, and a *Paeonia rockii* acquired at Chelsea Flower Show – also bear witness to a happily out-of-control plant addiction. These now occupy the built-in shelves originally intended as outdoor seating in the terrace. A driftwood log – reminiscent of a Viking longboat in shape, and a lucky find on Ross Sands, Northumberland – has found a second life as a planter, home to *Aeonium arborem* and other succulents.

As if the garden wasn't populated enough already, a rambling rose from a neighbour's garden is beginning to insinuate its way over the fence. Its appearance is both welcome and serendipitous,

since Paul and Gordon are recent converts to the joy of roses, having just this year added a David Austin rose, 'A Shropshire Lad' to their plant portfolio. The garden is run with minimal use of chemicals and Paul and Gordon swear by the worm juice produced from the wormery in their tiny basement front garden as their in-house plant food. Slugs are a problem that they navigate by avoiding slug magnets like hostas together with Gordon's early-morning slug patrols.

Supply sources are as eclectic as the garden's planting scheme. As well as Columbia Road, Paul and Gordon also use Beth Chatto's nursery, Langthorns Plantery and Great Dixter. The couple are also fans of Crûg Farm Plants and Pan Global Plants.

Luckily as Gordon and Paul's knowledge and interest in gardening has grown over the years, further outlets for their plant passion have presented themselves. Newly created tree pits on Rees Street have become grateful recipients of their surplus

plants, while both men are closely involved with the community-gardening effort in nearby Arlington Square. This formerly neglected public square has been taken in hand by the local residents' association (of which Gordon is Chair), and its team of energetic volunteer gardeners have planted more than 40,000 plants, trees, bulbs and shrubs in the square, since 2011. Gordon and Paul have also found themselves in demand as garden designers.

Arlington Square and 5 Rees Street have both opened to the public for the NGS several times in recent years, with 5 Rees Street attracting over 200 appreciative visitors during their last summer opening. Gordon and Paul thoroughly enjoyed the experience and are already hatching plans for next year's event – the perfect excuse for some new plants perhaps?

Hampton Court Flower Show

GARDENER'S DIRECTORY

Allotments

Alric Avenue Allotments Association
www.alricallotments.com

Barnet Allotment Federation
www.barnetallotments.org.uk

Belmont Lane Allotments & Leisure Gardens
www.belmontlane-allotments.co.uk

Bensham Manor Allotments
www.benshammanorallotments.org.uk

Bexley Council Allotments
www.bexley.gov.uk/allotments

Clifford Road Allotments (Barnet)
www.crallotments.org.uk

Croydon Council Allotments
www.croydon.gov.uk

Ealing Allotments Partnership
www.ealingallotmentspartnership.co.uk

Eltham and Avery Hill Gardens Society
www.eahgs.org.uk

Fulham Palace Meadows Allotments Association
www.fpmaa.com

Hackney Allotment Society
www.hackneyallotments.org.uk

Harland Avenue Sidcup Allotment Society
www.hasas.org.uk

Harrow in Leaf
(umbrella organisation for allotment and horticultural groups in Harrow)
www.harrowinleaf.org.uk

Hillingdon Allotment & Horticultural Federation
www.hahf.org.uk

Kent House Leisure Gardens Association
www.khlga.com

London Allotments Network
www.londonallotments.net

Manor Gardening Society at Pudding Mill
www.mgs-puddingmill.org

North Finchley Allotment Society
glebelandsallotments.org

One Tree Hill Allotments (Southwark)
www.othas.org.uk

Park Hill Allotments (Croydon)
www.parkhill-allotments.org.uk

Roehampton Garden Society
www.roehamptonallotments.co.uk

Romford Smallholders Society
www.romfordsmallholderssociety.org.uk

Rosendale Allotments Association (Dulwich)
www.rosendale-allotments.org.uk

Royal Paddocks Allotments (Hampton Court)
www.paddocks-allotments.org.uk

South Croydon Allotment Society Ltd
www.south-croydon-allotments.org.uk

Spa Hill Allotment Society Ltd
www.spahill.org.uk

West Ham Allotments
www.westhamallotments.org.uk

Windmill Allotments (Brixton Hill)
www.windmillallotments.org.uk

Woodhouse Allotments (Barnet)
www.woodhouseontheweb.org.uk

West Harrow Allotment & Garden Association
www.harrowinleaf.org.uk/whaga.html

Woodside Addiscombe & Shirley Leisure Gardens and Allotment Society
www.awslg.org.uk

Community Gardens, City Farms & Nature Reserves

Bankside Open Spaces Trust
Junction of King James St & Library St, SE1
www.bost.org.uk
T: 020 7261 1009

Brockwell Park Community Greenhouses
Brockwell Park, SE24 0PA
www.brockwellgreenhouses.org.uk
volunteer@brockwellgreenhouses.org.uk

Bromley by Bow Gardens
Corner of St Leonard's St & Grace St, E3 3BT
www.bbbc.org.uk
T: 020 8709 9700

Brooks Farm
Skeltons Lane Park, E10 5BS
www.brooksfarm.uk
T: 08456 122 122

Cable Street Community Gardens
101 Matilda House, St Katherine's Way, E1W 1LF
www.cablestreetcommunitygardens.co.uk
T: 020 7480 5456

Calthorpe Project Community Garden
258-274 Gray's Inn Road, WC1X 8LH
www.calthorpeproject.org.uk
T: 020 7837 8019

Camley Street Natural Park
12 Camley St, N1C 4PW
www.wildlondon.org.uk
T: 020 7833 2311

Capel Manor College
Bullsmoor Lane, Enfield, Middlesex, EN1 4RQ
www.capelmanorgardens.co.uk
T: 08456 122 122

Community & Environment Project Office (Edmonton)
Vincent House, 2e Nags Head,
Ponders End, Enfield, EN3 7FN
www.cepo.btik.com
T: 01992 701 438

Coram's Fields
Guilford Street, WC1N 1DN
www.coramsfields.org
T: 020 7837 6138

Culpeper Community Garden
1 Cloudesley Rd, N1 0EG
www.culpeper.org.uk
T: 020 7833 3951

Deen City Farm
39 Windsor Avenue, Merton Abbey, SW19 2RR
www.deencityfarm.co.uk
T: 020 8543 5300

Devonshire Road Nature Reserve
170 Devonshire Rd, Forest Hill, SE23 3SZ
www.devonshireroadnaturereserve-org-uk.com

Eden at St Paul's Community Garden
Rectory Grove, SW4 0DX
www.stpaulssw4.org/project/eden-garden/
T: 020 7622 2128

The Edible Bus Stop
www.theediblebusstop.org

Forest Farm Peace Garden
Hazelbrouck Gardens, Hainault, IG6 2XL
www.forestfarmpeacegarden.wordpress.com

Freightliners Farm
Sheringham Road (next to Paradise Park), N7 8PF
www.freightlinersfarm.org.uk
T: 020 7609 0467

Growing Communities
The Old Fire Station, 61 Leswin Road, N16 7NX
www.growingcommunities.org
T: 020 7502 7588

Grow Mayow Community Garden
Mayow Park, Mayow Rd, Sydenham, SE26 4JA
www.growmayow.blogspot.com

Hackney City Farm
1a Goldsmith's Row, off Hackney Rd, E2 8QA
www.hackneycityfarm.co.uk
T: 020 7729 6381

Hammersmith Community Gardens Association
1 Melina Road, W12 9HY
www.hcga.org.uk
T: 07890 514 050

Heart Garden
Chumleigh Gardens, Burgess Park, SE5 0RJ
www.artinthepark.co.uk
T: 020 7277 4297

Heathrow Special Needs Farm
Bath Road, Longford, UB7 0EF
www.heathrowspecialneedscentre.org
T: 01753 680 330

Hounslow Urban Farm
Faggs Road, Feltham, TW14 0LZ
www.hounslowurbanfarm.co.uk
T: 020 8831 9658

Hoxton Trust Community Garden
Hoxton Street, N1 6SH
www.hoxtontrust.org
T: 020 7729 1480

Kentish Town City Farm
1 Cressfield Close, off Grafton Road, NW5 4BN
www.ktcityfarm.org.uk
T: 020 7916 5421

King Henry's Walk Garden
King Henry's Walk, N1 4NX
www.khwgarden.org.uk
T: 020 7923 9035

Lambourne End Outdoor Centre
Manor Road, Lambourne End, Essex, RM4 1NB
www.lambourne-end.org.uk
T: 020 8500 3047

Meanwhile Gardens
156-158 Kensal Road, W10 5BN
www.meanwhile-gardens.org.uk
T: 020 8960 4600

Mudchute Park & Farm
Pier Street, E14 3HP
www.mudchute.org
T: 020 7515 5901

Newham City Farm
Stansfeld Road, E6 5LT
www.activenewham.org.uk/newham-city-farm
T: 0300 124 0123

Oasis Children's Nature Garden
Corner Larkhall Lane & Studley Road, SW4 6SP
www.oasisplay.org.uk
T: 020 7498 2329

Phoenix Garden
21 Stacey Street, WC2H 8DG
www.thephoenixgarden.org

Poets Corner Garden
1 Chaucer Road, Acton, W3 6DR
www.facebook.com/
poetscornercommunitygarden/

Roe Green Walled Garden
Roe Green Park, off Kingsbury Rd, NW9 9DT
www.bhcg.btck.co.uk/RoeGreenWalledGarden
T: 020 8206 0492

Roots & Shoots Wildlife Garden
Walnut Tree Walk, SE11 6DN
www.rootsandshoots.org.uk
T: 020 7587 1131

St Mary's Secret Garden
50 Pearson Street, E2 8JD
www.stmaryssecretgarden.org.uk
T: 020 7739 2965

Spitalfields City Farm
Buxton Street, E1 5AR
www.spitalfieldscityfarm.org
T: 020 7247 8762

Sunnyside Community Gardens
Jct Sunnyside Road & Hazellville Road, N19 3LX
www.sunnysidecommunitygardens.org.uk
T: 020 7272 3522

Surrey Docks Farm
Rotherhithe Street, SE16 5ET
www.surreydocksfarm.org.uk
T: 020 7231 1010

Sustainable Hackney
www.sustainablehackney.org.uk

Sutton Ecology Centre
The Old Rectory, Festival Walk,
Carshalton, SM5 3NY
T: 020 8770 5820

Sydenham Garden
28a Wynell Road, SE23 2LW
www.sydenhamgarden.org.uk
T: 020 8291 1650

The Gardens Community Garden
Doncaster & Stanhope Gardens,
off Green Lanes, N4 1HX
www.gardensresidents.blogspot.com
T: 020 8374 7721

Vauxhall City Farm
165 Tyers Street, SE11 5HS
www.vauxhallcityfarm.org
T: 020 7582 4204

Walworth Garden Farm
206 Braganza Street, SE17 3BN
www.walworthgardenfarm.org.uk
T: 020 7582 2652

Wellgate Community Farm
Collier Row Road, Romford, RM5 2BH
www.wellgatefarm.org
T: 01708 747850

Woodlands Farm Trust
331 Shooters Hill, Kent, DA16 3RP
www.thewoodlandsfarmtrust.org
T: 020 8319 8900

Community Orchards

The London Orchard Project
www.thelondonorchardproject.org

Hackney Harvest
www.hackneyharvest.com

Blondin Community Orchard
www.friendsofblondin.org.uk

Butterfield Green Community Orchard
www.shakespeareresidents.org.uk

Chinbrook Community Orchard
www.lewisham.gov.uk

Lambeth Walk Open Space Community Garden
www.rootsandshoots.org.uk

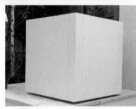

Garden Blogs and
Web Resources

www.blackberrygarden.co.uk
www.fennelandfern.co.uk
www.frustratedgardener.com
www.gardenersworld.com
www.growourown.blogspot.co.uk
www.guerrillagardening.org
www.outofmyshed.co.uk
www.oxoniangardener.co.uk
www.patientgardener.wordpress.com
www.realmensow.co.uk
www.rooftopvegplot.com
www.the-compostbin.com
www.thedahliapapers.com
www.themiddlesizedgarden.co.uk
www.theanxiousgardener.com
www.thegallopinggardener.blogspot.co.uk
www.thinkingardens.co.uk
www.throughthegardengate.co.uk/blog
www.twothirstygardeners.co.uk
www.urbanvegpatch.blogspot.co.uk
www.vegplotting.blogspot.co.uk
www.verticalveg.org.uk
www.weedsuptomeknees.wordpress.com
www.wellywoman.wordpress.com

Garden Events

February

RHS Orchid Show & RHS Botanical Art Show
www.rhs.org.uk/shows-events

RHS London Early Spring Plant Fair
www.rhs.org.uk/shows-events

March

RHS London Greener Gardening Show
www.rhs.org.uk/Shows-Events

**Chiswick House and Gardens
Annual Camellia Show**
www.chgt.org.uk

April

Spring Gardening Show, Capel Manor
www.rhs.org.uk/Shows-Events

May

RHS Chelsea Flower Show (p.46)
www.rhs.org.uk/shows-events

Chelsea Fringe (p.53)
www.chelseafringe.com

**International Sunflower Guerrilla Gardening
Day (p.117)**
www.guerrillagardening.org

June

Open Garden Squares Weekend (p.170)
www.opensquares.org
www.londongardenstrust.org

Grow (p.112)
www.growlondon.com
A contemporary garden and lifestyle fair

July

RHS Hampton Court Flower Show (p.123)
www.rhs.org.uk/shows-events

September

City Harvest Festival
Spitalfields City Farm
www.spitalfieldscityfarm.org

RHS Wisley Flower Show (p.258)
www.hcga.org.uk/events

October

RHS London Autumn Harvest Festival
Lindley Hall
www.rhs.org.uk/shows-events

RHS Cyclamen Autumn Show
www.rhs.org.uk/shows-events

HOUSE PLANTS

Battersea Flower Station

Garden Centres

North

Alexandra Palace Garden Centre
Alexandra Palace Way, N22 7BB
www.capitalgardens.co.uk
T: 020 8444 2555

Boma Garden Centre
51-53 Islip Street, NW5 2DL
www.bomagardencentre.co.uk
T: 020 7284 4999

Camden Garden Centre
2 Barker Drive, St Pancras Way, NW1 0JW
www.camdengardencentre.co.uk
T: 020 7387 7080

North One Garden Centre
The Old Button Factory, 25 Englefield Rd, N1 4EU
www.n1gardencentre.co.uk
T: 020 7923 3553

Sunshine Garden Centre
Durnsford Road, Bounds Green, N11 2EL
www.sunshinegardencentre.co.uk
T: 020 8889 4224

West

Battersea Flower Station
16 Winders Road, SW11 3HE
www.batterseaflowerstation.co.uk
T: 020 7978 4253

The Chelsea Gardener
125 Sydney Street, SW3 6NR
www.chelseagardener.com
T: 020 7352 5656

Clifton Nurseries
5A Clifton Villas, W9 2PH
www.clifton.co.uk
T: 020 7289 6851

Rassells of Kensington
78-80 Earls Court Road, W8 6EQ
www.rassells.com
T: 020 7937 0481

W6 Garden Centre
17 Ravenscourt Avenue, W6 0SL
www.w6gardencentre.co.uk
T: 020 8563 7112

World's End Nurseries
441-457 King's Road, SW10 0LR
www.worldsendnurseries.com
T: 020 7351 3343

South-West

Neals Nurseries Garden Centre
Heathfield Road, SW18 3HR
www.capitalgardens.co.uk
T: 020 8874 2037

Sheen Garden Centre
Adrian Hall Garden Centres,
181-189 Upper Richmond Road West,
East Sheen, SW14 8DU
www.adrianhall.co.uk
T: 020 8876 3648

South-East

Alexandra Nurseries
Estate House, Parish Lane, Penge, SE20 7LJ
www.alexandranurseries.co.uk
T: 0208 778 4145

Alleyn Park Garden Centre
77 Park Hall Road, SE21 8ES
www.alleynpark.co.uk
T: 020 8670 7788

Bexley Garden Centre
1-3 Basildon Road, Abbey Wood, SE2 0ET
www.bexleygardencentre.org.uk
Tel: 020 8311 5212

Hortus
26 Blackheath Village, SE3 9SY
www.hortus-london.com
Tel: 020 8297 9439

Secret Garden Centre
70 Westow St, Crystal Palace, SE19 3AF
www.thesecretgardencentre.com
Tel: 020 8771 8200

Shannons Garden Centre
99-105 Standstead Road, SE23 1HH
www.shannonsgardencentre.co.uk
Tel: 020 8291 1502

East

Growing Concerns
2 Wick Lane, E2 2NA
www.growingconcerns.org
Tel: 020 8985 322

Outskirts

Bexley Garden Centre
57 North Cray Road, Sidcup, DA14 5EU
www.bexleygardencentre.org.uk
Tel: 020 8309 1442

The Garden Centre
Snakey Lane, Feltham,
Middlesex, TW13 7ND
www.adrianhall.co.uk
Tel: 020 8751 7600

Wood's of Berkhamsted Garden Centre
High Street, Berkhamsted, Herts, HP4 1BJ
www.capitalgardens.co.uk
01442 863 159

Petersham Nurseries
Church Lane, 143 Petersham Road,
Richmond, TW10 7AG
www.petershamnurseries.com
Tel: 020 8940 5230

Squires Garden Centre
Common Road, Stanmore, Middlesex, HA7 3JF
www.squiresgardencentres.co.uk
Tel: 020 8954 4628

Squires Garden Centre
Sixth Cross Rd, Twickenham, Middlesex, TW2 5PA
www.squiresgardencentres.co.uk
Tel: 020 8977 9241

Squires Garden Centre
Halliford Road, Shepperton, Middlesex, TW17 8SG
www.squiresgardencentres.co.uk
Tel: 01932 784 121

Ruxley Manor Garden Centre
Maidstone Road, Sidcup, DA14 5BQ
www.ruxley-manor.co.uk
Tel: 020 8300 0084

London Horticultural Societies

Allotment & Kitchen Gardens
*Belmont Lane Allotments & Leisure Gardens
(London Borough of Barnet)
www.belmontlane-allotments.co.uk*

Bensham Manor Allotments
www.benshammanorallotments.org.uk

Camberwell Gardens Guild
www.camberwellgardenguild.org.uk

Chiswick Horticultural & Allotments Society
www.growchiswick.org

De Beauvoir Gardeners Hackney & Islington
www.debeauvoirgardeners.org.uk

Dulwich Society (garden group)
www.dulwichsociety.com/garden-group

Ewell Horticultural Association
www.ewellhortassn.co.uk

Flowers & Plants Association
www.flowersandplantsassociation.org.uk

Fulham Horticultural Society
www.liapod.co.uk/fhs/

**Hampstead Garden Suburb
Horticultural society**
www.hgs.org.uk/hortsoc

Hampstead Horticultural Society
www.hampsteadhorticulturalsociety.yolasite.com

The Hardy Plant Society Middlesex Group
www.hardy-plant-middlesex.org.uk

Harrow in Leaf
www.harrowinleaf.org.uk

Highgate Horticultural Society
www.highgatehorticulturalsociety.org.uk/

Islington Gardeners
www.islingtongardeners.org.uk

Kew Horticultural Society
www.kewhorticulturalsociety.org

Lambeth Horticultural Association
www.lambethhorticulturalsociety.org.uk

London Permaculture
www.londonpermaculturalists.ning.com

London Permaculture Network
www.londonpermaculture.com

Newton Park Horticultural Society
www.newtonparkhs.co.uk

Roehampton Garden Society
www.roehamptonallotments.co.uk

Roxbourne Horticultural Society
www.harrowinleaf.org.uk/roxbourne.html

Royal Horticultural Society
www.rhs.org.uk

Spa Hill Organic Gardening Group
www.spahill.org.uk

Upminster & District Horticultural Society
www.upminsterhorticulturalsociety.co.uk

Warlingham & District Horticultural Society
www.warlinghamhorticultural.co.uk

Whittingham Gardening Club (Waltham Forest)
www.whittinghamgardeningclub.blogspot.com

Organisations

Allotments Regeneration Initiative
www.farmgarden.org.uk

Alpine Garden Society
www.alpinegardensociety.net

Association of Garden Trusts
www.gardenstrusts.org.uk

British Beekeepers' Association
www.bbka.org.uk
For more beekeeping resources, see p.22

Capital Growth
www.capitalgrowth.org

The Cottage Garden Society
www.thecottagegardensociety.org.uk

E A Bowles of Myddelton House Society
www.eabowlessociety.org.uk

**Federation of City Farms &
Community Gardens**
www.farmgarden.org.uk

Green Chain Walk
www.greenchain.com

The Hardy Plant Society
www.hardy-plant.org.uk

The Herb Society
www.herbsociety.org.uk

Garden History Society
www.gardenhistorysociety.org

Garden Organic
www.gardenorganic.org.uk

Greenfingers
www.greenfingerscharity.org.uk

Japanese Garden Society
www.jgs.org.uk

Linnaean Society of London
www.linnean.org

London Children's Flower Society
www.londonchildrensflowersociety.org/

London in Bloom
www.londoninbloom.co.uk

London Middlesex Master Gardeners
www.londonmiddlesexmastergardeners.com

London Wildlife Trust
www.wildlondon.org.uk

Mediterranean Garden Society (UK branch)
www.mediterraneangardensociety.org

**National Council for the Conservation
of Plants & Gardens**
www.nccpg.com

National Gardens Scheme
www.ngs.org.uk

**National Society of Allotment &
Leisure Gardeners Ltd**
www.nsalg.org.uk

National Trust
www.nationaltrust.org.uk

National Vegetable Society
www.nvsuk.org.uk

**Naturewise London
(permaculture, forest gardens)**
www.naturewise.org.uk

(NCCPG) Plant Heritage
www.nccpg.com

The Old Lawnmower Club
www.oldlawnmowerclub.co.uk

Perennial: Gardeners' Royal Benevolent Society
www.perennial.org.uk

Professional Gardeners' Guild
www.pgg.org.uk

Project Dirt
www.projectdirt.com

Royal Horticultural Society
www.rhs.org.uk

Seedy Sunday
(seed exchange event in Brighton & Hove)
www.seedysunday.org

Society of Garden Designers
www.sgd.org.uk

Soil Association
www.soilassociation.org

Sydenham Garden
www.sydenhamgarden.org.uk

Thrive
www.thrive.org.uk

Trees for Cities
www.treesforcities.org

Woodland Trust
www.woodlandtrust.org.uk

Over 200 private, secret and unusual gardens and green spaces open to the public for one weekend in June. Located across London, gardens range from the historic and traditional to the new and experimental, including private gardens, roof gardens, community allotments, and gardens belonging to historic buildings, institutions, cafes, schools and shops.

Organised by the London Parks & Gardens Trust to celebrate the capital's unique urban, green space network.
www.opensquares.org

Bibliography

London's Parks & Gardens – Billington, Jill (Frances Lincoln, 2003)
The Allotment Book – Clevely, Andi (Collins, 2006)
Gardens of England, Scotland and Wales, A Guide and Gazetteer – Evans, Hazel (George Philip Ltd, 1991)
Directions for the Gardiner and other Horticultural Advice (edited Maggie Campbell-Culver) – Evelyn, John (Oxford University Press, 2009)
A Garden from a Hundred Packets of Seed – Fenton, James (Penguin 2001)
London's Natural History – Fitter, Richard (Collins 1945)
London's Pride: The Glorious History of the Capital's Gardens – Galinou, Mireille (ed) (Anaya Publishers Ltd, 1990)
The Story of Gardening – Hobhouse, Penelope (Dorling Kindersley, 2002)
The Cable Street Gardeners – Kelly, Chris (CK Editions, 2005)
The London Town Garden, 1700-1840 – Longstaffe-Gowan, Todd (Yale University Press, 2001)
Flora Britannica, The Concise Edition – Mabey, Richard (Chatto & Windus, 1998)
The Gardener's London – Macleod, Dawn (Gerard Duckworth, 1972)
London Gardens: A Seasonal Guide – Parker, Lorna (Watling Street Publishing 2004)
Forgotten Fruits – Stocks, Christopher (Random House, 2008)
A Little History of British Gardening – Uglow, Jenny (Chatto & Windus, 2004)
Allotments – Way, Twigs (Shire Publications, 2010)
The Brother Gardeners – Wulf, Andrea (William Heinemann, 2008)

Image Credits

Index

About us:

Metro is a small independent publishing company with a reputation for producing well-researched and beautifully-designed guides on many aspects of London life.

In fields of interest as diverse as shopping, bargain hunting, architecture, the arts, and food, our guide books contain special tips you won't find anywhere else.

How to order:

The following titles are available to buy from our website (P&P free)

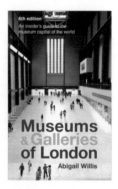

www.metropublications.com

London's Hidden Walks Series

" *A wonderful way to explore
this sometimes secretive city.*"
Robert Elms, BBC London 94.9FM

LONDON'S CITY CHURCHES
SEE THE SCORCH MARKS OF THE GREAT FIRE, OR VISIT AN ALTAR BY HENRY MOORE

LONDON'S HOUSES
FROM WORKHOUSE TO ROYAL PALACE, COME IN, CLOSE THE DOOR AND STEP BACK IN TIME...

LONDON'S MONUMENTS
FROM BOUDICCA AND BYRON TO GUY THE GORILLA

LONDON'S PARKS AND GARDENS
COVER MORE THAN TWENTY-FIVE PERCENT OF THE CAPITAL – THAT'S A LOT MORE GRASS BETWEEN TOES THAN ANY OTHER CITY IN EUROPE

LONDON'S CEMETERIES
SPEND THE DAY WITH KARL MARX, ENID BLYTON, KEITH MOON AND MANY MORE